Modern
Bird
Hunting

Modern Bird Hunting

Hunter's Information Series™
North American Hunting Club
Minneapolis, Minnesota

Modern Bird Hunting

Copyright © 1990, North American Hunting Club

All rights reserved.

Library of Congress Catalog Card Number 89-63989
ISBN 0-914697-27-7

Printed in U.S.A.
     5 6 7 8 9

The North American Hunting Club
offers a line of hats for hunters.
For information, write:
     North American Hunting Club
     P.O. Box 3401
     Minneapolis, MN 55343

Contents

Acknowledgments

Upland bird hunting is a sport steeped in tradition. In that same tradition we bring to you *Modern Bird Hunting*. The efforts of the authors combined with the behind the scenes work of the NAHC staff have made this work really worth the time to read.

Thanks to: Publisher Mark LaBarbera, Associate Editor Dan Dietrich, Editorial Assistants Karyl Dodge, Debra Morem and Tara Graney, Vice President of Products Marketing Mike Vail and Marketing Manager Linda Kalinowski.

Steven F. Burke, President
North American Hunting Club

Photo Credits

In addition to examples of their own talents, the authors have included photographs from: Chris Dorsey, Dan Dietrich, Federal Cartridge Co., Hornady Manufacturing Co., Mark Kaiser, Mark LaBarbera, Olin/Winchester, Russ Nolan, Pennsylvania Fish & Game Commission, Remington Arms Co., Leonard Lee Rue Enterprises, Tim Lewis Rue, South Dakota Division of Tourism, Ron Spomer, Irene Vandermolen, William Vaznis, Robert Whitaker and Dr. John Woods. A special thanks to Dean Peters for supplying the artwork for this book.

About The Authors

Hunting coats laden with carefully counted and categorized shells hung across the banister in the back hall. Meticulously cleaned and oiled shotguns were cased and waiting in the corner behind the door. In the kennels, three enthusiastic springer spaniels whined to get going.

But in the kitchen there was a pouting teenager. He was sitting backwards on a kitchen chair with his chin resting on top of its vinyl upholstered back. His tear-dampened stare was fixed out the big bay window. The rain wasn't letting up.

The lad was trying to look between the falling sheets of water, hoping to see the slightest hint that the storm might pass. But to the west loomed nothing but mile after mile of gray sky and falling rain.

The noon opener of the Wisconsin pheasant season was less than five minutes away, and 13-year-old Bill Miller couldn't believe he was sitting at home. My God!...This was pheasant season!

In the living room, calmly stretched out in the La-Z-Boy reading the paper, was Bill's dad. At the moment, he seemed to Bill like the most ridiculously stubborn man in the world. Why, getting a little wet wouldn't melt the guns, dogs or hunters, would it?

But what Bill failed to notice was that the Red Wing boots were already laced tightly around his dad's ankles and the lanyard of the dog whistle was already looped around his dad's neck. Though he had to put on the facade of fatherly wisdom which dictated "no birdhunter in his right mind would go out in weather like this," inside he wanted to have his nose pressed against the kitchen window, too. After all, this was the pheasant season opener!

That restrained, but obsessive love of birds, dogs and shotguns, passed from father to son, is what started co-author Bill Miller on his lifelong trek through North America's uplands. The first steps were taken at the age of five when Bill thought he convinced his dad he could keep up with the men and the dogs. Of course, his dad wasn't fooled, and really didn't mind carrying Bill on his shoulders half the day. They were together and hunting birds.

At age 12 Bill passed the required hunter safety training to carry a gun, and from then on the passion was fanned to a brighter flame by grouse, woodcock, pheasant, waterfowl and deer hunts all over Wisconsin. The family farm butted up against the Kettle Moraine State Forest which provided a 40,000 acre bird-rich backyard for close-to-home hunting.

In eighth grade, Bill discovered he wanted to be an outdoor writer. Nurtured by a steady diet of books like Mel Ellis's *Run Rainey Run*, Nash Buckingham's *'de Shootin'est Gent'man* and Jim Kjelgaard's *Irish Red,* Bill couldn't imagine becoming anything else. Early on he geared his education in that direction, frustrating teacher after teacher with English, history and even German class compositions based exclusively on topics related to hunting; no matter how farfetched! In high school, he even made his parents get special permission to enroll him in a junior/senior journalism class as a sophomore so he could write hunting and fishing stories for the school paper!

And Bill's fever for hunting continued to heighten through the teen years. In the days BDL (before driver's license), his mother was often forced from warm beds in the wee hours of the morning for transportation to marshes, woods or cornfields when dad couldn't go. High school friends with whom Bill hunted, often found him waiting on their doorsteps as much as an hour before he said he would be there. For duck hunting trips, the friend's parents' boat would already be hooked up and the decoys loaded. For bird hunts, the dogs would already be exercised and in the car waiting.

But the glory days came to a temporary end when Bill attended college at the University of Wisconsin—Eau Claire. Living away from home in a dormitory that didn't allow guns put a crunch on his hunting activities, but was a necessary evil if he wanted to become an outdoor writer. He majored in broadcast journalism and wrote his own minor program in environmental communications. It included courses in wildlife biology, recreational geography and geology. In his senior year at UWEC Bill co-hosted and produced "Chippewa Valley Outdoors" a

Bill Miller

weekly half-hour outdoors television program which aired on a local cable channel.

After his graduation in 1984, Bill joined the staff of the North American Hunting Club as associate editor of *North American Hunter*. He became managing editor, then editor and assistant vice president as the Club grew to a quarter of a million members.

After graduation, the doors of hunting opportunity were flung wide open. Since 1984, Bill has hunted all kinds of game in more than a dozen states and Canadian provinces. In his career he has taken white-winged doves, mourning doves, ringneck pheasant, bobwhite quail, sharp-tailed grouse, ruffed grouse, woodcock, Hungarian partridge, chukar, snipe and turkey along with many species of ducks, geese and big game.

He is avidly involved in various forms of competitive shooting including trap, skeet and sporting clays. In 1988 he competed in the first ever Sportsman's Team Challenge with fellow NAHC team members Steve Burke and Bob Allen. In 1989, Bill took first place in the 12 gauge shotgun event at the inaugural American Outdoorsman Of The Year Decathlon Championship and finished eleventh overall. He has competed in informal live pigeon shoots in the United States and Mexico.

To be able to afford his shooting addiction, Bill reloads thousands of rounds of shotshell ammunition each season. As the guest of North America's largest sporting firearms and ammunition manufacturers at new product unveilings, he is among the first outdoor media representatives to test new products entering the market.

Though his chores around the homestead tend to be neglected during the bird seasons, Bill's home is in Chaska, Minnesota where he lives with his beautiful wife, Laurel, and his sometimes overly-energetic springer spaniel, Gunner.

Some things never change. Take, for instance, the first day of pheasant season in Iowa. It has stayed pretty much the same for 50 years: high school buddies, five years on the good side of their twentieth class reunion, along with brothers, cousins and uncles, all milling around a fogged-over pickup truck sipping hot coffee and anxiously counting the minutes to the magic hour.

For a young Tony Caligiuri, the annual opening morning of pheasant season brought greater awe than the night before Christmas. His dad carried him piggy-back across drainage ditches and corn rows on that first opener more than 25 years ago and Tony has been a confirmed upland bird hunter ever since. He has hunted from the Arctic Circle to the interior of Mexico and in more than 20 states in between, searching for the most perfect point and the fastest covey rises across North America.

Tony Caligiuri

Growing up in Iowa, he enjoyed the next-to-unbelievable pheasant hunting of the 1960s and early '70s, when seeing more than one hundred roosters on a frosty November morning was a common occurrence. About the same time, bobwhite quail began their population explosion in southern Iowa and Caligiuri discovered his favorite of all the upland birds. With the addition of Huns, ruffed grouse and the occasional flight of woodcock, Iowa was mecca for the teen-aged upland hunter. In fact, the abundance of hunting did much to influence his decision to attend college in his hometown so he could still hunt, sometimes seven days a week during the easier semesters.

Fresh out of journalism school, Tony flirted with the idea of becoming a newspaper reporter, but quickly found out that a public relations desk in the outdoor products industry was more exciting. He freelanced his first story at age 22 and has published more than 200 since then. His articles and photographs have garnered many awards including two Best of Shows and a National Merit Award for outstanding college journalism.

Moving to Oklahoma in the early 1980s, Tony found another upland bird hunter's paradise: doves in almost every field and ranches that regularly produced 15 coveys a day of wild bobwhites. Besides Oklahoma opportunities, western Kansas was just a quick drive away, with its diversified shooting for such new found treasures as scaled quail and prairie chickens.

It was at this time that he discovered the Midwest doesn't hold a monopoly on good pheasant hunting. While driving through western Oklahoma on the way to a Kansas quail hunt, he stopped along the highway to stare in amazement at the most ridiculous sight of three ranch hands loading limits of pheasants into the back of a pickup truck, in a blizzard no less!

After that revelation, the wide open spaces of western Kansas, Oklahoma and the Texas panhandle became regular ringneck hunting grounds. Caligiuri still believes that the number of pheasants that can be found there is the best kept bird hunting secret in all of North America.

In love with the long seasons and romance of southern bird hunting, he moved to Texas in 1984. Back then, there was still enough rain to support a good population of bobwhites in the western Texas cow country, and south Texas was being overrun with scaled quail, or just plain old "blues" as the locals preferred to call them.

Texas quail hunting was different from the simple Saturday trips of boyhood Iowa. It became more of an applied technical science with special guns, special vehicles and trailers that held a dozen pointing dogs. It was here that the co-author formed concrete opinions on such things as double barreled shotguns, English pointers and lifelong hunting techniques. There were so many birds that theories were quickly and easily proved or displaced.

It was also in Texas where he met his wife, Ginny, who shares his enthusiasm for upland hunting and dogs. Currently residing in Arizona, the co-author and his wife enjoy an abundance of quail in three varieties, in addition to hunting for white-winged and mourning doves. He still manages to get back to the Midwest each year for a pheasant opener or two and makes Texas a regular stop on the quail circuit.

But no matter where he has lived and hunted birds, he has always been a traditionalist at heart. He maintains a love for the pump guns and doubles that American manufacturers turned out with such pride prior to the years of World War II, and for homegrown pointing dogs who aren't always steady to wing and shot, but seldom miss a bird.

Today, Tony Caligiuri writes almost exclusively for *North American Hunter* magazine, where he holds the privilege and title of Editor-At-Large.

Dedication

Bill's Dedication
 For my dad, who taught me about dogs and birds and other important stuff. And for my mom and my wife, who put up with it.

Tony's Dedication
 To my dad, who took the time and patience to show me what upland bird hunting and good sportsmanship was all about. And to my wife, whose understanding and support allows me to continue chasing pheasants, quail and the like all over the country.

Foreword

Outside it is still warm, not the kind of weather that one would expect during November in Iowa. Just the same, it is hunting season. All the upland seasons are in full swing, and the heat has made for some fairly tough hunting. But, it is hunting season, a time when the mind is easily swayed by thoughts of fine shotguns, frosty mornings in a picked cornfield and the annual reunions of old hunting pals.

Several million Americans hunt upland game each year; it is a time-honored tradition. The volumes that have been written the past half-century on the subject of birdshooting would fill a small library. Some would ask why we need another one, and that may be a valid question. But every once in a while young writers come along destined to make lasting marks on the outdoor world. In the case of *Modern Bird Hunting*, two of those extraordinary talents have combined experience and wit to produce an edition that is not just another hunting book.

The volume you now hold in your hands not only deals with the biological characteristics of every upland species in North America. It also shows you how to hunt them, where to find them and what shotguns and accessories to take with you. The authors are hunters who write from experiences gained in the field, and when they talk about bird hunting, whether ptarmigan on a grassy slope of a glacial undercut in the Yukon or doves in a hand-cut grain field deep in Mexico, they have been there. They have researched the past to give us some perspective on how our sport has evolved and they drive home the role of the hunter and the anti-hunter in a final chapter that looks forward to the future.

In between, they take you along on hunts for quail, pheasants, grouse and all the other upland birds across the country, both common and imported. They go from the Northwood grouse forests to the cow pastures of Texas, reliving trips with old friends, and starting off on adventures with new ones. Few of the best places are left undiscovered, and they take you along to a couple of out-of-the-way places as well.

Take the chapter on doves. Not only do we learn the pertinent facts about our most popular upland bird, we find out what it is like to hunt them in the U.S. and in Mexico. In the chapter on guns we take a look back at both the old classics and workhorses along with the new generation of today's upland guns.

The transitions from chapter to chapter are remarkably smooth for a book with joint authors. But then again, Tony Caligiuri and Bill Miller come from very similar backgrounds. They grew up hunting from the time they were old enough to walk and went into adulthood knowing that they would be writers. They each write with a unique style that blends careful research and personal anecdotes into chapters that are easily read and well-rounded.

Those of you who, like me, can't wait for opening day each year, those who merely exist sometimes for ten months to live fully for two months in the fall, will see much of themselves in this book. There is something for hunters everywhere. Those just beginning will get an in-depth overview of all the aspects of wingshooting. For the veterans who know everything already, well, they just might let you in on a secret place that you haven't yet discovered.

Many might say that the golden days of bird hunting passed 50 years ago. After reading this book, I'm inclined to believe that each and every day in the field should be a golden day, for success shouldn't always be measured by a full limit of birds. Success is being with good friends, seeing the horizon of someplace new and feeling the sharp wind of a December day. Success is watching a dog point and hold his first covey after you've trained him from a pup. Success is living in a country where all can hunt and enjoy the outdoors. Success is being able to dream.

Because not all shots are wide open and perfect, and because not all dogs mind like they should, we have our dreams. And dreams inspire books. Books can be educational and books can be entertaining. Seldom can a book be both. This is one of the rare ones.

Bob Allen
"Wingshooting" Columnist
North American Hunter

1

Our History Of
Hunting Upland Birds

Assuming upland bird hunters have a religion, North America must surely be Mecca. Our pilgrimages range from unplanned afternoon jogs in northeastern woodcock woods to month-long treks through the West where seven species of quail hide out like the lost cities of Cibola.

Every bird hunter knows the excitement of firing up the truck in the pre-dawn of opening morning. The mixed aroma of pointing dog, Hoppe's No. 9 and last night's fast food taco hanging in the cab. He knows the small town filling station attendant who wishes him luck and the plump cafe waitress who warns him about the "cholesterol in them eggs."

The small villages, grainfields, coverts and hills across North America can be vastly different. Yet, in a sense, they are much the same. Every town, from Billings to Baton Rouge, holds lease on a favorite cafe. Every Midwest cornfield harbors the still green remains of a two-row picker. Every stand of New England grouse timber has played stage to the practiced dance of a setter named Belle. And each fall, when the doves flock up out toward Yuma and the combines wind down west of Wichita, comes the bird hunter.

Wingshooting, however, wasn't always this way. Before our fathers and grandfathers hunted for sport, the first settlers hunted upland birds to put meat on the table.

The Earliest Days Of Wingshooting

When the founding fathers first came to this continent in 1620, they left behind a place quite different. In Europe, game belonged to the land-owner. Hunting there was a privilege. Imagine, then, how they reacted to North America, a continent bursting with big game, upland birds and waterfowl.

Stories abound of those early years. Pigeons were so numerous they broke tree limbs. Woodcock hunters had relays of dogs and an assistant at their side to reload. James Audubon reported that more than 100 woodcock were harvested using this technique–*in one day*. Turkeys and other birds were caught in clap-nets. Grouse, more often than not, could be bagged with a stick. Waterfowl came in to decoys provided by native American Indians.

Birds and big game were plentiful. Hunting was a necessity. It was a way to fill the larder, to survive. Hunting, quite simply, was as vital to the formation of North America as log cabins and wagon trains.

With only a scattering of settlers and ample wildlife for all, game regulations and harvest limits were far from the minds of those early set-tlers. Contrary to what they had left in Europe, game in North America belonged to everyone. There was plenty.

And plenty of land. Enough, in fact, to support farmers, settlers, wildlife and even wildlife that wasn't native to North America.

As early as 1733, people attempted to transplant pheasants to North America. That first attempt, made by Governor Montgomerie in New York, failed. Subsequent attempts in New Jersey by Benjamin Franklin's son-in-law and in New Hampshire by Governor Wentwort also failed. Today, however, they are considered as American as the pro-verbial apple pie.

In those days, wagon trains moved west. Scandinavians and Ger-mans and Englishmen, plow in hand, homesteaded. Mountain men and explorers, muzzleloader in hand, took to the rugged passes and rivers, exploring this continent. Elk, buffalo, deer, grouse, turkey, woodcock and pigeons provided food for all.

In the early 1800s a typical day in the field would find upwards of 50 woodcock, 25 quail and a handful of grouse in a single man's bag–*within 50 miles of New York City*.

When the timber was cut and crops planted, ideal habitat for game birds like quail and mourning doves was created. Originally only inhab-iting those areas rejuvenated by a fire, bobwhite quail found a perfect home near the edges of farmers' fields.

Early bird hunters did their wingshooting with heavy, long barreled, smoothbore muskets. In the early 1800s, a few English gunsmiths started to produce double barrel shotguns in standard gauges with twin flintlock hammers. About the same time, shooting birds for sport in Europe became popular. By the mid-1800s, breechloads and the first pin fire shells appeared. These early European breech-loaders are the basis for today's modern upland guns.

Wingshooting For Sport

The bird hunting in England and Europe, however, was nothing compared to what could be found in North America. With new developments in firearms and hunting techniques came the second era of North American upland hunting: wingshooting for pure enjoyment.

This second phase, lasting from about 1850 to the turn of the century, is perhaps the most important to us as modern day hunters. It is this period that brought on many of the engineering, manufacturing and social developments that have formed the sport as we know it today.

After the Civil War, enterprising gunsmiths, both here and in England, discovered that the bore of a shotgun could be adjusted to control the size of the shot pattern. For the first time, hunters had a relatively safe bet for hitting flying targets. Mule-drawn wagons loaded with southern gentlemen and pointers criss-crossed southern plantations, and writers started penning articles about quail and grouse shooting. Vacations were commonly planned around bird hunting trips.

It was also during this time period that the first wingshooting games appeared. An ex-market hunter, named Captain Adam Bogardus, patented a trap that threw glass balls into the air. Using his invention Bogardus broke 1,000 glass balls in 101 minutes during an exhibition in 1877. Refinements were gradually made to include the clay birds that all of us have broken at one time or another.

The first successful introduction of pheasants to North America was completed in 1882. Roughly two dozen pheasants were transplanted by the American Consul General in Shanghai to a farm in Oregon. The pheasants took a stronghold in that state and supplied many of the original stocking efforts in the Midwest.

Smokeless powder added another measure of reliability and by the turn of the century, American gunmakers were highly emphasizing the upland gun. It was the end of the second phase of North American upland hunting, but the beginning of the modern age of wingshooting.

North America's Modern Age Of Wingshooting

With this modern age of wingshooting came the modern age of firearms design. The man responsible for what we all know now as the shotgun was a brilliant gunmaker and father of 10 from Ogden, Utah named John M. Browning.

Up until the turn of the century, double guns, both English and American, were about the only options available for upland shooters. While the sport of American wingshooting was coming into its own, American shotguns were largely copies of British models. John Browning changed all that, pioneering and perfecting three designs that can be found in every serious hunter's closet.

Browning's first pump action shotgun was manufactured by Winchester as the Model 93, then refined a few years later to the take down version Model 97. While the 97 hammer gun was a dandy for the times, it is better known as the forerunner of "America's Gun," the Model 12.

Most hunters and shooters agree that the Model 12 is one of the finest firearms ever produced. Available in all modern gauges, and in .410 as the Model 42, the Model 12 is highly regarded as a hunting gun, skeet gun and trap gun. Produced for half a century, thousands of Model 12s are still in use.

Browning considered his most difficult invention to be his recoil operated autoloading shotgun. Granted a patent on October 9, 1900, Browning took the gun to Winchester for manufacturing. In one of their self-admitted greatest blunders, Winchester rejected the design. Discouraged but persistent, Browning took the gun to Remington. On the day Browning was to meet with Marcellus Hartley, Remington's president, Hartley died of a heart attack.

Standing, shocked and lost, on a New York City pier, Browning gazed at an ocean going steamer and decided to take the design overseas to Belgium. Fabrique Nationale D'Armes de Guerre in Liege, Belgium accepted the autoloader without hesitation and another upland favorite began showing up in the cornfields and briar patches of North America.

One of Browning's last projects is also one of the queens of American upland guns, the Browning Superposed. At 70 years of age, while personally supervising the production of the beautiful over/unders, Browning died in Belgium. When the ship that bore his body docked at stateside, a full United States Military Guard of Honor was there to meet it.

Though the all-American gun may be the repeater, we have also carried on a long-lived love affair with the side-by-side double. Good doubles haven't really changed in the past 70 or 80 years, except they are harder to find. Once the forging birthplace of most of the good, affordable side-by-sides, American craftsmen produce scant few of them today.

Pheasants were successfully introduced into North America in 1882. Two dozen were transported from China to Oregon, and this population supplied the original stocking efforts in the Midwest.

While the English and Europeans were hot on sidelock guns, American gunmakers have generally produced box-lock guns such as the Winchester Model 21 and the Parker. Once the finest of their kind, today both are seen more in collections than in the field. Ditto on the beautiful Foxes, L.C. Smiths and Ithaca doubles. But when you can find one, there are few things more satisfying than folding a pair of birds on a covey rise with a pre-war work of art.

Perhaps they are just symbols of bygone days when old men with files turned out some of the finest firearms in the world. Today, you'll find few craftsmen who are content to labor long hours over a bench to feel the satisfaction of producing a true work of art. A few U.S. concerns still have some double guns manufactured in Japan and stamped with a famous American name. Although they look the same, alas, they are not. For now, all most of us can do is dream.

While we're on the subject of nostalgia, how about a peek into yesterday's prices for bird huntin' gear and guns.

In 1926 a pair of Bean's Hunting Shoes–still a favorite today–went for $4.50, a Filson hunting coat was $6.50, Hoppe's No. 9 was 10 cents a bottle and a nice Ithaca double gun could be had for 40 bucks. Dogs, however, were a different story. Even back then a good pointer or setter fetched a full month's paycheck.

There were several books on upland hunting already on the market and a catalog list from a 1920's sporting books house shows no less than 30 titles related to training bird dogs. The automobile opened up the farms to otherwise city-held hunters and wingshooting was more popular than ever.

However, something bad was happening.

The Development Of Our Conservation Spirit
Three decades of industrial expansion followed the Civil War, benefiting the country economically, but depleting much of the habitat previously used by wildlife. Once teaming with wildlife, North America had quickly become a place that some feared would soon be void of game animals. Grouse populations were in trouble, as were bobwhite quail. The prairie chicken was near extinction. Farms were abandoned and dove populations fell.

President Theodore Roosevelt, himself an avid hunter, was not going to let this happen. Together with Gifford Pinchot (who was largely responsible for making "conservation" a public issue), he established the National Forest System and the National Park System. He directed every state to establish a conservation department and hunting seasons. Hunt-

Until the turn of the century, double guns were the mainstay for upland hunters. An American named John Browning changed that with the introduction of the pump, autoloader and Superposed over/under.

In the 1920s and 1930s, the automobile opened the farms to otherwise city-held hunters. Back then, an Ithaca double cost $40, a good pointer or setter a full month's paycheck.

ing licenses would be sold, and the money used to manage and promote wildlife populations.

Stocking, rather than habitat management, was the most prevalent game management philosophy at that time. State conservation departments searched for rugged game birds to introduce in their regions.

Chukar partridge were imported from the Himalayas. In deserts and badlands this bird thrived. Today, it is hunted throughout the arid Southwest and West.

Hungarian partridge were imported from Hungary. This bird, accustomed to the harsh winters and summers in Hungary, took well in several states and provinces.

The 1960s were the golden age of wingshooting in North America. Pheasant hunting, in particular, was spectacular. More than 60,000 hunters made annual pilgrimages to South Dakota for ringnecks.

Further protection was afforded game birds with the signing of the U.S. Migratory Bird Act of 1913. This act stopped all netting and similar commercial operations of migratory birds. People were rethinking the impact of commercial and market hunting.

During the Depression, the U.S. government put people to work rebuilding the land. The Civilian Conservation Corps was one such organization that employed people in the 1930s and rebuilt many tracts of land. In several states, thick sections of evergreens were planted, boosting available habitat for game and non-game birds.

The Pitman/Robertson Act taxed firearms ammunition and put the money directly back into conservation. Duck Stamp programs not only helped out waterfowl but the upland birds as well, and the North American hunter learned a new word–conservation. The next phase of upland hunting had begun, and American hunters enjoyed their most golden years of the sport from 1930 to 1970.

The Golden Age Of Wingshooting

A look at the history of pheasant hunting during this time period is typical of the quality of hunting found in many midwestern states:

During the years of World War II, South Dakota boasted populations of 40 million birds and the annual bag ran more than five million. The daily bag limit of 15 birds came easy. Seasons and bag limits became accepted regulations, opening days became time honored traditions. Local economies were bolstered by the hundreds of hunters who arrived each fall dressed in waxed cotton and canvas. The motels overfilled, the cafes ran out of food and the gas stations pumped their tanks dry.

Even during the early 1960s, 60,000 to 70,000 nonresidents still came to the pheasant capital to hunt ringnecks. A soil bank program provided for plenty of cover to keep numbers stable. And South Dakota wasn't the only place that had plenty of birds. Iowa, Nebraska, southern Minnesota and Kansas had their share of ringnecks too, only less attention was focused on the out-of-the-way hotspots.

Growing up in Iowa and seeing 250 birds streaming out of the end of a slough ditch was an every Saturday experience. When we woke up at 4 a.m. on opening morning, it seemed as if half the neighborhood was also getting ready to go. The traffic out of Des Moines would be bumper to bumper for 20 miles out of town. The half hour from 7:30 to the magic opening hour was the longest time in the world, even longer than the night before Christmas.

I remember the thick sandwiches and hot chocolate that knocked the frost off the November mornings, and the birds. It always seemed to take all day to kill a limit when it should have taken only a few minutes.

Today, more than 10 million bird hunters take to the fields and forests. Although not the "golden age" it once was, 30,000 hunters still make that pilgrimage to South Dakota.

Quail hunters in the South enjoyed exceptional bobwhite numbers and hunters in the Southwest discovered an untapped resource in the mountain and valley quail. The golden age of wingshooting was widespread and longlasting, but the 1960s brought in the sixth phase in the history of upland hunting.

The Decline Of Wingshooting

Intensified farming practices and habitat losses, combined with blizzards, made tough going for the pheasants and a series of droughts in some of the quail states cut the once liberal shooting and hunting way back. Dove numbers simply tumbled. The traffic in Huron, South Dakota is no longer bumper to bumper, but thanks to new crop reserve programs and organizations such as Pheasants Forever, future wingshooting reminiscent of the 1940s is not far-fetched.

Thirty-thousand nonresidents still come to South Dakota each year, making pheasant hunting a $30 to $35 million dollar industry. The average upland hunter spends $168 per year on his sport. All totaled, upland hunters contribute $1.8 billion to the economy each year. The pheasant, as it has been for 40 years, is still the king of the corn pile. The big birds get chased by 3.7 million hunters each year. Quail hunters number 3.2 million and the rest of the upland hunters make up about 2.5 million.

Throw in the dove shooters, and upland hunters number more than 10 million nationwide. We've come a long way since the time when setters sat instead of pointed. Some areas might harbor fewer birds and the grouse are gone from New York City, but upland hunters are more conscious than ever. We are entering the seventh era of North American upland hunting.

Present Day Wingshooting In North America

This phase of history is the most important. Hunter numbers are decreasing, the anti-hunter numbers are increasing and the birds seem to be holding their own. As a whole, we are becoming more sophisticated. We have recognized what we need to do and are taking steps to correct past mistakes.

With any kind of luck, 250 pheasants in one ditch will be a common sight again. It's possible. But for the time being upland bird hunting still ain't bad.

2

Today's Upland Shotguns

There are two different ways to look at shotguns for hunting upland birds. Neither is right. Neither is wrong. They are just different.

The hunter with the first view looks on his gun as a hunting tool. Nothing more. Nothing less. The shotgun is simply a means to an end in pursuing his game. Just like a craftsman maintains and takes care of his tools, this hunter recognizes the importance of maintaining and caring for his shotgun.

Though this hunter's gun is likely to be in good condition and always functioning properly, it is not coddled. It is a workhorse and when it ceases to function properly it is replaced. Period. No emotion, no sentiment.

Many good, very good, hunters have this attitude about their guns. Even past coach of the Minnesota Vikings, Bud Grant, who is as well-known among sportsmen for his passion for hunting as he is among gridiron fans for fielding great football teams, has this attitude. At a cocktail party during a firearms trade show Bud was asked if any of the hundreds of new guns he saw that day had caught his eye. Bud's reply was terse: "I've been shooting the same gun for years. I'm a hunter, not a shooter."

That's clearly the attitude of a man who sees a shotgun as a tool to get the job done. Another like him is NAHC Member Chuck Barry of Houston, Texas. Chuck is president and owner of Texas Hunting Products, which makes decoys and accessories for waterfowlers and upland bird hunters. He's also an avid hunter.

His favorite shotgun is a battle-scarred Ithaca Mag. 10 semi-auto. He even occasionally dove hunts with that bruiser just to get the feel of it before goose season opens. As much as he dotes on that gun, he's also been known to throw it, uncased (which is legal where he hunts), in a pick-up and tear off to some rice field the geese decided was better than the one in which Chuck was waiting. His gun, as much as he loves it, is a tool to get the job done...end of discussion.

The second hunter's view is of the upland shotgun, any shotgun for that matter, as a piece of fine art. It's a thing of beauty. It's important to him that it look as beautiful in the gun cabinet as it handles in the field. To his way of thinking, it's a nearly animate object that can caress and be caressed. Perhaps it has only been carried in the field once or twice, but to this hunter that particular gun embodies the aura and the memories of those golden October days.

This hunter is likely to own at least several, probably many, shotguns. And most are probably not bargain basement models purchased at the local department store.

One such NAHC Member is Bill Hanus of New Mexico who deals in fine bird guns, both foreign and domestic. In simply watching Bill handle guns and listening to him talk about them, you can read his affection for them. Watching him on the skeet range and sporting clays course, you can most certainly tell he knows how to use them, too. His is a love of admiration *and* familiarity.

Considering these two far ends of the spectrum, the only logical discussion of shotguns for upland bird hunting has to cover those things which the two factions have in common. Believe it or not, there are some.

Balance & Fit

Next time you want a good chuckle, stroll into your local discount store and ask the pimply-faced kid behind the sporting goods counter to show you a shotgun with good balance. He'll probably turn around and grab whatever he has overstocked. He'll extend the index finger on his right hand and settle the gun on it with his left hand. Then he'll inch the gun back and forth until it hangs on his one finger without any other support. With the gun gently swaying on his rigid digit he'll say, "Ah, look at the balance on this beauty."

In reality, you could ask for a bamboo lawn rake with balance and the hardware salesman could do about the same thing. The stereo salesman

Like father like son. NAHC members Mike (left) and Omar Boeselager choose one gun for all their wingshooting duties. Both carry Remington 1100 autos and shoot them well as indicated by this bag of pheasants.

could sell balanced speakers the same way. Or the local butcher—"Boy, look at the balance in this honey of a ham bone."

All that resting a gun or any object on a single finger shows is that you've located a point where the weight on each side of the fulcrum is about even. Meaningless as this gesture is, you'd be surprised how many people who should know better "test" the balance of a shotgun this way.

In shotgunning jargon, balance refers to how a gun feels. How is the gun's weight distributed? How does that distribution effect performance for the individual shooter?

Basically, shotguns can have one of three types of balance or weight distribution. A shotgun can be muzzle heavy, butt heavy or center heavy. One type of balance is going to feel better to some shooters depending on their personal shooting style and the type of shooting they plan to do with the shotgun. One type of balance is most useful in a specialized set of circumstances.

Muzzle Heavy Balance.   What kind of shooters prefer muzzle heavy shotguns? Top competitive shooters in all shotgun shooting games (read the world's best shotgunners), that's who. Trap guns tend to be muzzle heavy. Skeet guns are muzzle heavy. Sporting clays guns are on the muzzle heavy side.

In the hunting field, muzzle heavy shotguns have long been the mainstay of serious duck and goose hunters.

Why are weight-forward shotguns preferred by so many? It's because they promote steady swing and good follow-through for shooters who rely mostly on the swing-through method of pointing a shotgun. That is, tracking from behind a moving target, swinging the barrel through the target, pulling the trigger when the right lead is achieved, and then *continuing the swing with a steady follow-through.*

A muzzle heavy shotgun tends to force good follow-through habits. In the case of a steadily moving target in relatively open terrain, that means more hits.

The best way to get a good idea of this is with an exaggerated example. Imagine you have a fairly flexible yardstick in your hand. You're swinging it to and fro in front of you. It's easy to do, isn't it? The momentum of the light stick is not difficult to stop. You can stop or alter the direction of the stick's movement quite easily.

Now, run the far end of the stick through an apple. Try to duplicate the hasty start and stop movements you made with the empty yardstick. It's much more difficult, if not impossible. The weight at the end of the stick creates greater momentum which tends to keep the end of the stick moving in the direction it was started.

NAHC member Bill Hanus appreciates fine shotguns as works of art and craftsmanship as well as tools embodying the memories of crisp autumn mornings.

That increased momentum is what makes a muzzle heavy gun easier to swing smoothly. Or, better said, harder to swing erratically!

Butt Heavy Balance.   Now reverse the yardstick and hold it with the apple end about six or eight inches behind your hand. Try to swing the bare end of the stick with smooth and steady momentum. Don't let it jerk from point to point. Don't let it move up and down from the line of swing from point A to point B. Difficult to do, isn't it?

What the far end of the stick does do easily is move *quickly* from place to place. The weight of the apple behind your hand helps you speed up the movement of the distant end of the stick.

The weight to the rear of a butt heavy shotgun does the same thing. It tends to help you move the barrel very quickly and, for the shooter who relies exclusively on the snap-shooting style of wingshooting, this can be of some benefit. Snap-shooting is, of course, the system in which you pick a point the appropriate distance ahead of a moving target and fire at that point. The closer the target is, the easier it is to estimate that point. So the faster the barrel can be brought to bear on a target, the better. This is the forte of the butt heavy shotgun.

Center Heavy Balance.   Though most hunters will lay claim to a favorite style of shooting, the best wingshots are those who adapt to the situation. Through practice, they've developed the skill to instantly assess the flight of a target and determine what kind of shot is called for. It isn't a conscious process in which the brain says, "Oh, this bird is departing quickly through the trees. I had better make a snap shot." It's more of an instinct, a reflex.

Because the gun must provide the characteristics necessary for the wingshooter in any situation, classic upland bird guns have center heavy balance. In shooting circles, this is more commonly known as "between the hands balance." This means that the weight of the gun is centered between the shooter's hands as he shoulders the gun. It is really a compromise that allows the shotgun to be the most versatile for the shooter who is skilled enough to take advantage of it.

Shotgun Fit.   Balance and fit really boil down to how a shotgun "feels" in your hands and at your shoulder. A shotgun that feels good instills confidence, and that's half the battle of becoming a good wingshot. The best way to figure out what feels good is to shoot a lot of different guns, stock configurations, etc. But short of a session with a professional stock builder and his "try gun" there are a few tips to assessing the fit and balance of any shotgun.

A session in front of a full-length bedroom mirror is in order.

Start with the shotgun's top half or comb. It must be such that when the shooter's cheekbone is pressed firmly against it, his eye is looking

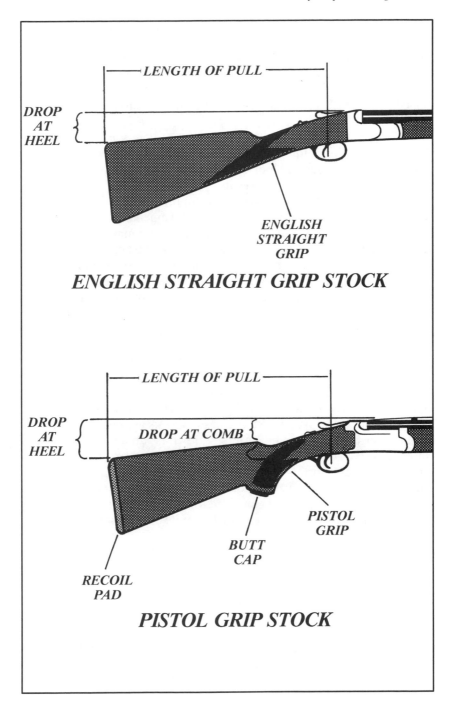

LENGTH OF PULL

DROP AT HEEL

ENGLISH STRAIGHT GRIP

ENGLISH STRAIGHT GRIP STOCK

LENGTH OF PULL

DROP AT HEEL

DROP AT COMB

PISTOL GRIP

BUTT CAP

RECOIL PAD

PISTOL GRIP STOCK

straight down the barrel, past the front bead.   In essence the wingshooter's eye becomes the rear-sight, much like an archer's when he's aiming an arrow. The point at which the shotgun meets the cheek, and therefore the angle at which his aiming eye views the front bead, must be absolutely consistent from shot to shot if accuracy is to be obtained. An ill-fitting comb will make this consistency difficult to achieve.

With your eyes closed, mount the gun as you would in the field. Make sure you're holding the gun comfortably before you open your eyes. Open your eyes and look at how your aiming eye is positioned in relation to the rib of the gun. Try this several times.

If, when you open your eyes, your pupil is consistently out of line with the rib, you may need to have comb adjustments made. If your eye appears to the outside of the rib or barrel, the comb may be too thin. To the inside, it may be too thick. Likewise if your eye appears too low behind the receiver, the comb is too low. If you can see lots of the rib and your eye appears high, the comb is too high.

It's easy to make a comb higher or wider with the addition of tape or moleskin. If you overcompensate, it's easy to remove, too. However, reducing height requires sanding and refinishing, and once it's done, it's gone. Proceed with caution.

Length of pull or stock length is measured from the butt to the trigger on a parallel line with the gun's bore. The time-honored method of testing length of pull is to position the trigger finger on the trigger as you would if you were going to fire the gun. Bend your arm at the elbow and bring the butt into position so that the stock rests against your forearm. The butt or back of the recoil pad should come up about half-an-inch short of the base of your biceps. If you'll only shoot the gun while wearing a lightweight shirt, then the butt can come to rest on the base of the biceps, but having it come up short allows for the heavier clothing you may wear while shooting the gun. And for ease in mounting a gun under all situations, it's better that the stock be a mite on the short side than the long side.

To test length of pull in the mirror, stand sideways to the glass and mount the gun. The thumb on your trigger hand should be about an inch from your nose.

When shortening or lengthening the stock be careful not to alter the pitch of the gun. Pitch is the angle at which the stock is cut off at the butt, but strangely enough, it is measured at the muzzle. You can easily tell how much pitch your gun has by setting it in a doorway. Set the gun down on the doorjamb, butt flat on the floor with the trigger side away from the wall. Slide the gun toward the wall until the breech section

Balance and fit really boil down to how a shotgun "feels" in your hands and at your shoulder. A shotgun that feels good instills confidence, and that's half the battle of becoming a good wingshot.

touches. The pitch will be the distance from the center of the barrel to the wall.

If the barrel stands out from the wall, your gun has down pitch. If the barrel is parallel with the wall you have zero pitch. Most shooters require about $1^1/_2$ inches of down pitch, depending on the shape of the shoulders. Down pitch also helps keep the gun on the shooter's shoulder.

Another dimension of stock design that contributes greatly to feel is "cast." Cast is the horizontal angle of the stock in relation to the centerline of the barrel. Most production shotguns today are made with no cast. That is to say that the stock is in a straight line with the center of the barrel or barrels. Therefore the gun could be used with equal results by a right-handed or left-handed shooter. However, some of the finer production doubles and most custom guns are built with cast. This form of ergonomics makes a gun fit the body position of a shooter better.

In viewing a shotgun for a right-handed shooter with a dominant right eye from above the butt end, the stock would appear to bend to the right. That's called "cast on." For a left-handed shooter with a dominant left eye, the stock would bend to the left. That's called "cast off."

The amount of cast dictates the position of the eye in relation to the center of the rib, much like the thickness of the comb on a gun with no cast. The advantage of cast is that it can be manipulated over a far greater range even compensating for a right-handed shooter with a left dominant eye.

Gauge Selection For Upland Birds

It's probably impossible, but it certainly would be interesting. The results sure would be telling. The results, that is, from a survey to reveal how many woodcock have been taken by duck/goose hunters on their way in and out of the swamp.

The survey would also tell how many of them were carrying 10 gauge or 12 gauge shotguns, sporting 3-inch shells with number 4 or larger shot. I know personally of a couple of bobwhites that fell to steel BBB 3-inch goose loads as a tired Texas goose hunter slogged up to an overgrown fence line and the covey took to the air on the far side.

I'll bet the numbers would surprise a lot of upland purists who feel the only sporting gun for quail or woodcock is a 28 gauge side-by-side choked skeet and skeet.

Yep, it sure would be interesting and prove the point that virtually every species of game bird, web-footed or upland-loving, has been taken with every gauge and configuration of shotgun. What it wouldn't prove

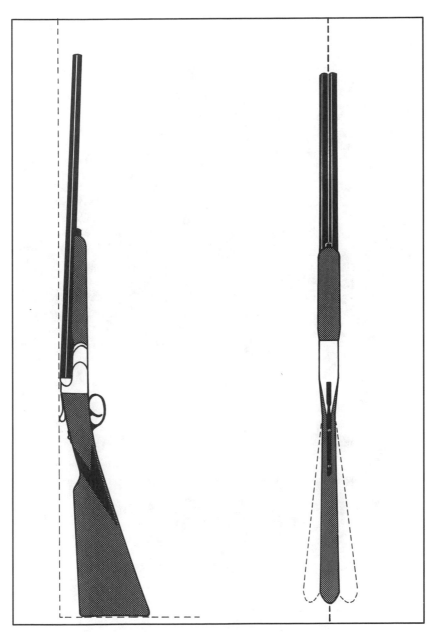

To check a shotgun for pitch, place the butt on the floor and slide the breech to a square door jam. The distance from the wall to the middle of the barrel is the amount of pitch.

Some shotguns are built with cast. That is an angle to the stock. This is an early version of the science we know today as ergonomics.

A great deal of consideration must go into selecting the proper gauge for your upland bird hunting. Species, conditions, your physical build and your own preferences are all factored in. However, your ability to make clean, one-shot kills with the shotgun is of greatest importance.

A lot of upland birds have fallen to guns less than perfect for the task at hand. Co-author Miller took three pheasants on a driven bird hunt to test Remington's 10 gauge semi-auto complete with 32-inch barrel.

is that a 3-inch-barreled 10 gauge is the best choice in guns for woodcock hunting.

Without a doubt, the 12 gauge is the hunter's gauge. It is also the target shooter's gauge. And the sporting clays enthusiast's. The 12 gauge is everybody's gauge...especially the meat hunter's.

NAHC Member Bill Hanus operates the aptly named Bill Hanus Birdguns out of Silver City, New Mexico. BHB is sort of a field wingshooter's dreamland. Bill deals fine shotguns, lines up imports that nobody else can get and even commissions specially designed guns that best suit the needs of many discriminating American wingshooters. If it's got two barrels, smooth bores and is used in "civilized shooting" Bill can get it for you at a price that few others can touch.

Anyway, Bill dotes on his middle gauge hunting guns. He loves to hunt with 16s, 20s and 28s, but, he admits, for raw efficiency nothing matches a 12 gauge.

"For meat hunting, it remains a mystery to me why anyone would want to shoot anything other than a 12 gauge shotgun—at anything!" Bill says.

"If the name of the game is killing, the 12 gauge has no equal. Although the AK-47 and the Uzi grab the headlines in the drug wars, the last paragraph will probably be written with the short-barreled 12 gauge pump carried in the front seat of police patrol cars. With one 00-buck up the spout and more in the tube, and given across-the-street ranges, America's street cleaning and alley sweeping firepower is already in place.

"As a combat weapon, the 12 gauge has a long and noble history. The Winchester M97 Trench Gun of World War I was the only weapon that drew cries of 'unfair to civilized warfare' from the Kaiser's High Command (who, by the way, had brought poison gas and the Maxim machine gun to the party).

"And during the Korean misunderstanding, the weapons of choice for those in front-line fox holes was five or six 12 gauge pumpguns loaded with 00-buck. Against charges of drug-crazed, screaming Korean ground troops, the standard operating procedure was to stand up, hold back the trigger and pump, hosing down the oncoming horde. When the bolt slammed home on an empty chamber, the guys fell down in the hole, picked up another loaded shotgun and repeated step one. There is absolutely no doubt that for close encounters of the worst kind, in alley or jungle, the 12 gauge is Number One. Primo. The best."

"Same thing goes in a wilderness survival situation," says NAHC Shooting Advisory Council member J. Wayne Fears. "There is no other single gun with the power and versatility of loads to keep your survival camp larder full. From North America's biggest bear to lemmings on the tundra, you can't do better than the 12 gauge to keep you well fed."

All of this heaped on top of the endorsement of every writer who has penned the answer to the rhetorical question, "If I could only have one shotgun...?" It certainly would seem a mystery why any other gauge was ever created.

But there is one vital component that is left out of this equation—the joy of wingshooting. The challenge and the self-imposed handicaps that

The 12 gauge is the gauge for the one-gun hunter. These pheasants were taken with a Winchester 101 Lightweight 12 gauge.

make upland bird hunting a sport and not a trip to the meat market. Why, with that gruesome history of the 12 gauge in mind, it almost seems boorish to release all that fire-power at a fragile target like a woodcock. Yes? No? Maybe?

The first responsibility of any hunter is to equip himself to make fast, clean and, most importantly, humane kills. The gauge of the shotgun has to be up to the task at hand. It's for that reason alone the 12 gauge is the premier gauge for hunting the upland bird covers of North America.

On birds with a tenacity for life, like cock pheasants, on birds that regularly offer long range shooting, like hard-hunted, late-season Huns, on just plain big birds, like the prairie chicken and sage hen, the well-built, properly fitted 12 gauge shotgun is without peer. It is without question, the shotgun of the "one gun" hunter. And with the tremendous variety of factory loads that can be purchased and the even wider array that can be handloaded, it certainly can be called upon to "do it all" for the North American upland bird hunter.

The Golf Bag Approach
But there are certainly those hunters who prefer to take the "golf bag" approach to hunting guns. That is to select from a collection of shotguns a gun tailored to the type of shooting most likely to be encountered on a particular trip afield.

For example, the "golf bag" hunter might own a 20 gauge auto he shoots well around dove fields, where action is fast and furious and low recoil is a must. For grouse, woodcock and early season quail he may prefer to shoot a 28 gauge side-by-side choked skeet one and skeet two. When the quail are warier in December, he may switch to an improved and modified 16 gauge over/under. For cornfield pheasants he carries a 12 gauge pump, the first repeatin' gun he ever owned. And on...and on...and on.

There obviously comes a point at which this idea becomes little more than an excuse to own another beautiful shotgun, but then, there's nothing wrong with that either. The sky is the limit as long as the hunter is committed to practicing with each new acquisition. He must be familiar with each gun in his collection so that he can be confident of making fast, clean, humane, one-shot kills.

Of course, there *is* one other limiting factor on the size of a bird hunter's "golf bag." That is the number of imaginative ways in which he is able to sneak new guns into the house past a non-hunting spouse.

The Other Gauges

The middle and small gauges are the forte of the "golf bag" hunter. Each suits a purpose no other fills quite as well. There are few hunters who understand this as well as NAHC Member Bill Hanus. And today, you'll find few hunters who can match his outgoing affection for these "little" guns.

This section on "The Other Gauges" is really Bill's—so here goes:

"It seems to me that over the last half century, events have conspired to challenge the small gauge shooter. The small gauge aficionado has to contend with four creeping problems.

"The first is the magnumization of the small gauge. American shotshell makers have worked hard on the theory that 'more is better' as far as shotgun shells are concerned. This has had the effect of 'promoting' power and payload to the next larger gauge—12 gauge power in a 16, 16 gauge power in a 20, 20 gauge power in a 28, and 28 power in a .410!

"The added recoil has not been compensated by improved efficiency. However, most reloading tables offer excellent hunting loads in 16 gauge one-ounce loads, 20 gauge seven-eighths-ounce loads and 28 gauge three-quarter-ounce loads. I don't consider the .410 much of a hunting gauge, but it is pretty hard to improve on the one-half-ounce skeet load at 20 yard ranges.

"Second is the evolution of the soft shot 'promotional load.' This cheap ammunition often sold by the mass merchandisers is usually loaded with the dregs of the shotmaking process.

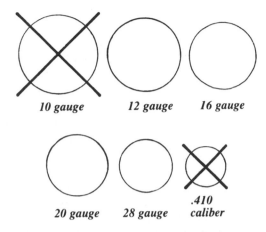

10 gauge   12 gauge   16 gauge

20 gauge   28 gauge   .410 caliber

The gauges the upland bird hunter should consider are the 12, 16, 20 and 28. The 10 is too much for practical use on upland birds. The .410 isn't enough gun to assure humane, one-shot kills.

"At the moment of ignition (when you pull the trigger) about 20 to 25 percent of the shot at the bottom of the shotcup is deformed—and goes wandering off into space when it leaves the muzzle.

"At 15 yards, soft shot doesn't matter much. But at 45 yards, trying to pick up a pheasant flushing at the end of the cornfield, you're out of luck.

"Hard shot (three to six percent antimony) does not deform easily, so the result is more pellets in the target at every range. Copper and nickel plating is almost always used on hard shot these days, and has the effect of adding an extra bit of velocity and an additional five to eight yards of effective killing range. Premium shells always cost more, but they really are a commodity in which you get what you pay for, especially when you're hunting with a middle gauge gun. The smaller the gauge you shoot, the more difference this makes.

"The third paradox with which small gauge hunters must contend can be a scourge or a boon depending on how well you understand it: Today's plastic wads equal tighter chokes.

"The plastic wad in common use today makes shotgun shells extremely efficient. It not only helps cushion the shot column at the point of ignition, but it prevents the individual pellets from being abraded and deformed on their passage along the barrel walls. This results in more pellets in the target area, almost as if you had tightened the choke. It could easily result in your improved cylinder/modified gun shooting closer to skeet two and improved modified.

"The problem is compounded by the fact that many foreign shotgun makers use choke constriction standards based on cardboard, fiber wad shells of 50 years ago!   In the case of one of these foreign guns firing today's premium American shells, it is possible that your improved cylinder/modified gun shoots modified/full or full/extra full patterns!

"This presents two potential disasters for the small gauge shooter: A) plastic wads can bulge a full choke barrel at the muzzle end, and B) you'll miss a lot of birds you would have otherwise killed! Those that are hit will probably be mush!

"Fortunately, this problem is one that can be easily solved by your gunsmith. He can open your chokes to any constriction you wish. Have him lengthen the forcing cones at the same time. It is also possible to move the point of impact up to nine inches in any direction by boring an elliptical choke. I have several of my grouse/woodcock guns adjusted so that the right barrel shoots six inches high at 16 yards in order to pick up a rising bird while it is visible roosting on my front sight. Second barrel shoots dead on.

"By the way, Dick Gonser (Skeetmaster, P.O. Box 10, Glendora, CA 91740, phone: (818) 963-4751) does all my choke work, and I have no hesitation in recommending him to my fellow NAHC members.

"Good chokes maximize the efficiency of the plastic wad in small gauge guns.

"Finally, as a small gauge bird hunter, I detest steel shot. It is the curse of the upland bird hunter, wingshooters in general. In small gauges it is unsafe and unsatisfactory. It has the potential to permanently rack a lot of wonderful old upland bird guns and make it impossible to safely shoot many of today's fine side-by-side doubles. *Never shoot steel shot in a small gauge shotgun you plan to pass on to your heirs!*

The 16 Gauge. "Within the past few years, many shotgun writers have rediscovered the 16 gauge—but no one summarizes the case for the 16 gauge one-ounce load better than my friend Rich Grozik in his book *Game Gun:*

> *Within normal shooting ranges, few upland bird situations require more than one ounce of shot; the 16 gauge with $2^3/_4$-inch chambers was designed specifically for one-ounce loads. Shot charge in relation to bore diameter for the 16 gauge in the one-ounce load is excellent. Such "square loads" minimize shot deformation from bore scrub and take full advantage of properly choked barrels. Quail hunters...have long heralded the virtues*

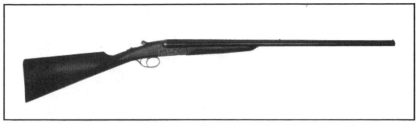

*Bill Hanus considers the 16 gauge the ultimate upland bird gauge. That's why he se-
lected it when Precision Sports asked him to design a side-by-side to carry his name.*

*of the 16 gauge side-by-side, and many a woodcock and grouse
has been brought to dog as well by the open-choked twin tubes of
the 16. Loaded with ¹/₂ drams-equivalent of powder, the one-
ounce 16 gauge shotshell is pleasant to shoot and deadly effective on upland birds.*

"Although American makers seem reluctant at present to offer a one-
ounce load for the 16, the English maker—Lyalvale Express—shells are
now being imported and are available in the following configurations:

Lyalvale 16 Gauge High Velocity High Antimony Shells

Length	Loads	Available Shot Sizes
2¹/₂-inch	⁷/₈-ounce	7¹/₂, 9
2¹/₂-inch	1-ounce	6, 7¹/₂, 9

"This 2¹/₂-inch ammunition can, of course, be used in modern
2³/₄-inch chambered guns as well as thousands of pre-1930 made shotguns with shorter chambers of 2¹/₂ inches or 2⁹/₁₆ inches.

"My own high regard for the 16 gauge is demonstrated by the fact
that when Precision Sports invited me to design a "dream" birdgun to
carry my name, I picked the 16 gauge for the first run. The vital statistics
on the original Bill Hanus Birdgun were: 25-inch barrels factory choked
Skeet 1 (.004 constriction right barrel) and Skeet 2 (.010 constriction left
barrel). In the Bill Hanus Birdgun II we are offering barrels of 25 or 27
inches, but keeping the same choke constrictions. The gun is also available in 28 gauge now, too. The result is a well-made gun of exceptional
quality (it carries a lifetime operational warranty) for less than $900!

"To summarize, the 16 gauge comes highly recommended and offers impressive credentials for the middle gauge shooter's consideration. It's an old love affair offered anew."

The 20 Gauge. "Weighing in at a couple ounces on either side of six
pounds, the 20 gauge gun is an upland hunter's delight. Although virtu-

ally all modern 20 gauge guns are chambered for 3-inch shells, the 20 performs at its best with three-quarter- or seven-eighths-ounce hard shot loads. It is interesting to note the number of competitive skeet shooters who prefer to shoot their 20 gauge guns in 12 gauge events, rather than take the punishment of the larger gauge over a prolonged period.

"Wide load selections are offered by almost all ammunition makers, and 20 gauge hulls are a delight to reload, both durable and easy to obtain. Waterfowl considerations aside, if you want to settle on one gauge for your shooting, the 20 is an easy choice. With three-quarter- or seven-eighths-ounce loads, it makes a perfect gun for women, young shooters and anyone who wants to do without unpleasant recoil and heavy weight.

"A quick look at shotgun and shotgun ammunition sales charts will confirm: the 20 gauge is everyone's favorite 'little' gun."

The 28 Gauge. "I probably sell as many 28 gauge shotguns as anyone in the country, but rarely to a young shooter. Maybe you have to have a couple of decades of hunting experience under your belt to appreciate the virtues of the 28 gauge. That's too bad, because it is a great gun for shooters of all ages!

"In any case, the 28 gauge is significantly different from all other gauges, and understanding the differences makes one appreciate the 28 gauge all the more.

"Shotgunning differs from all other sports in that it is a three dimensional affair. A shotshell pattern may be so many inches high and so many inches wide; but most shooters forget that the shot string might be *12 or 14 feet long!*

"This holds true for the 12 gauge, the 20 gauge and the .410, but the 28 gauge is the greatest exception to the rule. And because of its shorter shot string, eight to nine feet with good loads, it enjoys all the knockdown power of its bigger brothers. If you do your job and properly position the shot string in relation to the moving bird, that bird is hit nearly as hard and as often by the 28 as it is by the 12! Hit with either one, he's just as dead!

"The 28 gauge is the most underrated of the gauges. A 28 gauge gun on a 28 gauge frame is a delight to shoulder, swing and carry. My standard reload is of three-quarter-ounce of $7\frac{1}{2}$ shot—nickel-plated if I can get it. It works well on everything from ducks over decoys to all kinds of upland birds. In fact, the only two turkeys I ever shot, I got with a *single shot* from a 28 gauge carrying that load...but that's another story.

"I consider the 28 gauge, along with the 16 gauge to offer the most in shooting satisfaction. Someday you'll own a 28 gauge and you'll wonder why you waited so long to enjoy this shooting pleasure."

The 28 gauge is not only a great gun for women and youngsters. It's a practical hunting gauge for any upland hunter who doesn't like recoil.

And A Little Bit More

Thanks, Mr. Hanus, for a job well done.

You'll note that Bill's endorsement of the middle and small gauges stops short of the .410 bore; and justly so. The .410 is not a hunter's shotgun. Most certainly it is not a beginner's gun. With the scanty one-half-ounce loads that the .410 shoots most efficiently, it's too difficult to hit anything, much less make a sure-kill shot on an adrenaline-pumped game bird. It is completely understandable why a novice hunter so equipped would quickly become disgusted and give up. Some nimrod has equipped him with a rig that expert wingshots would pull from the closet for some added challenge!

In the "golf bag" hunter's arsenal, the .410 exists for two reasons. The first is that the .410 is a great training gun for the advanced marksman. It is completely unpunishing to shoot and if you reload, it costs only pennies to keep in ammunition. Clay targets don't suffer if they aren't hit well, so the .410 is perfectly permissible at the range. And when you can go out to the skeet range and consistently break 'em all with a .410 on your shoulder, you'll tear 'em up in the woods with any hunting gauge you choose.

Second reason for the .410 to exist is beauty. Anyone who's seen a fine side-by-side or over/under .410 doesn't need more explanation. It's much like looking at a petite young maiden. No one with an ounce of decency could deny her allure.

Which Action For Upland Birds?

It's a pretty safe bet to say that virtually every species of upland game bird has been taken with every shotgun action. But again, that doesn't prove that the semi-auto is the best bird gun. Nor does it prove the double or the pump or the single-shot is best. Even more than in gauge selection, the choice of action is based on personal preference, on what "feels" good. The only fair way to critique the merits of each for the hunter looking for a new gun or thinking of experimenting with something different is to simply discuss their advantages, disadvantages and allure.

Side-By-Side Double Guns. There comes a time in most every man's existence when he sets out to find the one component he hopes will make his life complete. He seeks a lifetime companion who will share intimate moments that wouldn't be the same if shared with another. He looks for one with beauty and grace and lines he can admire in the light of the hearth on long winter nights.

We are, of course, talking of the upland bird hunter's search for a side-by-side double barreled shotgun that he can call his own. A gun to

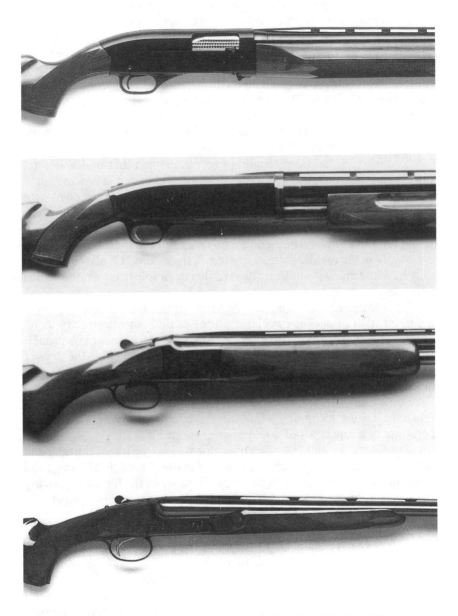

Some upland hunters consider each of these actions his "best" birdgun. If he shoots it well, he's right! From top to bottom, these actions include: auto-loading, pump, over/under and side-by-side.

have and to hold, and to carry into the grouse coverts and pheasant fields. A gun to cradle in his arms on long walks through New England bogs and piney Southern plantations.

There still resides in the memory of a few living hunters a time when a side-by-side of acceptable quality could be had for a price that wouldn't require a second mortgage on the homestead. What wonderful days those must have been. The hunter who sets about such a quest today will find the search more difficult, but not impossible.

But what really makes the side-by-side double-barrel shotgun the gun most often identified as a "bird gun?"

Tradition. It has been around longer than any other multi-shot action. It has had the most chance to develop and gain a following. In a sport so steeped in tradition it's only logical that the oldest type of gear would be so revered.

But all the sentimental glop aside, the side-by-side double has a lot going for it as an upland bird gun. Well designed and built side-by-sides, especially in the middle gauges, are really light guns. Of all the actions, they have the greatest tendency toward that desirable between-the-hands balance.

Double guns have the advantage of offering longer barrel lengths in a shorter overall package because a long action isn't necessary as on pumps and semi-autos. With highly efficient modern smokeless propellants, the additional barrel length isn't as essential as it was in the days of blackpowder, but it can eke a few extra feet per second even from modern hunting loads.

Some hunters find the wide plane presented by the side-by-side barrels to be an aid in sighting a moving target in thick cover—a situation common to many types of upland wingshooting.

The safety on double guns is often located on the top of the tang and is truly ambidextrous, which can't be said of many models of pumps and semi-autos—especially the older ones. Because of the far fewer moving parts generally found in double guns, they are considered the most reliable of all multi-shot actions.

Side-by-side shotguns come in three flavors: double-trigger, single non-selective trigger and single selective trigger. The single non-selective option offers the least versatility. When you take off the safety and pull the trigger, the barrels fire in the order determined by the gun's maker, period. The single selective design lets you decide which barrel to fire first. That can be an advantage, especially if one becomes adept at instantly making barrel selection based on shooting situation—very few (read almost none) shooters develop that skill. Double triggers offer eas-

Proponents of side-by-sides say that the wider sighting plane helps them get a target faster. Maybe; maybe not.

ier instant selection of barrel, thus choke, but for the inexperienced dou-
ble-shooter, follow-up shots often turn into follow-up cursing.

If you do select a double-trigger gun, always go with a straight stock
design. Straight or English stocks, rather than a pistol grip or semi-pistol
grip, better position the back hand for moving from trigger to trigger.
Trying to get back to the second trigger on a pistol-gripped double can be
an exercise in digital contortionism.

In really well-built doubles, much of the kick is designed out of the
gun, but there is no mechanical means to deaden recoil as there is in the
semi-auto. So, the recoil-sensitive shooter either needs to look at a small
gauge double or another action.

The greatest disadvantage of the modern side-by-side double barrel
shotgun is price. Few really well-designed and well built side-by-sides
can be found for less than $1,000. Those that can, like the Bill Hanus
Birdgun series are available on special order only.

Over/Under Double Guns.   America is a country of rifle shooters.
Look at the guns that live in legend here. Kids everywhere watched
movie good guys fight movie bad guys with Winchester lever actions. In
tales of World War II it was always the hero and his rifle that saved the
day.

American rifles are exclusively single barreled affairs, so it isn't
hard to see that when a rifle shooter looks down the barrel of a shotgun he
wants something that is at least a little familiar. That's probably why single barrel shotguns are numero uno in popularity among American bird
hunters.

Target shooters, the guys whose greatest satisfaction in life is to see a
smoked clay target, prefer the narrower sighting plane, too. The single
barrel would appear to promote better accuracy, but in reality any advantage in this area is between the shooter's ears. A good side-by-side is
"tuned" to shoot both barrels to the same point of impact—the one
you're looking at down the *single* rib between the barrels. But then,
there is nothing wrong with an advantage in the mind of the shooter.
Anything that gives a wingshooter confidence will do wonders to improve his shooting.

What the over/under really does is to take almost all the advantages
of the double barrel and put them into a gun that offers the rifle shooter
that old familiar single tube sight picture. That's exactly why it's em-
braced so enthusiastically by more and more American upland bird
hunters.

An added advantage of the over/under is that they are more moder-
ately priced and more readily available than good side-by-sides. An upland hunter can easily buy a Browning or a Beretta stacked-barrel double

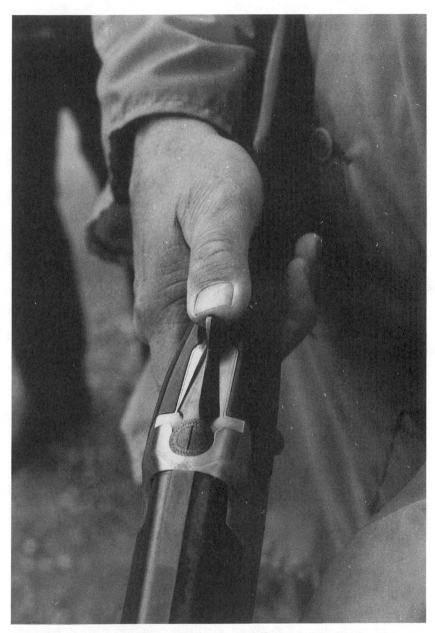

Production line doubles with tang safeties are truly ambidextrous shotguns. However, never forget to wrap your thumb around the grip after the safety is off. To do so could result in a nasty bruise or cut.

for substantially less than $1,000 and expect to own a well-built gun that will perform for years to come.

The only instantly recognizable disadvantage of the over/under is the radius necessary to load or eject shells. Because the gun has to be broken so far open for the shell from the lower barrel to clear the action, loading for follow-up shots is slowed and more space is required to perform this task. This poses a problem when shooting from a cramped blind or butt.

Some side-by-side devotees will tell you that the large, deep forend of the over/under doesn't promote good field shooting technique or feel as opposed to the tiny forend on an upland side-by-side. However, that's strictly a matter of personal preference based, again, on the intangibility of "feel." Most over/unders tend to be on the heavy side compared to side-by-sides of comparable gauge, too.

Pump Actions. The pump action is an American phenomenon, truly suited to the needs of the all-around hunter on this side of the Atlantic. If you only own one shotgun for all your hunting, it should probably be a 12 gauge pump with 3-inch chambers.

Shells for such a gun could be loaded to cover all types of upland bird, waterfowl, small game and big game hunting in North America. The action is far from fragile. In a pinch, it will ram home and fire shells that would leave lesser guns hopelessly jammed. The pump action is among the most likely to stay reliable through the worst Mother Nature can dish out, even the underrated vagaries of dust and freezing rain.

Should you need five shots, in some cases more, they're ready and waiting. With a modicum of practice the pump shooter can turn loose accurate shots as fast as his semi-auto toting crony.

Fathers looking for a son's or daughter's first gun could do far worse than to start the youngster's shooting career with a pump shotgun. They have all of what it takes to help instill basic shooting skills and discipline in the beginning shooter. They tend to be the least expensive of all the multi-shot actions, which is important if junior decides hunting isn't for him. Even the best pump guns, the household name brands, run quite a bit less than doubles or semi-autos of the same quality.

Today, many manufacturers are custom tailoring pumps especially for the upland bird hunter. These upland guns often feature straight stocks, shorter barrels and reduced overall weight. They are certainly a pleasure to carry all day, but some wingshooters find them whippy when it comes to pointing. For lots of snap shooting they're fine, but they make open country, swing-through shots more difficult.

The advantage of a straight stock on anything but a side-by-side, double trigger double is debatable. There is less to them than pistol-grip

The pump action makes a great lifetime gun. It's rugged and reliable.

stocks, so they do have the advantage of lightness. That helps balance the bobbed barrels on these guns. If you're interested in trying something new, the switch from pistol-gripped stock to straight stock is easier to make than the vice versa exchange.

All in all, the pump action is a great, all-around shotgun. It offers versatility and reliability above all others. It just doesn't have a lot of pizzazz.

Semi-Automatics. Load it. Point it. Pull trigger. Pull trigger. Pull trigger. Pull trigger. Pull trigger.

You've just zapped five shots from a semi-automatic shotgun in a lot less time than it took to read that paragraph. Now the gun lays in your hands with its maw wide open asking for more ammunition to do it again.

On the surface, the great thing about the semi-auto is simplicity. If the shotgun is properly maintained, it does what it is supposed to do with the slightest nudge of your index finger. No barrels to select, no triggers to change, no forearm to pump between shots. The semi-auto leaves you free to concentrate on the primary task at hand—hitting what you are shooting at.

The semi-autos of yesteryear were weighty propositions that turned an all-day pheasant hunt into a weight-lifting marathon. But today, semi-autos, like pumpguns, are being built with the needs of the hiking hunter in mind. These lightweights offer the same bona fide advantages and questionable attributes as upland pumps.

Where the semi-auto tends to falter is in reliability. They'll consistently work well in the field, if the hunter is willing to spend the time at home, or in the hotel room, or in the camper, to meticulously clean the gun and see that all parts are in good repair. They provide the most field convenience of any action at the expense of some inconvenience at the cleaning bench. The upland bird hunter who honestly lives by the credo which says, "At the end of the hunt you take care of the dog first, your gun second and yourself last," will live long and prosper with a semi-auto shotgun.

Although more expensive than a pumpgun of like quality, the semi-auto offers the beginning shooter the welcome advantage of low recoil. Semi-autos use some of the energy which other guns channel into kick to cycle the action. This has the effect of dampening the push at the shooter's shoulder. Even the veteran wingshot finds that a welcome plus around a busy dove field.

Follow-up shots with a semi-auto are fast. But it takes practice to make them count. (These birds were taken on a hunting preserve where both roosters and hens are legal game.)

Choke & The Upland Birdgun

In all texts on shotgunning, a great deal of emphasis is placed on the pattern of shot that shotguns throw. And rightly so. It is this pattern of shot that breaks targets and kills birds.

The pattern of shot thrown by any given shotgun is a function of many variables. These include the constriction of the shotgun's barrel, the amount and type of powder in the load, the capacity and measurements of the hull, the type and size of shot, the wad or shotcup, and even the atmospheric conditions under which the shot was fired.

Hypothetically, the most efficient pattern a shotgun could throw would consist of one pellet. The gun that throws that pattern is called a rifle. If it were possible for the wingshooter to direct a tiny, single projectile to the base of a flying upland bird's skull on every shot, then the whole discussion of shotguns and patterns would not be necessary.

The rifle throws the super-ultimate pattern. But since the super-ultimate pattern cannot be directed accurately enough shot after shot, what's next?

Perhaps the ultimate pattern would consist of only eight pellets. Though not directed with pinpoint accuracy, each of these eight pellets would always strike the target, and all eight would arrive on target at precisely the same moment.

Two pellets in the "ultimate pattern" would always take the flying bird in the head. Two more would enter the vitals—the heart and lungs. The remaining four pellets would be evenly divided to break at least one of the flying bird's wings and one of its legs.

"Breaking down" an animal is most often thought of as the realm of the rifleman after dangerous big game, but it certainly applies for the upland bird hunter. By breaking a wing and a leg, the perfect pattern would eliminate the possibility of a bird gliding out of sight before it falls or running away after it hits the ground, if the bird were not instantly killed by the pellets to the head or vitals. Breaking down upland birds is especially important for the hunter who is without the services of a good dog. The easiest birds to find are ones that stay where you drop them.

Unfortunately, even this hypothetical "ultimate" pattern is just that. It doesn't exist. So the upland bird hunter has to search out the next best thing.

To really understand choke and how it effects success in hunting, the hunter needs to realize the difference between a pattern's spread and its density.

"Spread" is the total area that a pattern of shot covers at a given distance. For example, the spread of a full choke gun at 25 yards might be

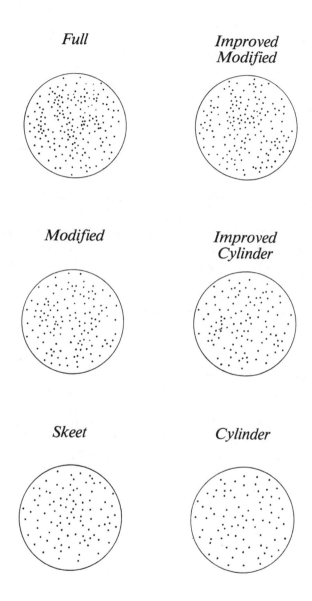

Pattern spread and density are two considerations which the upland bird hunter must keep in mind.

20 inches. That is, the majority of shot from the fired shell will strike in a 20-inch diameter circle at 25 yards.

"Density" is the measure of how much shot falls into an area of specified size at a specified distance. A full-choke gun may give a pattern 80 percent density at 40 yards. This means that 80 percent of the pellets from the load are still within the boundaries of a 30-inch circle at 40 yards.

When famed wingshooter and Trap Shooting Hall of Fame Inductee Bob Allen talks about chokes and patterns he tells the story of a successful Louisiana farmer who sent his son to Georgia Tech for an education. After about a week, the father called his son to ask how he was doing and what he had learned.

The son replied proudly that during the first week he learned the formula πr^2.

The father abruptly said, "Get on home, boy. I ain't payin' them $4,000 a year to lie to you! Pie are round; cornbread are square!"

What in the heck do pie and cornbread have to do with shot patterns? Bob goes on to explain:

"Go back to sixth grade math and you might recall that πr^2 is the formula for the area of a circle. What it shows us is that the difference between a 24-inch pattern and a 30-inch pattern is much greater than we think.

"The area of a 24-inch diameter pattern is 452 square inches; the area of a 30-inch diameter pattern is 707 square inches. At first glance that appears to be only a six-inch difference, but in reality it makes for a whopping 36 percent difference in killing effectiveness."

That means that the chances of a target being struck are more than one-third better if a pattern is just six inches larger in total area—if the part of the pattern through which the bird flies is dense enough to cause a hit.

Patterning Your Upland Birdgun

Shotgun manufacturers base choke on the amount of constriction they build into a shotgun barrel or choke tube. It's a mechanical measurement that is within standard specifications for the company. Such-and-such constriction is supposed to produce such-and-such results in patterning.

Sometimes they do. Sometimes they don't. So many variables come into play, that there is no way a shotgun manufacturer can account for them all. Their specifications for choke are based on their own testing and on the standards of the industry.

NO.	9	8½	8	7½	6	5	4	2	1	BB
SHOT SIZES **Diameter** **in inches**	.08	.085	.09	.095	.11	.12	.13	.15	.16	.18

BUCKSHOT **Diameter** **in inches**	No.4 .24	No.3 .25	No.2 .27	No.1 .30	No.0 .32	No.00 .33	No.000 .36

SHOT PELLETS PER OUNCE (Approximate)

LEAD				STEEL	
Size	Pellets	Size	Pellets	Size	Pellets
BB	50	6	225	BB	72
2	87	7½	350	1	103
4	135	8	410	2	125
5	170	9	585	4	192
				6	315

This chart indicates the diameter of various shot sizes and how many lead pellets of each size make up an ounce. The shot sizes of the upland bird hunter are 9, 8, 7½, 6, 5—and, maybe, 4.

Basically, that means the markings on a shotgun barrel or a choke tube are a relative thing. The barrel marked full will pattern tighter than the barrel marked modified, but whether it throws a true full choke pattern can only be determined by testing the gun with the loads it will shoot most often.

Various degrees of choke constriction are given the names Cylinder (no constriction), Skeet, Improved Cylinder, Modified, Improved Modified, Full and Extra Full.

Traditionally, the standard range for patterning shotguns was 40 yards. It's from this kind of testing that the industry developed its standards for choke constriction. At 40 yards an extra-full choke puts 75 percent or more of its pattern in a 30-inch circle. Full choke patterns 65-75 percent in the 30-inch circle. Improved modified holds 55-65 percent of the shot in the 30-inch ring at 40 yards. Modified choke will give a 45-55 percent accounting. Improved cylinder holds 35-45 percent. Skeet choke 30-35 percent. And cylinder bore, or no choke, only keeps 25-35 percent of the load in 30-inches at 40 yards.

To determine percentages on the pattern board, fire a shot from the off-hand position at a softball-sized spot on your patterning target. Tie a

Only when you are familiar with your shotgun, your loads, and the patterns they combine to produce can you expect consistent results in the field.

marker to a 15-inch piece of string, and at the board locate visually the center of your pattern. Hold the end of the string at that spot and with the string taut, draw a circle with the marker. The 15-inch length of the string gives you a 30-inch diameter circle. Next count the pellet holes in this circle. Circle each one as you count it to avoid counting any hole twice.

Determine the number of pellets in your load by multiplying the weight of the shot load in ounces by the number of pellets in each ounce. The following chart will be useful in determining the number of pellets per ounce for shot sizes commonly used for hunting upland birds:

Divide the number of holes you counted in the 30-inch ring on your patterning board by the total number of pellets in the load you fired. The result is the percentage you're looking for which can be used to determine the true choke of your gun, regardless of how it is marked.

If you're seriously interested in determining whether your shotgun performs as it is marked, this type of individual testing of each gun or choke tube is the way to do it. However, it takes a lot of tedious hole counting and number crunching to produce knowledge that isn't extremely useful.

Darn few upland birds are taken at 40 yards. It is far more important for the serious wingshooter to know the size and density of his pattern at the ranges he shoots his birds. To do that simply pattern your gun at ranges from 10-40 yards at five-yard intervals. The results will be revealing if you've never patterned your shotgun.

Practical Choke Chart
Pattern Diameter

Range	Imp. Cyl.	Modified	Full
10 yds	15 ins	12 ins	9 ins
15 yds	20 ins	15 ins	11 ins
20 yds	26 ins	19 ins	15 ins
25 yds	31 ins	25 ins	20 ins
30 yds	37 ins	31 ins	25 ins
35 yds	43 ins	38 ins	31 ins
40 yds	50 ins	45 ins	40 ins

(Actual patterns will vary (+/-10%) due to shot size, shot type, shotcup design and manufacturer's production methods.)

Effective Range

Even more variables are introduced to the equation when one begins to consider the maximum effective range for a particular choke. A great deal depends on the size and tenacity for life of the upland species you're after. Some will take a hit from just one or two pellets and call it quits. Others can carry off half a load to die hours or days later.

After patterning your gun *at hunting ranges*, common sense interpretation of the results will be the key to the effective range of your gun. The traditional rule of thumb for 12 gauge guns is that maximum effective range is the point at which 50 percent of the shot from a standard 1+1/8-ounce load is still inside a 30-inch circle.

A gun shooting within the standards of full choke will do this at 50 yards, modified at 45 and improved cylinder at 40. Those are maximum ranges for a 12 gauge gun. At any greater range, with lighter loads or in smaller gauges, all bets are off.

Limit your upland bird shots to 50 yards maximum! Opportunities to shoot even that far will be few anyway!

Remember, your gun has a minimum effective range, too. Shooting birds too close with a tightly choked gun results in wasteful destruction of delicious meat that should have been enjoyed on the dinner table.

Adding Another Dimension

When viewing load results on a patterning board or studying diagrams of shotgun patterns on paper, it is easy to think of a pattern of pellets in only two dimensions: height and width. In reality, a pattern has three dimensions. Since all the pellets in a load do not exit the muzzle at the same time and do not all travel at the same speed, the pattern also has depth. This is known as "stringing" or the "shot string."

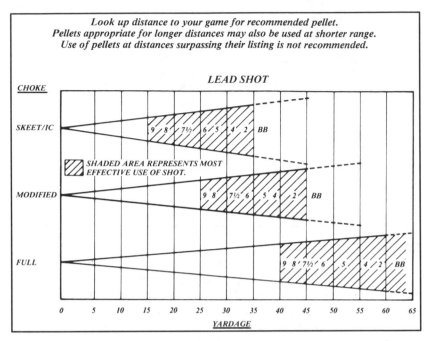

This chart gives you an idea of what patterns should be doing at the ranges upland birds are normally shot.

When you look at a pattern on a piece of paper, you can't tell in what order the holes were made, but it is important to keep it in mind. Especially at ranges out around 40 yards and beyond, holes in depth can exist through which a bird could fly. Though two pellets may have struck the pattern board only two inches apart on the plane of the paper, one could have arrived at the target far enough behind the other that a moving target the size of an upland bird crossing at an angle to the pattern could have slipped between the pellets.

There isn't a lot the upland bird hunter can do to his gun to shorten the shot string. However, selection of high quality loads can shorten the shot string tremendously and mean more and harder hit birds.

Point Of Impact

Without patterning his shotgun, it is also impossible for the upland bird hunter to tell where his gun is shooting. Just like the rifleman sighting in his firearm, a shotgunner needs to know where the point of impact is when he "has the sights lined-up."

Don't forget that a shotstring has depth. Though holes in a pattern board may look as though no bird could fly through, that's not always the case.

The point of impact from a shotgun is where the center of the pattern falls at a given distance. It may be right on target, but it could just as well be high, low, left, right or any direction from center. Even after shooting their guns at a six-inch circle marked on the patterning board and seeing the results from themselves, many hunters refuse to believe that the guns center patterns anywhere but where they are aiming. But pellet counts and percentages don't lie.

The reason many hunters can hit what they are shooting at with a shotgun with an off-center point of impact is because they've become used to their guns. Trial and error shooting over years has imprinted on their brain what the sight picture should look like to score a hit with that gun. At least those shooters can honestly say that they are familiar with their shotguns.

Some shotguns are designed to throw the center of the pattern high of the line of sight. The most common example is the trap gun. The stock and rib designs on these guns are coordinated to throw the center of the pattern high. This allows the trap shooter to apparently have his target floating on top of the front bead when he pulls the trigger, yet actually have enough lead on the rising target to center it in the pattern.

It doesn't take much imagination to see how this could be useful to hunters after game birds whose normal flush is up and away from the hunter. Unfortunately, unlike trap targets, the flight of game birds is not completely predictable, and the hunter would be under pressure to remember to compensate even more on diving birds and incoming targets. So in the long run, you're better off learning with a gun that centers its pattern where you point it, then sticking with that gun.

To check point of impact draw a six-inch circle on the pattern target. Take a standing off-hand shooting stance at the distance indicated earlier as proper for your gun's choke constriction. Fire at the target.

Do not shoot from a benchrest or a rifleman's prone or sitting position. That's not how you'll normally be shooting at upland birds, and what you are trying to determine is how the gun will center its patterns in field use.

After one shot, go downrange and circle the pattern. Also circle the area near the center of the pattern that seems to have the densest concentration of pellet holes. How does the center of the pattern and the pattern as a whole compare to your six-inch circle? Is it centered? If so, you're lucky. If it's not centered, how far off is it? In which direction? Think back to shots you missed with the gun. Have there been some misses you swore were going to be hits that sent twigs falling ahead, behind, above or below the bird?

The ultimate upland birdgun is one which its owner shoots well most of the time. And at least once in a while, it shoots like a magic wand.

Even if your testing shows that your gun does not center its pattern on the line of sight, it's not a problem if you've learned to compensate for the gun and hit consistently with it. The problem comes up when you borrow a gun or buy a new one. If it doesn't shoot the same place your old one did, you'll have trouble hitting with it.

Correcting the situation is a "pay me now or pay me later" situation. You can either have your gun fixed by a gunsmith to center the pattern where you point it and relearn to shoot it or alter all your future guns to shoot the exact same place your old one does.

Changing point of impact is tricky business, best handled by a gunsmith who is completely familiar with this type of work. This is one type of shotgun alteration where you want to be sure to check a smith's references. Good ones have often built a reputation on specializing in this type of work.

Point of impact can be altered by changing the stock design, altering choke constriction, realigning barrels, back boring or any combination of these specialized customizations.

The Best Birdgun

"The best birdgun is the one you shoot the best and enjoy shooting the most." Sounds like the words of an "expert" who really doesn't want to take the time to answer your questions. However, with a couple of qualifiers, no truer string of English words has ever been put together.

One major qualifier is that the gun must be up to the task of making one-shot, humane kills consistently. We owe that to the birds. We must be aware of our firearms' limitations and choose shots within those restraints.

Beyond that, any shotgun you enjoy shooting (that includes carrying) is suited to upland bird hunting. Have fun.

For the wingshooter who wants more, here is an overall profile of what makes a good upland bird gun. A lot of great guns fall inside these parameters.

1) A "lifetime" upland gun should be able to fire more than one shot without reloading. A single-shot is a fine beginner's gun because of the measure of safety its limited capacity affords, but no bird hunter should go a lifetime without the chance to take a legitimate double on ruffed grouse or quail.

2) The best upland birdguns feature open choke(s) whether provided by a fixed choke barrel or by interchangeable choke tubes.

Think about the majority of ruffed grouse, woodcock and bobwhites you've shot. At what ranges were they really taken? Really? We have a bad habit of remembering the few fantastic long shots we make and forgetting the more common, close ones we miss.

Cylinder, Skeet, Improved Cylinder and Modified are the upland bird hunter's chokes.

3) The best upland birdguns can be carried all day. That may mean they are "light"; it doesn't mean they are ill-balanced. And remember, a 20-year-old hunter's estimation of light can be a lot different than that of a 50-year-old hunter.

4) Every time you pick up your birdgun, it should feel like an extension of your body. It should point as easily as you point your index finger. And at least twice in its owner's hunting career, the upland birdgun of a lifetime should shoot more like a magic wand than a combination of wood and steel.

To some upland bird hunters, all of that is embodied in a single gun—a tool for hunting. For others it is a cabinet full of guns meant for show as well as go. Whichever it is for you, enjoy it. That's what bird hunting is all about anyway.

3

Loads For
The Upland Hunter

L ife must have been much simpler for the upland bird hunter whose wardrobe consisted of a single loincloth and whose hunting arsenal was whatever tree limb or bone he could fashion into a club.

Simply pick up a stick, heft it to check its balance, swing it a couple of times to get used to the feel, then set off for a day's hunt.

It does make one wonder, though, if the caveman bird hunter saved those clubs from hunt to hunt. Did he build a rack to display them on the cave wall? Did he keep them well polished and look longingly at them when bad weather prevented him from hunting? Did he get disbelieving stares from his non-hunting spouse when she posed rapid-fire questions, "Why in the world do you need all those clubs?!? You can only use one at a time anyway, right? Hmmm? Am I right?"

Well, maybe cave-dwelling bird hunters didn't have it so good anyway.

Today's hunter is indeed fortunate. He has available to him the widest and finest array of hunting tools in the history of mankind. That certainly goes for shotguns, and even more so for the shells that go in them.

Whether you prefer to do all your upland bird hunting with just one or two shotguns or the golf bag approach, you can buy or build ammunition that will tailor your shotgun to best fit any specific hunting situation.

The Modern Shotshell

There is an unavoidable similarity in shotshells on the American market today. Perhaps that is simply because we have come so far and there is little room for improvement.

No matter whose brand name is going on a line of shotshells, the manufacturer has to offer a product that a large number of consumers will find useful. For example, if very few people are shooting 16 gauge guns, then there is no sense in putting a lot of research and development money into new 16 gauge loads.

Likewise, safety and liability are major concerns. Shells must follow the standards of gauge and length to be marketable. If a manufacturer were to offer something odd or unusual, you can bet your bottom dollar that some guy out there won't read the package warning and will end up in the emergency room with the doctor picking shot out of various parts of his anatomy. Even under the debilitating effects of anesthesia he would be plotting his lawsuit!

All modern shotshells are built from five basic components: the shell case, the primer, powder, the wad or shotcup and shot.

The Shell Case. When you buy shotgun shells, the shell case is what you see. Today, it is almost always plastic with what appears to be a brass head. Most often now the head is really steel plated with brass. Some, notably the Activ brand, are externally all plastic with no metal showing.

Over the years, some standardization has come into existence. On most currently manufactured brands available in the United States, 20 gauge shotshells are yellow and 16 gauge shells are purple. This is an important safety measure to reduce the chance of slipping one of these smaller shells into a 12 gauge gun. The results are potentially life-threatening!

Shells for 12 gauge guns still come in a variety of colors, and it is doubtful this will change. Each manufacturer has a traditional color to which they cling. Remington wouldn't be Remington without green shells, Federal has its rich wine color and Winchester 12 gauge hulls are the familiar AA red. Activ is a relatively new manufacturer on the scene and isn't known for a particular color. Some of their 12 gauge hulls are red, some are tan.

Color of the hull certainly doesn't effect the performance of the shell, but it is imperative that you know what you are putting in your gun! Color-coding helps, but don't rely on it! Shells for 28 gauge and .410 shotguns are often the same color and could easily be mixed up! Shell cases are never color-coded for length, and though chances of an accident resulting from this are slim, we're all much better safe than sorry! *Know what shells you are putting in your shotgun!*

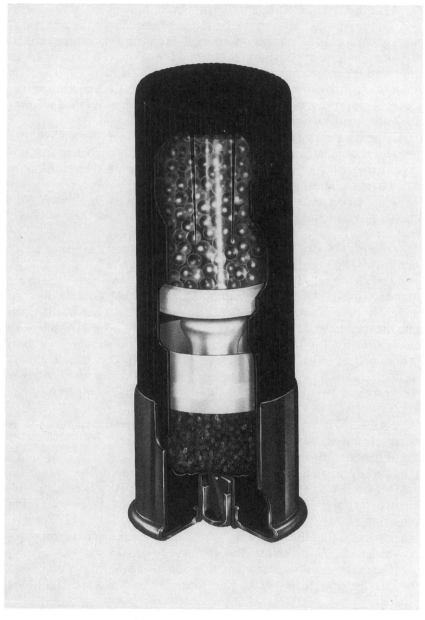

Though the "look" of shotshells from various manufacturers is different, the basic components of the modern shotshell perform the same function no matter whose label is on the headstamp.

Traditional plastic shotshells are produced through one of two methods. Thinner-walled, less expensive, but less reloadable hulls are created through a process called "poly-forming." Poly-formed shell cases usually consist of three parts: a strengthened plastic tube, a fiber or paper base wad and the metal head. This is the type of case most often seen on the less expensive promotional loads distributed by the major manufacturers. This process is also known as the Reifenhauser method of shotshell case manufacturing.

A process called "compression-forming" is more expensive, but produces hulls that have thicker case walls and last through many reloadings. In these shells, the case is all one piece and the metal head is simply fitted over the already closed end of the shell tube.

The pioneer and most famous compression-formed hull is the Winchester AA, but today Remington and Federal also have their own versions.

Often this type of hull is reserved to a manufacturer's target line and/ or top-shelf hunting loads.

Activ shotshells feature the only "all-plastic" case readily available to today's North American upland bird hunter. Though outwardly they appear to have no-metal construction, a piece of steel mesh is molded into the shell head. This is not only to strengthen the head to handle with ease extraction from the most brutal action, but to maintain a uniform primer pocket for subsequent reloadings. Though other manufacturers have tried to make a go of "all-plastic" shotshells in years past, Activ is the first to really have gotten a foothold in this highly competitive market.

Primers. The primer in a shotshell is like the ignition in your car. It is what sets the whole act in motion.

When the firing pin in your shotgun, the equivalent of your auto's ignition key, hits the primer, it causes a small explosion. The mixture inside the primer is the only component of a shotshell that is an actual explosive. It is detonated by the force of the primer cup, which your firing pin dents, striking a pointed anvil inside the primer. The outside case of the primer is called the battery cup and gives its name to the type of primer which is used in all shotshells—the battery cup primer.

The sparks resulting from the explosion inside the primer move into the shell through the flash hole. They immediately contact and ignite the powder.

Read that carefully. Primers explode. Smokeless powder burns. Primers contain explosives. Smokeless powder is highly combustible in a tightly contained area.

Co-author Miller on a Winchester factory tour examines a handful of AA hulls in the early stages of the compression forming process.

Modern primers are reliable even after the abuse they take bouncing around in a hunting jacket pocket for a couple of seasons.

Powder. In dealing with factory loads, you really have little to say about what powder is inside the shotshells you are buying. It is formulated by the manufacturer in huge quantities to provide consistent performance in a certain load.

On the outside of factory-loaded shotshells you will find an indication of the shells power, but it is given via an antiquated system most modern hunters will agree has outlived its usefulness—the dram equivalent.

The dram is a measurement for blackpowder. In charging a muzzle-loading shotgun of old or a blackpowder shotgun shell you would have said, "I'm pouring in three drams of powder," just as today's handloader can tell you how many grains of a particular powder he uses in a load.

Dram equivalent is a comparison of the velocity of a modern smokeless powder load to an old blackpowder load. For example, if you have a box of hunting loads that say $3^3/_4$ dram equivalent, it means that the shells in this box will generate the same velocity and "punch" that an old blackpowder load with $3^3/_4$ drams of powder would have.

(Warning! Never load firearms meant for smokeless powder with blackpowder loads and never load firearms meant for blackpowder with smokeless powder!)

The modern hunter should be thinking of velocity in the terms of feet per second coupled with the amount and size of shot in a particular load. This combination most accurately tells him whether or not he'll receive killing performance on the species of bird he is after.

The handloader has a myriad of powders from which to choose. Each is designed specifically for a velocity range and particular type of load. The best way to make the proper selection is through consulting several up-to-date shotshell loading manuals.

Wads. The modern shotshell wad is a difficult thing to describe because it comes in so many shapes and performs so many important functions in the load.

What can be said is that, across the spectrum of brands, the modern wad is plastic. In years past it might have been felt, cardboard or some other experimental fibrous material.

In seasons gone by, the fiber-type wad was nothing more than a disc that separated the shot from the powder. Its main purpose was to act as a seal to build pressures as the powder ignited and the gases were looking for room to expand. An "over shot wad" or "over shot card" was used in lieu of a crimp to hold the shot in the shell.

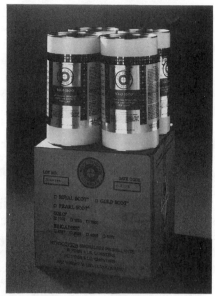

Even today, advances in smokeless powder are made each year. For example, American handloaders now have access to nitrocotton powders from the Scot Powder Company.

The modern wad still acts as a seal, but its other functions are even more important in producing consistent, efficient patterns.

The modern wad can also rightly be called a "shotcup" because it actually is a cylinder in which the shot sits in the shell and in which it travels down the barrel of a shotgun. This protects the shot from deformation which occurred in loads of old when the pellets scrubbed directly against the barrel. Having a layer of plastic between the pellets and the barrel wall also reduces "leading" which was quite frequent with the old loads. Today, the buildup of lead on shotgun barrel walls has been replaced by a coating of plastic, but with proper solvents the plastic is much easier and less messy to remove, and it doesn't need to be removed nearly as frequently.

The modern plastic wad not only reduces pellet deformation caused by the shot charge moving down the barrel, but wad bases are designed to dampen the shock of the hot gases impacting the rear of the shot column. The base still acts as a seal to hold back gas and increase pressure, but the suddenness, the jarring of the impact is reduced. This helps prevent the pellets from compacting together and deforming their perfectly spherical shapes.

The plastic cylinder in which the shot travels down the barrel is slitted lengthwise in several places. As the wad exits the barrel, the walls of the shot cup peel back like the petals on a flower. This allows the shot pattern to open up and travel unimpeded downrange. The more length-wise slits in the plastic wall, the faster the pattern is allowed to spread when it leaves the muzzle.

You'll often see this shotshell component fall to the ground a short way downrange, especially if the wad is a dark, solid color. Examination of a spent wad and comparison to a new wad will give you a better idea of its purpose and how it works.

Some loads, particularly heavier hunting loads, are not loaded with what you would consider a "wad" by these parameters. In these loads a separate plastic disc is inserted into the hull over the powder. A flat piece of plastic is then formed into a cylinder and inserted into the shell. This protects the shot from the barrel walls while traveling to the muzzle.

In some specialized handloads, other components are added to shot-shells to achieve specific results. For example, to load shells of a particu-lar gauge with a reduced shot charge, it is necessary to drop old-fashioned fiber wads into the bottom of the shot cup or place them on top of the shot to take up excess space. Using these "filler wads" or "filler cards" is the only way to get a proper crimp on these reduced payload handloads.

To create shotshell loads which spread shot more rapidly upon exit-ing the barrel, "spreaders" or "spreader wads" are sometimes used by handloaders. The line of components from Pattern Control Shotshell Wads offers an $1 1/_8$-ounce wad with a plastic post formed into the center of the shotcup to achieve this rapid spread. Ballistic Products, Incor-porated's line features X-shaped cardboard spreaders which hand-loaders set vertically in the shot cup to achieve rapid spread. Such altera-tions can make a tightly choked barrel shoot more open patterns for different hunting applications.

Only experienced handloaders should undertake such specialized projects, and then only after consulting reliable handloading resource materials provided by the component manufacturers!

Shot. Because of the important role each component in the modern shotshell plays, it is difficult to designate one as the most important. Truly, if one fails, the whole system will fail. However, because it is the one variable over which the sportsman buying factory loads has the most control, shot could be considered the most crucial component. Likewise it is the shot which makes contact with the target and ultimately collects the bird. That fact alone makes an understanding of this component vi-tally important for the upland bird hunter.

All shot is not created equal. Boy, is that an understatement!?! Not only are there a wide variety of shot sizes and payloads available to the upland bird hunter, but quality varies from brand to brand and load to

Careful monitoring and upkeep of equipment is crucial to the production of quality shells at the Winchester shotshell plant in East Alton, Illinois. Huge batches are the reason ammo makers can create such consistent loads.

load. Today, there is a selection of coatings available, too. To choose the proper load for each hunting situation, the hunter must understand what shot should do, and how it does it.

As we've seen, the most important attribute of a good hunting shotshell load is consistency. Shot has the greatest influence on that consistency. Specifically, hardness of the shot is of the most importance. The harder the shot, the greater its resistance to deformation as it travels down the barrel of the gun. The rounder the shot is when it leaves the muzzle, the more aerodynamically stable it is as it travels toward the target. This stability begets consistent, albeit tighter, patterns.

The previous chapter discussed proper control of pattern density through barrel constriction, so let's concentrate on pattern consistency.

Recall, the hypothetical ultimate pattern—eight pellets all striking pre-determined kill-points of a flying upland bird. All eight pellets arrive on target at precisely the same instant—in other words, they are all travelling in a two dimensional plane (the pattern as height and width, but is only as deep as the diameter of the pellets).

To theoretically achieve this feat, each time the gun was fired, the pellets would have to leave the barrel with absolute consistency meaning absolute aerodynamic stability. Not possible in the real world.

However, also recall the next best thing—a pattern through which a target could not fly without colliding with several pellets. A perfectly spaced, perfectly efficient pattern. Again this is not achievable in the real world, but the harder the shot, within reasonable limits, the closer we can come to achieving this ultimate pattern.

Hard shot lends itself to more efficient patterns in two ways. First, each pellet which remains aerodynamically stable will more readily assume a more consistent position in the spread or width of the pattern. Secondly, flattened or otherwise deformed pellets slow down more quickly and fall away from the rest of the pattern. This lengthens the shotstring and creates those three-dimensional openings in a pattern that birds somehow have a habit of finding. Hard shot shrinks the size of those holes.

Three basic types of lead shot are available to the upland bird hunter. The least expensive factory hunting loads contain a grade simply called "hard" shot, meaning it contains more than one half of a percent antimony. (Antimony is the metalloid used to make lead shot hard.) Reloaders will recognize its common name, "chilled" shot. Actual antimony content is controlled by the manufacturer to gain specific hardness appropriate to the use for which a batch of shot is intended.

The next level of shot is extra-hard shot. This grade usually contains six to seven percent antimony and is loaded in top of the line target loads and field loads. Its consistent and tight patterns best meet the extreme demands of competitive shooters. To reloaders it's available as "magnum" shot.

Coated or plated shot is extra-hard lead shot electroplated with nickel or copper to offer the greatest resistance to deformation. It provides the most consistent patterns to the greatest ranges and is preferred by the most demanding competitive clay target shooters—those competing in International Trap. Plated shot also offers some distinct advantages to the upland bird hunter. On thick-skinned, long range targets like late-season pheasants or prairie grouse, you can't beat coated shot loads.

On tough, feathered targets, plated shot offers better penetration. Because it remains more aerodynamically stable it retains velocity further down range, therefore it retains more energy or "knock-down" power.

Plated shot also offers another advantage over plain lead on all upland species. Because of the smoothness and slipperiness of the plated surface, this shot doesn't ball up feathers around individual pellets and push them into the bird. Shot travels faster and more unimpeded to the

When hunting in Mexico you'll be required to use ammunition manufactured and purchased there. The brands and boxes may look familiar, but quality is inferior to American-made ammo.

vitals. Kills are cleaner, and cleaning the birds becomes less of a chore, because you don't have to dig out globs of feathers from the meat. More meat is preserved, too.

As you move up the grades of shot, the prices go the same direction. The main reason premium hunting loads cost more than promotional loads is the higher grade of shot they contain. A few trips to the patterning range will quickly convince a hunter that for the number of shells he shoots at upland birds in a given season, the increase in price is well worth the better results.

Choosing The Proper Shot Size

Imagine that you are a captured spy and that you've been given a choice of your torture. You can have a single 50-pound anvil dropped on your body, or you can have five 10-pound anvils dropped to hit various parts of your body simultaneously. In either case the weights will be dropped from one altitude. What's your choice?

In making your decision you have to figure that if the 50-pound anvil hits your head or chest, your vitals, the force of that great weight is probably going to kill you. But you also realize it is only a single anvil. It may just graze your arm or leg and cause very little damage at all.

On the other hand, if all those 10-pound anvils hit you simultaneously, there is a pretty good chance that at least one will make contact with a vital. The question is will it have enough energy built up to cause fatal damage?

Well, that kind of cloak-and-dagger decision is one that few upland bird hunters will ever have to make. But in effect, every time we select a shotshell for a bird hunting foray we are making that same decision about the effect of the shot on the birds.

In any given shotshell payload, there is a finite volume. That finite volume will contain fewer pellets of large diameter than it will pellets of smaller diameters. Naturally, individual pellets of a larger diameter will weigh more than individual pellets of a smaller diameter made of the same material. Call these the laws of shotshell nature, but add some more.

The payload from a specific shotshell load will start on its way at the same speed regardless of the size of the pellets comprising the payload. However, beyond the muzzle lighter (read smaller) pellets slow down faster than heavier (read larger) pellets. Loss of velocity also means loss of energy or "knock down" power.

Another analogy in handyman's hardware terms might ask which hurts more? Getting your thumb in the way of a 16-ounce claw hammer travelling at full-swing, spike driving speed or the same hammer travelling at carpet-tack-tapping speed?

So this is the trade-off that must be considered. Will surer, cleaner kills result from harder hits by fewer pellets or by a greater number of hits each transferring a smaller amount of energy? The answer is—it all depends.

It depends on the "toughness" of the upland bird you are hunting— both its physical characteristics and its tenacity. Pheasants, for example can be very "tough" birds in both ways. They have lots of feathers, they can be relatively large, and that long tail often tempts the hunter to center his pattern too far back. Pheasants are prone to ignore being wounded, they seem to either hit the ground dead or running, and they are masters at camouflage despite their gaudy plumage. Woodcock on the other hand are not usually "tough." They are thin-skinned and lightly feathered. When hit, they fall to the ground and seldom move whether they are dead or alive. When only winged, instead of running and hiding themselves, they'll jump straight up and down in one spot helping you to find them.

It depends on the ranges at which most birds will be shot on a particular hunt. Of course this will vary from shot to shot, but look at the average of what you're expecting for the hunt. Even the type of dog you are hunting over can change the ranges at which shots will be taken. Pointing dogs usually offer closer flushes with the hunters prepared for birds to fly. Birds generally flush a bit farther ahead of flushing breeds and the shots can't always be anticipated as readily.

It depends on the situation in which shots will be taken. For example, will most of the shots be taken at birds travelling away such as in quail hunting over pointing dogs, or will this be a driven bird hunt in which case most birds will be taken with incoming shots? Some situations like dove hunting around crop fields will offer an equal number of both.

In general, the belief is bigger birds, longer range birds and birds taken while moving away from the gun require the larger shot sizes. Smaller birds, at closer ranges coming toward the gun are best taken with smaller shot sizes. Generally.

North American upland bird hunters really need only concern themselves with shot sizes 5, 6, 7 1/2, 8, 8 1/2 and 9. It's too bad that number 7 shot, an extremely versatile and useful size can't be added to that list, but at the time of this publication, it is not commercially available to the hunter in factory loads or as a readily available reloading component. The charts in this chapter provided by ammunition manufacturers can help narrow down the choices.

Referring back to that ultimate pattern that would put two pellets in each of the bird's vitals, the question of shot-size selection becomes a little clearer. Always use the smallest size of shot that will provide sufficient energy to ground the bird. The smaller shot offers more opportunities per load to achieve those "perfect hits."

Factory Loads

The rifleman is in a situation different from that of the shotgunner. To achieve maximum performance from his hunting tool, he must turn to his workbench and his handloading tools. Even in this day and age when ammunition manufacturers are turning out "premium" and "supreme" loads which are actually top quality handloading components assembled at the factory and come close to duplicating handload accuracy, the handloader can still eke out a fraction of an inch better accuracy. He can search the bullet charts and powder catalogs to customize his rounds for his very specific purpose for his specific rifle.

Fortunately, or unfortunately depending on your viewpoint, most of the upland bird hunter's best loads are coming right out of the factory gates of Olin, DuPont, Federal and Activ. Fortunate, because these superior quality shells are easy to obtain for anyone who wants to use them. Unfortunate, because without reloading ammunition, the shotgunner loses the benefit of familiarity with what goes into a good shotgun shell, and ultimately with the performance of his gun.

Compared to the rifleman who can probably recite verbatim the velocity and energy of his pet round from muzzle to infinity, few shotgunners have even an inclination of the muzzle velocity of their hunting loads, much less what effect that has down range.

Honestly, you could probably hunt successfully for years without that knowledge *if* you conscientiously stock the shelves of your ammo closet season after season with the best ammunition the factories are turning out.

Repeat, *the best* ammunition the factories are turning out! That does not mean the cheapest!

Inexpensive factory loads will kill upland birds, they do every season. But these so-called "promotional" loads will not give you the most consistent performance from your shotgun nor grant you the greatest confidence in your abilities. These less expensive shells are often called "dove and quail," "duck and pheasant" or "rabbit and squirrel" loads. Sometimes they are given a completely different brand name and sold at a bargain basement price.

There are reasons why these shells cost less. One is usually the shell case. On promotional loads these are often made of less expensive mate-

Load And Shot Size Options For Upland Birds

Species	Amount of Shot (oz.)	Shot Sizes
Pheasants	1, 1-1/8, 1-1/4, 1-1/2	4, 5, 6, 7-1/2
Bobwhite Quail	7/8, 1, 1-1/8	7-1/2, 8, 9
Western Quail	1, 1-1/8, 1-1/4	6, 7-1/2
Doves	7/8, 1, 1-1/8	8, 9
Ruffed Grouse	7/8, 1, 1-1/8	7-1/2, 8, 9
Hungarian Partridge	1, 1-1/8, 1-1/4	6, 7-1/2
Chukar Partridge	1-1/8, 1-1/4	6, 7-1/2
Prairie & Mountain Grouse	1-1/8, 1-1/4	5, 6, 7-1/2
Woodcock	7/8, 1, 1-1/8	8, 9

rials and through less expensive methods. This reduces reloadability of the hull—often not a factor in choosing hunting shells.

The second difference is that promotional loads usually carry a payload of less expensive, low antimony shot. The higher the percentage of antimony in lead shot, the harder it is. Low antimony shot is softer and deforms more easily under the forces of being launched from a shotgun barrel.

This is important to the bird hunter. Deformed pellets fly erratically. This can create holes in a pattern—holes which at best a bird could fly through unscathed; holes which at worst could reduce the number of hits on a bird and leave it wounded in the field.

The wingshooter can't even count on promotional loads of the same brand to be consistently loaded with the same components. For example, if a manufacturer has an overrun of a particular type of powder that can't be used up any other way, they might concoct a promotional load to use it up. Rest assured that before it leaves the factory the load will be proven safe for the weakest of shotguns, but it may end up in the same "dove and quail" box that contained a different load recipe on the last lot run.

You don't need to play guessing games on an upland bird hunting trip you've been waiting for all year. Don't settle for promotional loads for hunting. If you can't buy anything else at your usual source for shells, look elsewhere and tell your regular supplier he should start stocking premium grade shotgun ammunition.

If you insist on saving a few dollars, do it when you go target shooting. If your shells cause misses or marginal hits on clay targets, nothing is hurt except your pride.

Target Loads From The Factory

Some of the very best shotgun shells available to the bird hunter today are factory target loads. It's easy to understand why.

Target shooters from weekend pop can flingers to All-American Trap & Skeet shooters comprise the fastest growing segment of the shotshell market. Mike Jordan at Olin/Winchester says that a large and growing portion of the company's total shotshell output is devoted to top quality, target oriented loads. From any manufacturer's standpoint, it is a must that the shooting public consider his target loads the best.

To present that image, ammunition manufacturers want top-notch competitors winning major shoots with shells carrying their logo. This kind of winning publicity sells shells to would-be greats whose heroes win with a particular brand of shell.

Now winning over a top-gun-type shooter to your brand of shell is a difficult assignment. Clay target shooters who are really serious about

Watching boxes of target loads come off the loading line at the Winchester factory is awe-inspiring to the handloader. Manufacturers place a great deal of importance in the quality and consistency of their target loads.

their game have spent long hours at the patterning board finding out whose factory load (required in major competitions) produces the most efficient and consistent pattern in their competition guns. They've tested velocities, various choke/shell combinations and anything else they can think of. At this level of competition, where breaking hundreds straight is the norm, every miss is viewed with great suspicion. Because these super-shots hit so much more often than they miss, there is every reason for them to honestly believe that a miss could be the result of an inconsistent shell.

To win over the winners, ammo makers need to supply them with shells that incorporate the very best design and components. That means hard shot, consistent patterns and consistent velocities. And all of those are exactly what hunters need in good hunting shells.

Target loads from the pip-squeak $1/2$ ounce payload of the $2^1/_2$-inch .410 through the heaviest 3 dram 12 gauge $1^1/_8$ ounce trap loads offer much of what is needed for North American upland bird hunting. Shot sizes for factory target loads are exclusively numbers $7^1/_2$, 8 and 9. These are the best shells available for birds like quail, dove, ruffed grouse, woodcock and even pheasants under some conditions.

Top-Shelf Hunting Loads From The Factory

For those special birds and hunting conditions that require greater oompf than target loads provide, the factories are turning out some equally fine heavier loads. These include Federal's Premium line, Winchesters Double X loads and Remington's Express and Premier shells. All of these are available in the other shot sizes which upland hunters need from time to time, like numbers 4, 5, 6.

Many of these loads are buffered. This means that granulated plastic is mixed with the shot to further reduce deformation. Also to reduce deformation, the shot in premium shells is often coated with nickel or copper.

Another unexpected shotgunning sport from which the upland bird hunter has gained some good loads is turkey hunting.

Technically, the wild turkey is most certainly an upland bird, but it is not ethically shot on the wing, making it beyond the scope of this book.

For the most demanding long-range, tenacious bird situations, turkey loads like the three-inch 12 gauge carrying $1^3/_4$-ounce of number 6 shot or even 2-ounce of numbers 4 or 5 have a bona fide, albeit limited, application in the upland fields. Because of the sky-rocketing number of turkeys and turkey hunters, a great deal of research has gone into developing better loads for shooting these tough-to-keep-down birds. The result is some very high-tech loads giving exquisitely dense and powerful

Hunters can learn a valuable lesson from the demanding standards of competitive shooters. Demand the best shells for your hunting applications. For hunters, sporting clays are shedding a lot of light on the benefits of top-quality shotshells.

patterns to maximum ranges. The late-season, public land pheasant hunter and the stalker of tough birds like the sage hen have been a beneficiary of these advances.

Handloading Hunting Shotshells

All of this is not to say you can not or should not handload shells for hunting upland birds. You can most certainly get satisfactory results and a special satisfaction from hunting upland birds with shotshells you've built yourself.

Unless you shoot a lot of hunting loads in a year, you won't notice a considerable savings by loading your own. A 25-pound bag of shot yields 400 one-ounce loads. A one-pound canister of powder could be enough for 250 shells depending on the load. It may take several seasons for the average hunter to get back the money that he put into buying those components.

But for some hunters there is a savings. Dove hunters in particular are known to expend a lot of shells for each bird brought to bag. For them, handloading might be an economical boon if they hunt often. You can also save some money on hunting loads if you get together with some friends to split the cost of the bulk components. The only difficulty is getting a group to all settle on one load!

The biggest reason the hunter should be a handloader is not to save money on shells expended in the field, but to make regular target practice easier on the budget. The most important aspect to improving percentages in the field is practice on clay targets. The more you shoot, the better you'll be at it. Of course there is a limit to the physical talent and mental concentration each of us possess, but we won't even come close to straining that upper end by getting out to shoot once a week.

Handloading puts that frequency of practice within reach of more pocketbooks. Dick Placzek of Hornady says, "If you're an avid trap or skeet shooter, or a devoted bird hunter, it's easy to turn out low cost reloads in a hurry. And you'll save big bucks over factory ammo! Reloading gives you an immediate return on your investment. Comparisons from year to year show a *steady* savings between 30 and 50 per box!"

Here's what Hornady found in a recent price check for a 12 gauge $2^3/_4$-inch box of $1^1/_8$ ounce loads:

Retail price per box $5.75
Cost of components to reload one box $2.50
Savings per box $3.25

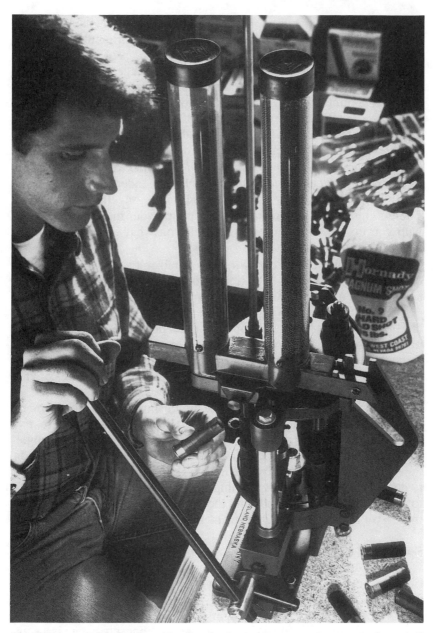

Handloaders can produce good hunting loads, too. Just remember, to equal top-shell factory loads, you need to do your homework.

That's a 57% savings on just one box of shells! Imagine if you make the time to shoot just one box of shells per week during the summer to keep your shooting skills in shape. On a dozen boxes of shells, you save $40.00. That almost pays for one of the less-expensive single-stage reloaders and a couple of shot and powder bushings!

For the hunter who decides to take advantage of the benefits hand-loading has to offer, there are a number of ways to dive into it. The simplest, least expensive and therefore probably the best way is to purchase a single-stage shotshell reloader and a good book on shotshell reloading. One really good one is *The Handbook of Shotshell Reloading* authored by Kenneth W. Couger and edited by Richard Henderson. It's published by SKR Industries, Inc., 233 W. Twohig, San Angelo, Texas 76902. These items, along with manuals from the powder manufacturers, will help you decide on loads to try and tell you what components you'll need.

Study your manuals carefully! Shotshell reloading is not compli-cated, it simply requires attention to details. With some reading and some care you'll soon be rolling your own like a pro.

Only if you are into frequent target shooting or reloading for a siz-able group of hunters should you consider a progressive reloader. They no doubt offer the advantage of speed to the shooter who is going through many rounds of a specific load, but they are slow and more com-plicated to switch from load to load. Single-stage presses can be conven-iently converted from recipe to recipe as you wish.

That's why on the workbenches of target shooters who do a good bit of hunting, you'll often see two shotshell presses. The progressive pumps out round after round of their favorite target load and the single-stage does the short run work of giving them tailor-made hunting rounds.

When it comes to quality, the most a shotshell handloader can hope to do is match the best that is coming from factory production lines. The top-end factory target rounds and the premium field loads are so good, there isn't much room for improvement.

Specialty Loads

The shotshell handloader can do one thing for himself that the facto-ries won't do. That is produce specialty loads tailored to specific hunting situations.

One of the most renowned experts in this area is Dave Fackler who operates "Ballistics Products" in Long Lake, Minnesota. Dave is a shot-shell reloading fanatic from the word go and his company has developed reloading recipes hunters can use to build loads for all kinds hunting situ-ations. You want a round for hunting in below zero weather; they've got

Orvis' specialty loads feature flattened shot to give faster spread to the pattern.

it. You want a load that will make your full choke shoot more like a improved cylinder; they've got it.

Ballistic Products has a reloading guide called *Advantages* and catalogs that offer specialized components and tested recipes for all kinds of shotshell reloading.

Notably, two highly specialized factory loads are available via importers. The first are 2¹/₂-inch shells from Lyalvale. These shells are loaded to operate in any gun with 2 ¹/₂-inch or longer chambers. This is a boon to wingshooters who dote on European shotguns made before World War II. And all shotgunners could do a lot worse than to take advantage of the light-kicking, hard-hitting attributes of these fine shells.

The second specialty load is currently available from Orvis. It takes the spreader load idea to a new realm for the early-season grouse and woodcock hunter who knows that shots have to be quick and wide or not at all.

Simply called the "Spreader Load," Orvis's new load uses flat, disk-shaped shot instead of conventional round pellets. The non-aerodynamic flat pellets widens the pattern of any shotgun, giving up to twice the pattern diameter of conventional shot at normal hunting ranges. Its purpose is for single flushing birds at ranges of 10 to 25 yards. The pattern spreads so quickly that these shells are not recommended for shooting covey birds if killing more than one bird per shot could put you over your limit.

Compared even to premium conventional shotshells, factory-loaded specialty ammunition is expensive, but as always it is a case of getting what you pay for.

Handloading's Greatest Benefit For The Hunter

Finally, another important benefit of handloading is that it teaches the hunter what goes into a good hunting shotshell. By becoming familiar with each component and each stage in the loading process, you come to better understand how a shotshell really works and why some work better than others. You understand what a wad is meant to do and why. You develop a visual concept of how many more pellets are in a one-ounce load of number 8s than a one ounce load of number 6s. You learn how different primers effect chamber pressure. All of this and more becomes second nature.

And you can't help but become a better hunter/shooter because of it.

Steel Shot For Upland Birds

Waterfowl hunters are facing the cold fact. If they wish to continue in their sport, they must make the switch to steel shot. As of 1991, that is the law of the land—everywhere in the United States.

Upland bird hunters now face the same threat. Legislation has been suggested in some states that would require the use of steel shot by all waterfowl, small game and upland bird hunters on heavily hunted public hunting areas. To date, thankfully, it has always been defeated. But as the percentage of the population who understand hunting continues to decline, the storm clouds thicken on the horizon.

The day of decision is already here for some upland bird hunters. Namely, those of us who like to go afield for a mixed bag hunt. Many of us have a very difficult time denying our canine hunting companion the joy of a watery retrieve when a wood duck busts from the stream that runs through our favorite woodcock cover. It's very difficult, too, to pass

If you want to hunt a mixed bag of upland birds and waterfowl, you must use steel shot loads for all of the hunt.

up a big greenhead that jumps from a slough that is known to also hold pheasants.

But as tempting as those shots are, if we take them with lead shot, then we are breaking the law.

In fact, even if we have lead shotshells in our possession when we take those shots, we are still liable to get pinched. So much for the idea of carrying a few steel shells and loading them before dropping off a popple ridge into the creek bottom.

The only alternative for the take-'em-as-they-come hunter is to shoot steel at the upland birds as well as the waterfowl.

The first thing to consider is your shotgun. Can it handle steel shot without ill effects? Most can. Some can't.

This is particularly true of fine, old side-by-side double guns. Many times the barrels on these guns have thin walls that could be warped by the excessive use of steel shot. The best thing to do is check with the manufacturer of your gun to see what they recommend.

Assuming your gun is up to shooting steel, selecting the best load for your hunting situation is a whole new ball game. Because steel is lighter than lead it leaves the muzzle faster, but loses energy faster downrange. For waterfowl hunters whose shots often come at maximum range, this has meant increasing shot size by about two sizes to compensate for the energy loss compared to lead. This may not be as great a consideration for the take-'em-as-they-come combination hunter, because his upland shots are usually at less tenacious birds and his waterfowl shots are almost always short-range, jump-shooting opportunities.

With this in mind, the woodcock/wood duck shooter might want to try steel number 6 loads which is the smallest size shot in which steel is available. The higher velocity of steel shot means it reaches its target faster, and this has actually made it the preferred load of some upland bird hunters. Chuck Barry, president of Texas Waterfowl Products, is one convert.

A few years back, Chuck decided to shoot steel number 6 loads while dove hunting to tune up for the upcoming waterfowl seasons. Instead of having to develop a new "feel" for the steel loads, Chuck says his percentage on doves went up immediately! The reason being that on birds in good range, he actually had to lead less with steel than with lead. Pellets arriving on target faster also gave the doves less time to go into some fancy unanticipated maneuvers.

The pheasant/mallard shooter should probably stick with a load shooting number 4 steel, which gives similar down range performance to number 6 lead—a widely accepted shot size for close-range gunning on both these species.

In the meantime, it is important upland bird hunters do everything they can to fend off the under-informed, would-be good-doers who believe steel shot should be required for all upland bird hunting.

4

Clothing And Accessories
For Modern Bird Hunters

When I was growing up, the story used to circulate each hunting season about how my father, as a young man, moved out of the house after an argument with his mother over the practicality of specialty hunting clothes. It seems my grandmother, a frugal woman who raised eight kids through the Depression and a world war, didn't think much of spending hard earned money on clothes that could be worn only a few months each year.

The choice between looking dapper in the cornfield and giving up a free meal every night must have caused my father a bit of serious thinking. But evidently it wasn't too tough a decision, as 35 years later his hunting pals can still recall Dad walking around his empty new apartment checking out the water pressure and closet space, all the time dressed head to toe in new cotton duck. He was complete, with a Jones style cap, double-faced pants bloused out of shiny Red Wing sport boots and shell loops stretched tight with a full box of the latest high brass. It wouldn't have been such a sight had the outside temperature not been 90 degrees and the nearest bird season more than three months away.

The fact that my father's original Red Head coat and pants still occupy a nail in his basement is proof of the endurance found in quality hunting clothes. Back then, even though most items were well-made, there wasn't much variety. Everything was traditional hunter's brown.

Brush facing on pants was a double layer of the same material, or a stiff leather at best. Coats were heavy and cumbersome, boots needed constant maintenance to keep them even semi-waterproof. Gun manufacturers had yet to put their names on clothing lines and about the only place to shop was at the corner sporting goods store.

Today, hunting clothing has evolved more than the guns, the vehicles, the seasons, even the habitat. Colors are in, as are specialty fibers, space age plastics and high-tech laminates. Department stores carry racks of clothes and several former good ol' boys have become millionaires selling hunting togs through mail order houses. Contemporary variations of all the originals are endless, but the guidelines for the basics remain unchanged.

Footwear

A bird hunter can have a pretty good outing without a vest, brush pants or a hat, but a good pair of boots are essential. Nothing can ruin an otherwise great day like a pair of sore, blistered feet. An average eight-hour hunting day might see 10 to 15 miles pass underfoot. Depending on the terrain, that's plenty of walking to inflict some podiatric damage.

A pair of upland boots should be as light as practical while still being durable enough to provide adequate support without falling apart. Uppers should provide protection for the foot, and support for the ankles. The soles, regardless of material, should be thick enough to protect the bottom of the feet from jagged rocks and stone bruises. All hunting boots should have a heel. Heels dig in when coming downhill and keep a hunter from sliding.

Personal preference for upland hunting leans toward the moccasin-toe style boots that have been around for years. In the corner of my gun room are three pairs made by the W.C. Russell Moccasin Company in Berlin, Wisconsin. All were handmade to specific foot tracings and measurements at a price comparative to off-the-shelve models. These boots are comfortable, supportive and as waterproof as leather can be. If I'm going to be hunting in snow or extremely wet conditions I wear a pair of round-toe, Gore-Tex lined, big game style boots that lace all the way to the toe.

Boots that lace with eyelets up to the top are preferable over hooks as hooks have a tendency to bend or break and are always catching on brush or undergrowth. I prefer a crepe rubber type sole over the vibram lug style for most upland hunting as lug style soles have a bad habit of collecting mud.

Nothing can ruin an otherwise great day like a pair of sore, blistered feet. Upland boots should be as light as possible, yet provide support for the ankle and protection for the foot and sole. Most upland boots sport a rubber bottom and leather top (left), or a leather/cordura outside and Gore-tex liner inside (right).

Many of my shooting pals insist on shoe pac type boots with rubber bottoms and leather tops. This boot, while normally not as comfortable as an all leather boot, is super for wet conditions.

I'm not much for insulated boots because my feet have a tendency to heat up naturally. I don't need the help! But for hunters out in below freezing weather most of the time, insulated boots work well.

Leather boots will last many seasons when properly cared for and treated. Weather and water strip the leather of its original oils. Wet leather should be dried at room temperature. Heat burns leather fibers causing it to become brittle and break down, leaving the hunter with a pair of worn out boots. After the boots are dry, oil them with a quality leather dressing. Silicone treated boots should be retreated with a silicone spray or silicone polish.

Vests And Coats

After footwear, the most essential piece of bird hunting attire is a vest. A good vest consists of three basic elements. A game bag, shell loops and a mounting pad for the shotgun stock. One of the better known hunting clothes manufacturers likes to tout the saying, "A poor man can only afford to buy the very best." No time is this more true than when it comes to purchasing an upland vest.

An all-around upland vest should be constructed with a fairly sturdy, continuous fabric, crossing the shoulders with a wide strip of material. Though strap-type vests might be cooler in hot weather, I like the wide shoulder vests for their better weight distribution ability. A full vest also gives you a place to mount the gun when it comes time to shoot. A typical strap outfit can interfere with gun mounting, turning an otherwise good opportunity into a miss.

The game bag should ride fairly high, above the bottom of your butt. Besides the extra fatigue involved from carrying weight too low, the low-riding, detachable-type game bags hang up on brush and bounce against your thighs all day—not a pleasant way to carry five or six pounds worth of pheasants. The game bag should have a front loading entry. When the shooting is really hot, there's nothing worse than laying down your bird in the bag and then reversing the process again.

Game bags should be fully lined with coated nylon to keep blood from soaking through into your other clothes. Front pockets should be expandable with plenty of shell loops and low enough so as not to interfere with mounting the gun.

Contrary to popular belief, most gun writers can't shoot a limit of quail with a handful of shells. Shell loops are a must for me. I can't count all the times I've worked my way back to an out-of-the-way covey only to find that, after crawling under a fence or sliding down a creek bank, I'd lost all the shells I had started out with except the four or five I had securely slipped into the loops.

The anticipation to walk the frosted fields is still the same every hunting trip, only now I take the extra five minutes and fill all my available shell loops. Other nice features in vests, though not necessities, are inside accessory pockets that snap shut for a small knife or candy bar, and a high-riding lunch pocket where sandwiches won't get crushed.

Most serious upland hunters I know prefer a full orange vest. Often, the best hunting is in the thickest cover and it's nice to know that you can be seen. One exception is the dove hunting vest. Provided state game regulations do not require blaze orange, camo or olive drab is fine, but make sure everyone is posted a safe distance apart. Many hunters immediately field dress doves and put them on ice. While lugging around a

Most upland hunters prefer a full, wide vest, complete with game bag, shell loops and mounting pad.

cooler isn't always easy, a mesh game bag allows the birds to cool down and breathe.

Coats should have the same attributes as vests with plenty of movement in the sleeves such as those with bi-swing backs and pivot sleeves, since coats are worn under colder conditions than vests. I like those with corduroy collars and cuffs. A snap on the shooting shoulder side of the collar prevents it from interfering with gun mounting. The trend the past few years seems to be toward coats with zip-out liners of various weights. These are fine for hunters who tend to get cold and can be zipped out as the day gets warmer.

I'm one of those people who heats up quickly when I walk, so on days where the temperature doesn't get much below zero, I'm quite comfortable in just a flannel shirt and hunting coat, but I realize I'm the exception. The old layering system can't be beat when it comes to upland hunting. Dress with enough on in the morning, take it off as the day or weather warrants.

For 75 percent of my hunting I get by fine with a heavy shirt and a vest, adding a cotton turtleneck underneath if needed. For a real cold day when the snow and wind is blowing, I'll take a coat with a zip-in Thinsulate liner. Thinsulate provides warmth without bulk, making it great for a hunter on the move. Down and Quallofil are warmer but the bulk makes shooting and moving more difficult.

Pants And Chaps

Upland hunters need the lightest weight pants practical. A medium weight is a good compromise as the legs aren't difficult to keep warm. Blue jeans are better saved for Saturday night and wool is best for deer camp. Bird hunting britches constructed from sturdy cotton or Hunter Twill fabric and faced with a brush resistant material are almost a necessity in wild bird situations.

Hunter Twill is quiet, soft and tear resistant, and the only material that I've been able to coax through a full season. Cordura nylon makes a tough, brush resistant facing while still allowing adequate knee movement. The other desirable feature in upland pants is plenty of belt loops. As we get older our waist tends to widen a bit, and three or four belt loops won't do the trick!

Some hunters prefer chaps over brush facing on pants. Chaps are also great on wet days because you can slip them off easily when you get back to your vehicle for a dry ride home. Early season hunting in snake country can be made more enjoyable and secure with high density Cordura snake-proof chaps. When the briars and thorns are especially plentiful, heavy leather or cowhide facing gives the best protection, but these

Serious upland hunters prefer blaze orange vests and caps. Here's why. This hunter is easily camouflaged by the thick cover between him and his partner. The only exception is when dove hunting.

pants or chaps are tough to walk in and hell when they're soaked with water.

Hats And Gloves

Line up 100 upland hunters and chances are that within the group you will find similar shotguns, coats, pants and boots. But one thing you can be reasonably sure of is that out of the 100, no two hats will be alike. This is the one area where a little expressed individuality is acceptable.

In most situations, ear flaps aren't needed. When quail or pheasant hunting, the birds are often heard before they are seen, so the less that covers the ears, the better. High-tech uplanders favor the hats that slope from the crown forward, since the streamlining helps keep the hat from getting knocked off in the brush. The hat's bill should provide protection from the sun and have a dark underside to reduce glare. Some hunters prefer a cowboy hat or English style hat for upland hunting. These types of hats are good for keeping out the rain and sun but they fall off easily in brush.

Except for camo dove hunting hats, blaze orange is the only way to go for upland hunting hats. Not only do they let your hunting buddies know where you are, blaze orange is great for marking downed birds.

Warm weather hunting demands a ventilated cap or hat that provides protection from the sun and disperses heat. A moisture absorbing sweat-band keeps perspiration from running down the face and steaming up shooting glasses. Old fashioned straw hats can't be beat for keeping cool on a hot dove shooting day.

Just as keeping the head cool is important in hot weather shooting, keeping the head warm is necessary on cold days. Hunting hats for sub-freezing temperatures can be had with Thinsulate insulation and water-proof shells for snowy days. Flaps that flip up can be used to keep the ears warm when needed, then buttoned away when not needed.

Gloves are a sore subject with many upland hunters. No matter how well they fit, there is still that sensation of something foreign between you and your favorite shotgun. Personally, I veto them for any type of bird hunting. I lose a little control over gun mounting, and sliding a top tang safety takes a little more effort. However, there are days when Mother Nature demands more than a good old fashioned blow of hot air into cupped hands.

When I have to wear them, I choose a pair of close-fitting knit gloves with leather fingers and palms. If I were a tycoon and could afford to tear up the $40 cape skin variety, I might wear them, but as it is I usually try and get by with the lightest pair around. Most serious hunters I know keep them in their pockets most of the time anyway.

Blue jeans are better saved for Saturday night and wool is best for deer camp. Bird hunting britches should be constructed of sturdy cotton or Hunter Twill, faced with a brush resistant material.

Optics

Every bird hunter can benefit from a pair of quality shooting glasses. Besides the obvious safety factors, good lenses can reduce glare and increase contrast.

Twice, I have experienced eye injuries that have put me out of commission while shooting. The first time a gust of wind blew some clay target pieces into my face from a high overhead shot. After a night in the hospital flushing out my left eye, I should have learned. The second time the bolt on a rental gun was not quite locked up and powder gas whoofed into my right eye. That little episode cost me an afternoon of Sonora dove shooting.

Now, if I'm hunting birds I'm wearing shooting glasses. In addition to broken targets and powder gas, glasses keep branches from poking and help prevent tearing on cold windy days. The one drawback is fogging. Fogging can be prevented by selecting behind the lens frames that let air circulate between the glass and the face. This frame style has been popularized by Decot Hy-Wyd Rimless glasses.

Shooting glasses should have safety lenses such as the CR-39 hard resin type. The CR-39 lenses also have better refraction characteristics than glass because plastic is more porous. Plastic lenses can be coated to make them more scratch resistant. Wrap around temple pieces of the soft cushion variety keep the glasses from sliding down the nose.

Orange and yellow lenses have been favorites of upland hunters for years and are still good choices. As a rule, light yellow or orange increases contrast and sharpens detail on hazy and overcast days. They let in plenty of light which is safe as well as desirable. Light lenses force the pupil to contract, decreasing the amount of harmful light that can enter the eye. While dark lenses may appear to cut out brighter light, they actually offer less protection for the eyes.

The other optics that I always have in the truck are a pair of binoculars. Good binoculars can save lots of unnecessary walking. This trick was taught to me by my old bird hunting pal, Don Thomsen. When we were driving from farm to farm and saw a ditch or patch of cover that looked promising, Thomsen would pull over and give it a good going over.

More often than not we would find that, after closer inspection, the ditch cover was too thin to hold birds or that cattle had trampled a promising looking patch to bare ground. Once in a while we might stumble on a pair of cock pheasants working the edge in a field that we might have otherwise passed up. Binoculars are also great for watching a visiting song bird or spying on a big whitetail buck.

Warm weather hunting demands a ventilated cap (top) that provides protection from the sun, and disperses heat. Cool weather hunting requires a sturdy cap (bottom) that provides protection from the wind, rain and snow, and holds in heat.

Upland binoculars don't have to be anything special. Just about any model that magnifies and gathers light will work. My favorite is a pair of 8 x 30s that are always in my gear bag. They have saved a lot of non-productive walking and found a few bonus birds to boot.

Cameras, Film And Other Gear

More than anything else, bird hunting is made of memories. The gun powder drifts away with the wind, last year's favorite slough ditch gets plowed under, but pictures stay around forever.

Today's compact 35mm cameras make picture taking so easy, novices become experts overnight. They slip easily into a bird vest and are ready in a snap to take pictures of a dog on point, a hunting buddy or a brace of colorful birds. Compacts range from inexpensive, fixed-focus models to lightweight, full-feature models with auto-focus, film advance and telephoto capabilities.

Most light situations can be covered with 100 ASA speed print film. The higher the ASA, the less light the film needs to work. As the ASA goes up so does the grain in the print, so keep the 500 ASA film for after dark and special effects.

When taking the traditional "grip and grin" shots of hunters with birds, light the subject from the back or side and make sure the subject's face is not shadowed by a hat.

There are many other accessories that upland hunters can benefit from. Things like coolers and gear bags should be chosen to fit the individual situation.

The best friend a hunter can have is a friendly smile and a thank you for the farmer who lets him hunt. Appreciation will get you more opportunities than the most expensive suit of hunting clothes available.

5

Dogs For
The Upland Hunter

Woodcock! NAHC Member Dan Dietrich's first exuberant exclamation, "Birds!" left no doubt that the flight birds were here as a pair of timberdoodle landed a short distance ahead. As usual, the first flush of the day was so unexpected, no one thought of shooting.

Attracted by the shout, Gunner, my 16-month-old springer, pushed into the narrow strip of spruce where Dan had jumped the first two birds. Another came towering out.

The first pair, probably older, wiser birds, had stayed low and twisted through the cover. The third bird took the traditional route of woodcock and rose vertically to treetop height before leveling out. But before he could begin a horizontal escape, he collided with a load of number 8 shot among the treetops.

The first bird of the season was down!

It was also the first real, wild, un-set-up bird of Gunner's young career. He was the first of the party to reach it, but wasn't quite sure what to do with this bird. It didn't sit still like the dead pheasants and pigeons he was used to. Instead, this morsel was jumping a foot or more in the air every time he put his nose to it! It was puffing its feathers and trying to scare him away in a woodcock-kind of way.

Gunner didn't cower, but he wasn't going to dive in and put his lips around this one either!

In a moment, the human he'd come to look on as "Old Dad" was by his side. A little encouragement got Gunner to pick up the bird and carry it the last couple of feet. Sort of a retrieve, but not really.

The next woodcock jumped just a few yards farther along the edge of the swamp. It bore low out of the spruce and straight into the alder tangles, but for one split second Dan saw a chance. He swung his Remington 870 into line and jerked the trigger. No soap. Timberdoodle disappeared.

With birds seemingly everywhere, our trio of hunters and the dog headed in the general direction that the last woodcock had taken. The hunters stretched out in a line about 20 yards apart and began a slow slog through the alders. Gunner worked between them.

Not 10 yards into the brush, Gunner picked up a dead woodcock and like a pro brought it to "Old Dad." Gunner's first legitimate retrieve! And on a bird that no one would have ever picked up without the dog!

Apparently Dan's snap shot had actually taken the bird in the opening, but a second woodcock had attracted his attention as it flew on in the same direction.

Less than an hour's hunting on a tiny parcel of land in east-central Minnesota. Just one October golden moment for three hunters. But this tiny morsel of a hunt sums up everything that makes upland bird hunting and good bird dogs as inseparable as beer and pretzels. Special moments like a first retrieve and finding birds that would otherwise become food for foxes. That is hunting with a good dog.

More Success, More Fun

It's snobbish to say, "If you don't have a dog, don't hunt birds." That's the common line of guys who say, "If I couldn't run the dog, I wouldn't go hunting." Honest? Maybe. Practical? No.

Everyone who enjoys hunting can't own a dog. Modern lifestyles and living situations just don't permit everyone this pleasure. Does that mean they shouldn't be allowed to hunt? Certainly not.

What it does mean is that the hunter who goes after birds without a dog must come to grips with several realities. First, he is at a definite disadvantage to the hunter who owns a well-bred, well-trained dog. He's not going to find as many birds.

Secondly, he must understand that lacking the company of a dog, he himself assumes all responsibility for finding wounded birds. That's a task that is difficult under the best circumstances and can potentially eat up a lot of limited hunting time.

Thirdly, he must come to grips with the most unsettling consequence of dogless hunting. He is going to lose birds. Very few dogs find them

For some hunters, upland bird hunting and good bird dogs are as inseparable as beer and pretzels. Special moments like a first point, first retrieve and finding birds that would otherwise become food for foxes add a new dimension to upland hunting.

all, but even the most incompetent of the canine clan will find more crips than the dogless Homo sapiens.

The crux is you can successfully hunt upland birds without a dog, but you'll be a better hunter, bag more birds and enjoy your hunting more with a good dog than without one.

Puppy, Thy Name Is Potential

Every time a bird hunter brings a new dog into his family, the thought of registering the new addition with the name "Potential" should cross his mind. Of course, what kind of nickname does that leave for field work? "Potty," "Tent"...no, they just don't cut it. Maybe "Tial," (naturally pronounced like "teal"), but that sounds too much like "heel" and might be confusing for the dog.

But there's no doubt about it. "Potential" is the universal name that fits every bird dog puppy bred, born, weaned and taken home to excited children and a skeptical spouse.

The hunter's sense of that potential will wax and wane in the months and years ahead. It will be strongest when he's still at the kennel selecting the new pup from a squirming, frolicking mass of potential. Though he's looking at a creature that eats whenever it wants, sleeps whenever it wants and relieves itself wherever it wants, the hunter's mind is at least a decade of dog years ahead. Though his eyes see seven-week-old pups, the hunter's mind is wearing rose-colored glasses through which he can only see scenes of first retrieves, locked-up points and silky ears by a roaring fire.

The sense of potential will ebb while cleaning messes off the dining room carpet. It will plunge when puppy is more interested in what's under the porch than answering the whistle. It will be questioned when an irked spouse mentions suspicious-looking tooth marks on the legs of the family heirloom piano.

And then potential will soar again when pup wins his first wrestling match with a wing-clipped pigeon or makes that first tentative puppy point on a tethered grouse wing.

Though the emotions of the bird hunter/dog owner are wont to ride a roller coaster for the life of his hunting companion, reality is usually somewhere in the middle. Less exciting, but easier to live with.

Most dogs of good breeding have the potential to be at least semi-great. That's not always the case, because dogs are at least as individual and unpredictable as humans. But in general, it's probably a fair statement.

Whether a dog reaches its potential for semi-greatness or even goes beyond is a function of the ability of the owner/hunter to select a dog that

Co-author Miller with his sometimes overly-energetic springer spaniel, Gunner.

will best suit his kind of hunting. Then it's a function of the owner's willingness to exude bodily fluids, namely blood, sweat and tears, in helping his dog to become the best it can be. In other words, his willingness to *work with* the dog.

It is beyond the scope of this book to delve deeply into training methods to aid your dog in reaching his full potential. There are dozens of great books and superbly produced video tapes available on that subject. Instead, the following is written to help guide you in the selection of the right dog for your kind of hunting. This will also try to impart a trio of truisms which ensconce the hunter-gun dog relationship:

1) All dogs, even within a breed, are individuals.
2) The trainer has to be smarter than his pupil.
3) The amount of its potential a dog achieves is directly proportional to the effort an owner is willing to put into the training.

Which Dog For You?

Even if a hunter can bring a dog to its full potential, the hunter won't be satisfied if the dog he has selected is not well-matched to his style or type of hunting.

Selecting the right dog for the conditions you'll hunt most frequently is much like selecting a shotgun. Again, you'll find those hunters who prefer the one-dog-for-everything approach and those who would like to have a "golf bag" full of dogs. In this case, there are probably more hunters who would like to own a bevy of canines, but simply can't because of the restrictions of living in suburban North America.

Consider carefully the species, or type of species, you'll hunt most often. Are they tight sitting birds that hold well for a long-ranging pointer or are they running birds that require the disciplined quartering of a Lab or well-trained spaniel? Is the terrain open where you can see a dog on point for half a mile or is the cover you hunt most often so thick that you're lucky if you can see half a yard? Is the climate balmy all season or will you push cattail sloughs and willow thickets when the temperature hovers around zero and two feet of snow covers the ground?

Hunting dogs, like humans, vary in their adaptability. So if you really hunt all kinds of birds in all kinds of cover, try to choose one of the breeds that is more adaptable.

And finally, consider your personal hunting preferences. Do you enjoy hunting more over a dog that points birds or one that flushes birds? Well-trained pointing dogs generally offer closer shooting with the hunter more prepared for the shot. Flushing dogs tend to offer a more energetic, animated performance and work close to the hunters. They tend to be better retrievers, too.

Co-author Caligiuri with his German shorthair, Choc.

On the downside, pointing dogs generally don't make as good family pets as do flushing breeds and some pointing breeds tend to be flighty. Pointing dogs can be more time-consuming and demanding to train and require more "staged" live bird work at a kennel or shooting preserve. With a flushing dog, shots in the field tend to be longer and come with less notice. To be effective, the hunter with a flushing dog must keep his canine companion in sight at all times and stay alert to the dog's "birdiness."

In the last 50 years, upland dogs have become highly regional. Pointers still dominate the South, setters are most often associated with the grouse and woodcock coverts of the Northeast, the Continental breeds have adapted well to the Midwest and West and the spaniels are the favored dog with most Northwood's hunters.

All these considerations are generalities, stereotypes. Again, dogs are as individualistic as humans! However, it is these considerations which can help you decide which type of hunting dog you have the best chance of bringing to its full potential.

The Pointing Breeds

Tucked away in a corner of the sprawling main lodge at Hawkeye Hunting Club is Jerry Water's office. On the walls are inspiring oils of English pointers doing what they do best, pointing coveys of bobwhite quail or lounging around in the back of pickup trucks. Up the hill from the lodge are the kennels, where the actual models for the paintings spend their free time when they aren't out hunting.

Compared to most of the dogs around Center, Texas, they live an idyllic life. The hunting season can last up to six months, the birds are always plentiful and, even though pen-raised, they fly like hell. And though some of the finest dinners in the South are served in Hawkeye's dining room, and lunker bass swim in the surrounding lakes, it is not the food, the fish or even the birds that make Hawkeye an upland hunter's mecca. It is the pointing dogs.

Without pointing dogs, upland hunting would be pretty much a hit-and-miss proposition. Watching a Brittany work out a patch of South Dakota pheasant cover or witnessing a quivering pointer with a double snout full of bobwhite are some of the finest sights in life. They can turn an otherwise sour day into a lifetime of memories with just one solid point.

Upland bird hunting is the pointing dog's game!

I once had a bird hunting buddy who often stated that hunting birds without a pointing dog, "just wasn't hunting at all." Likewise, I had an-

When selecting a hunting dog, consider your personal hunting preferences. Pointing dogs offer closer shooting with the hunter more prepared for the shot; however, they don't make as good family pets as do flushing breeds.

other partner who swore that even if he could hunt all the quail in Texas he wouldn't get out of the truck if he couldn't take his dogs.

Even though pointing dogs are considered as American as a Filson vest or Winchester Model 12, all the dogs in the field today can trace their roots to east of the Atlantic. More precisely, almost all can credit their existence to the Spanish pointer and English pointer. Prior to the development of modern sporting arms, these original pointers were trained to pause at the scent of game long enough for the hunters to release sight hounds such as greyhounds or salukis. Through the years, the pointing breeds evolved into lighter, faster dogs who froze at the scent of game long enough for the hunter to flush the bird and shoot.

The dogs most familiar to American hunters would be those from the British Isles, including the English pointer, English setter, Irish setter and Gordon setter. The last 40 years have also brought on a massive rise in popularity of the Continental breeds, including the Brittany spaniel, the four German pointing breeds and the Hungarian vizsla. While the British breeds are more closely associated with quail and grouse, the Continental breeds are versatile pointing dogs that are used not only for bobwhites and grouse but for pheasants, mountain and desert quail, western grouse and even waterfowl.

The English Pointer. But for many, especially those diehard quail hunters in the South, a pointing dog simply means an English pointer. These men will readily tell you that anything else is just a pet, not a bird dog. Trained to properly hunt for the gun, as opposed to hunting in field trials, an English pointer can be top-notch. In fact, they are still the most popular of the pointing breeds. Pointers are strictly gun dogs, unlike Labs or setters, they are not particularly good pets and are a bit too high-strung for house dogs.

Pointers learn and train early and quickly. In the United States they have been largely bred for field trials, and many hunting dogs have a tendency to be wide-ranging. This is a fine trait if your chosen hunting terrain is a 1,000-acre cow pasture in west Texas. However, it can be a hindrance in the smaller hunting confines of the Midwest and Northeast. They sometimes have trouble with birds that don't hold, such as pheasants. But for the hunter who wants a hardworking, hard-charging companion, there are few better choices. With some time and proper training, contrary to popular belief, they can be adapted to close cover situations.

The Setters. On the other hand, the English setter is a friendly sort and is often regarded as the most beautiful of the pointing dogs. Up until the 1920s, they were also regarded as better hunters than the pointer. In fact, in the years before 1900, setters won almost every field trial ever ran in the U.S. Still, today many will argue that he is a better gun dog, the

For the hunter who wants a hard-working, hard-charging companion, there are few better choices than an English pointer. Pointers learn and train early and quickly. With time and proper training, they can be adapted to close cover situations.

pointer only having the advantage at trials because he ranges wider and works faster.

Today's setters are known as affectionate family dogs who work close, lock up tight on birds and retrieve well.

While the English were developing their own version of a setter, their neighbors in Ireland and Scotland were working with their own distinct dogs—the Irish setter and the Gordon setter.

Gordon setters, when bred as bird dogs, can be distinguished by a fairly keen nose and rugged endurance. They are solid pointers and good retrievers. Even though they reached their popularity with hunters late in the last century, there is now a renewed interest, especially with some select grouse hunters in New England.

The dog was named after the Duke of Gordon, a Scottish sportsman, thought to be the originator of the breed in the late 1700s. Gordons are primarily ground scenters, thoroughly working cover to pick up the track of game that has passed. To hunt in this manner, they must be steady and thorough in contrast to the fast-moving, pointing breeds that rely on winding or detecting scent in the air.

Ideally suited for pheasants or grouse, Gordons will work close on command, hunt hard in heavy cover and retrieve well. Not widespread, good pups can still be found from a few reputable breeders.

Another breed, once extremely popular with North American hunters, that has now fallen by the wayside is the Irish setter. Today, most are headstrong, stubborn and hard to control. In the late 1800s, the dogs were popular with quail and grouse hunters and made excellent showings at field trials competing against English pointers and setters. About the turn of the century, the dogs began to be bred primarily for the bench and their emphasis as a gun dog declined.

Today, a more compact version, known as the red setter is becoming popular in limited circles and they are proving to be quite a capable and versatile, all-around upland hunter.

*The Brittany Spaniel.*Over the past 35 years, the Brittany spaniel has become extremely popular with U.S. hunters. Showing up in field trials as early as World War II, today's Britts are primarily bred as close-working, on-foot gun dogs. The only spaniel that points, Brittanies are easily trained, work hard and have a style all their own. Versatile dogs, they can handle quail and pheasants with equal talent and are right at home in the Midwest states where both birds are found side by side.

Not known as especially wide-rangers, the dogs are better suited for the heavier cover of the northeast and Midwest than the wide open cow pastures of the South.

English setters are known as affectionate family dogs that work close, lock up tight on birds and retrieve well.

German shorthairs, like Caligiuri's, can point, trail both big and small wounded game and retrieve ducks and geese.

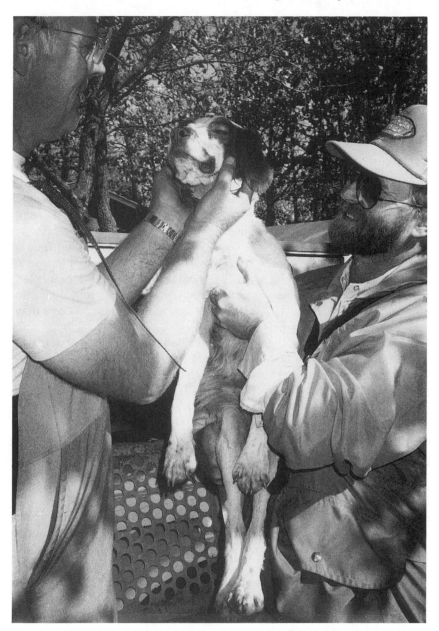

Brittany spaniels are close-working, versatile gun dogs that can handle quail and pheasants with equal talent. The only spaniel that points, Brittanies are easily trained, work hard and are better suited for heavy cover.

The Continental Pointing Breeds. German pointing dogs have been steadily increasing in popularity and versatility since World War II. The more common breeds include: German shorthaired pointer, German wirehaired pointer, pudelpointer, wirehaired pointing griffon, and weimaraner. Along with the Hungarian vizsla, the dogs are sometimes collectively referred to as the Continental breeds.

Relatively young breeds when compared to the more established English dogs, they are distinguished by cropped tails and what some hunters believe are more practical colors for hunting, especially in snow. The English pointer was favored by German nobility in the late 1800s, but they desired dogs with more versatile characteristics than the bird-hunting-only, wide-ranging pointers. Consequently, German dogs could be counted on to not only point, but also trail, both big and small wounded game, and readily go into the water to retrieve ducks and geese.

Undoubtedly the most well-known of the above-mentioned four is the German shorthair pointer. In its modern form the shorthair has been around since the 1880s. Experimental variations are well-documented 20 years prior to that. The dogs are thought to have been imported into the United States about 1920. However, some unpublicized dogs may have arrived as early as 1900.

German shorthairs range in color from solid liver and heavy ticked to almost pure white with few markings. They are characterized by an exceptionally good nose and close working style that makes them ideal for almost every upland situation and bird. They are particularly adept at hunting the mixed bag conditions in the Midwest and West and are the favored choice of Southwest gunners who hunt desert quail.

Shorthairs are hardworking, rugged and natural hunters. Not yet common as pets or bench breeds, most dogs are owned and bred by active hunters.

In contrast to the shorthair, the pudelpointer is the least known of the Continental breeds. The pudelpointer can find both English pointers and the standard poodle in his family tree. The first pudelpointers found their way to North America in the mid 1950s. More popular in Canada than the United States, pudelpointers are good pointers and retrievers, especially in the water.

Other recent emigrants include the German wirehaired pointer, the griffon (also trademarked by a wiry coat), the vizsla and the weimaraner. Like all Continental breeds, the dogs are characterized by all-around hunting traits and a seemingly stronger desire to retrieve.

Because of this, the shorthair, wirehair and vizsla are all popular as shooting preserve dogs. They are also the favorites of weekend hunters

German shorthairs are characterized by an exceptionally good nose and close working style that makes them ideal for almost every upland situation and every bird. Shorthairs are rugged, natural hunters, particularly adept at hunting mixed bag conditions.

who desire utility dogs that are fairly easy to train and that run within acceptable foot hunting range.

Flushing Dogs

When you talk about purebred flushing dogs for hunting upland birds in North America you're commonly discussing one of four breeds—the Labrador retriever, golden retriever, Chesapeake Bay retriever or the English springer spaniel.

There are some other fine flushing breeds around, namely the English cocker spaniel, Welsh springer spaniel, Clumber spaniel, Boykin spaniel, American water spaniel, Irish water spaniel, curly-coated retriever and the flat-coated retriever. They're around, but the average bird hunter is likely to go a lifetime and never see one in any of the coverts he hunts. That's how rare they are on this continent.

Why are these other breeds so rare? Well, some are too specialized in the types of game and cover they hunt well. Others are often too boneheaded to train quickly. Some have been bred for the bench so long that few have much hunting ability left. Several don't make great family pets. And some languish for no good reason other than that one of the four most popular flushing breeds does everything just as well or a little bit better.

The Labrador Retriever. The origins of the Labrador retriever are obscure. The most common legend, and legend is really all that exists, credits the origination of the breed to fishermen in the Newfoundland area of North America. From that beginning, the breed found its way back to Great Britain where it came into full bloom as a gunning dog. Then in the early 1900s it came back to American shores in rapidly increasing numbers. Today it ranks as the most popular breed of retriever and of flushing dog with American sportsmen.

Labs come in three flavors: black, yellow (not golden) and chocolate. The dog is one in the same. In fact, all three could be born in the same litter of pups.

No matter what color the fur on its back, the Labrador retriever is one hell of an upland bird hunting dog. From good hunting stock, a Lab is liable to have a great nose. Though it's specialty always has been and always will be retrieving, Labs are easily taught to quarter and work heavy cover for all species of upland birds.

Almost without fail, a Lab's disposition is wonderful. A Labrador retriever is the canine companion for a hunter and his family who are looking for a great hunting dog that will make a marvelous pet.

Many hunters consider the Lab about tied with the springer as *the* all around hunting dog. The Lab generally does a better job on retrieving

No matter what color the fur on its back, the Labrador retriever is one hell of an upland bird dog. The most popular breed of retriever and of flushing dog, Labs are easily taught to quarter and work heavy cover for all species of upland birds.

waterfowl, especially under harsh, cold conditions. A springer has the tiniest edge in the uplands if for no other reason than his animated, roll-with-the-punches style of hunting. A serious bird hunter could choose a good specimen of either breed for hunting anything feathered and look back with no regrets.

The Golden Retriever. If you'll agree that the Labrador is a great hunting dog who also makes a marvelous pet, then you'll understand that the golden is the canine companion of choice for a hunter and his family who are looking for a great pet that will make a marvelous hunting dog.

Without a doubt, the golden is the gentlest, sweetest of the retriever breeds. Like all dogs, they'll stay loyal to the family that loves them, but seldom is there a snarl or a growl for anyone from a golden. That's good for a family dog; bad if you lack patience for training. The man with a short temper will find it unfortunately easy to sour a good golden.

Of the retriever breeds, the golden is the upland specialist. Because of his fine coat and softer constitution, he's better suited to the uplands than the wetlands, especially when the weather turns rugged.

The beautiful golden retriever is believed to be of Scottish origin, dating from the same era as the Labrador. On this side of the Atlantic, it's that beauty and sweet disposition that has caused somewhat of a demise for the golden. A dog with those attributes is bound to be sought after by non-hunters as pets and show dogs.

When that happens breeding gets haphazard and hunting qualities can be lost.

This has been the sad case for some goldens in recent years. The hunter who is interested in owning a field-worthy golden retriever, or sporting dog of any breed, needs to carefully research the pedigree of the pup he's considering. Only from that document can you tell what kind of genetics you're getting. Then, just to be sure, try to line up a hunt over the dam and sire or a full-sibling from a previous litter. Then you'll know.

The Chesapeake Bay Retriever. "Tough!" In a word, that's what Chessies are all about. Tough in the field. Tough in protecting their families. Sometimes tough to train.

The Chessie is really a specialist. He's been bred through the years to be able to withstand cold wind and cold water. They were a breed developed by waterfowl market hunters not only as fierce, spirited retrievers, but as watchdogs for the homestead.

The Chesapeake is at its finest when the weather and the waves are at their worst. He loves to retrieve ducks and geese under conditions that leave lesser dogs whining in the corner of the blind. He does a fine job of retrieving on ol' terra firma as well, but is meant for swimming work.

English cockers are one of the seldom seen, but great, bird dogs.

Chesapeakes can be fine upland dogs as well. In fact, if you've got a good one and you want to see him have a good time, let him hunt pheasants or grouse instead of ducks and geese a day or two out of the season. NAHC Member, avid waterfowl hunter and devoted Chesapeake owner Bruce Horrell says, "Sonny (his Chessie) is absolutely crazy about hunting pheasants. After a hard season of waterfowl hunting, it's like watching a kid playing on the first day school lets out! They love it, and they're good at it!"

There are few upland bird hunting situations that require the attributes of a Chesapeake. Unless you pursue upland birds regularly and for long stretches in sub-zero temperatures, hunting them with a Chessie is sort of like gunning for woodcock with a 10 gauge Magnum. You have more dog than you need, and he's not the best choice to get the job done.

The Chessie has a great nose. He's the consummate retriever. He usually hunts naturally close and can be taught to quarter thoroughly. But he has two strikes against him for day-in, day-out upland hunting. First is his size. Chessies are big—they commonly weigh close to 100 pounds. Big dogs tend to tire more quickly than smaller dogs, and they have a hard time rooting into all the tight patches of thick cover through which smaller dogs seem to glide. Secondly, Chesapeakes tend to be aggressive in relating to people other than their owner and other dogs. Not necessarily mean, just aggressive. They tend to make very good watchdogs.

Again, *dogs are individuals as much as people!* Not all Chessies are aggressive. For instance, Bruce Horrell calls his "Sonny" a golden caught in a Chesapeake's body and with the Chessie's constitution. Find one like that, and you've got yourself a great dog—for all kinds of hunting!

The Springer Spaniel. It is believed that the early ancestors of the spaniels were the same Spanish dogs that were the long-ago progenitors of the pointing breeds. Generations of breeding are all it took to produce two such distinct families of dogs.

The exact origins of the springer are obscured by time. The first evidence of a distinct spaniel breed comes from the first century A.D. in the works of various writers and painters. Dogs of the spaniel type were known in Spain, France and England. About 600 years ago, spaniel-type dogs are known to have been in the field supporting the work of coursing hounds, falconers and huntsmen armed with nets.

The spaniel's job was to "spring" game; to flush it. Same as it is for the modern upland bird hunter. Springers, even in the days of yore, became recognized as such good hunters that one lord banned their use,

Every upland bird hunter deserves at least one day over a well-trained springer spaniel. While a Lab goes at hunting like a businessman goes about making money, a springer wears his emotions on his sleeve. This happy-go-lucky vagabond loves what he's doing, and his energy and ambition seem limitless.

claiming that their skills as hunters were unsportsmanlike and unfair to the game.

Though the English springer spaniel was not recognized as a separate breed in England until 1902, it is believed that the first springer-type dog came to the New World not long after the Mayflower. By the 1860s the dogs were commonly found in the company of hunters after upland birds and waterfowl in the marshes of New Jersey and New York.

The English springer spaniel was first officially recognized by the American Kennel Club in 1910, and in 1924 the English Springer Field Trial Association was formed.

Like many other breeds, the springer in North America has suffered the vagaries of breeding for the show ring, so much so that almost two distinct breeds have developed. In general, the show dogs are leggier, bigger dogs, while the hunting dogs are squatter, more compact and chunkier. And for the most part the field dogs have better noses and more brains.

Every upland bird hunter deserves at least one day in the field hunting over a well-trained springer spaniel during his lifetime. It's an experience not soon forgotten. For many hunters that one day turns into a life devoted to these addicting canines.

Compared to a springer, a Lab or a golden goes at hunting upland birds like a businessman goes about making money. It's what he loves to do, but he's not going to let anyone know it. In comparison, the springer is a happy-go-lucky vagabond. He wears his emotions on his sleeve. He loves what he's doing, too, but he doesn't care who knows it.

The springer's energy and ambition seem limitless, especially when his tired hunter is trying to nap in the October sunshine after a l-o-n-g morning's hunt.

Dogs Aren't For Everyone

A hunting dog is not a hunting machine. It can't be turned off for six to nine months out of the year when bird season is closed. A dog is dependent on its owner for food, water, shelter, sanitation and exercise...every day of its life. That's a commitment almost as big as raising children.

For the hunter who is prepared to make that commitment, a dog, of whatever sporting breed, is out there waiting. For the hunter who isn't, there is no shame in not owning a dog. He'll simply have to hunt with some different methods and make sure to do everything he possibly can to recover every bird he drops. That's a big responsibility, too.

6

Bobwhite Quail

L ife holds few sweeter sounds than the split-second roar of a bob-white covey rise. For many NAHC members the bobwhite quail is the most exciting of all upland birds. Steeped in tradition, whether in the horse-drawn wagon hunts of the deep South or a Thanksgiving get-together in Kansas, bobwhite quail reign over one of hunting's largest kingdoms.

During the mid-1970s, 10 to 15 million bobwhite quail were bagged annually. Today, more than three million hunters harvest upwards of 20 million birds each season, making bobwhites the second most hunted game bird in North America. (Pheasant hunting, of course, is the most popular.) Found primarily east of the Rocky Mountains and south of the Great Lakes, bobwhites are actively hunted in six distinct regions comprised of almost 30 states. In contemporary times, bobwhites have actually expanded their native range and many states have much better hunting today than they did in the proverbial good old days.

Bobwhites are handsome birds though not striking. Males have a pronounced white throat patch and white stripe above the eye, both bordered in black. Hens have a throat patch and stripe that is buff colored rather than white, making the gender readily apparent, though not necessarily so on the fly. The brown, black and tan shades over a bobwhite's back gives the bird excellent natural ground camouflage.

The weight of an adult bob ranges from five ounces to one-half pound, depending on region, weather, food and water. Bobwhites measure about 10 to 11 inches from beak to tail.

Gregarious birds, bobwhites communicate with their telltale "bob-bob-white" calls and a variety of danger and covey assembly calls. During most of the hunting season and throughout the winter, bobs will stay in coveys, breaking up each spring in preparation for breeding and nesting.

Prolific in seasons of favorable weather and climate, the bobwhite hen is an excellent mother, laying up to 15 eggs in a clutch. In some Midwest states where a harsh winter or spring blizzard can drastically reduce the population, surviving birds can bring the population back to stable levels in as little as one or two years.

Biologists believe that bobwhite populations peaked in the late 1800s. At that time the nation was also covered with hundreds of small farms. The small patches of varied cropland supplied a cultivated food source of corn, sorghum, wheat and beans supplemented with available natural food such as lespedeza, smartweed, various wild peas and sunflower seeds.

The hedgerows and small timber strips around the crop patches provided nesting and roost cover as well as water. Where these small crop fields can still be found, hunting is good. The birds move out at dawn to feed and hunting the edge of the feeding areas is often productive. Coveys can be caught going from food to cover and back again. Dogs are almost essential to productive quail hunting, both for local coveys and downed birds. Two or three hunters with a pair of dogs is generally considered ideal. Some birds are taken by hunters who are primarily after other species such as pheasants or rabbits, but the majority of birds are killed by dyed-in-the-wool quail hunters.

Which states have the best quail hunting is relative to a number of factors. South Texas has some tremendous hunting, but the ranches are locked to the average hunter. Likewise, western Oklahoma holds some of the highest concentrations of birds in North America, but almost every ranch is tied up by commercial operations or exclusive leases. Traditional farming states, such as Iowa and Kansas, may have fewer coveys per square mile but the hunting is often only a door-knock away.

Quail hunting across the United States can easily be broken into six regions. Within each region are similar types of habitat, seasons, bag limits, bird populations and landowner customs.

Steeped in tradition, whether in the horse-drawn wagon hunts of the deep South or a Thanksgiving get-together in Kansas, bobwhite quail reign over one of hunting's largest kingdoms.

Midwest

The midwestern region comprises 285,000 square miles and includes Nebraska, Iowa, Missouri and Kansas. This region is *the most overlooked of all the bobwhite hotspots.* The average annual bag for the four states runs about six million birds with Kansas and Missouri grabbing the lion's share. As a ratio of the annual bag divided by the square miles of the region, the quail quotient is 21.5 per square mile, one of the highest in the nation.

Most of the quail in the Midwest are found on privately owned farms, though some state-managed wildlife areas have excellent hunting. This is primarily row crop country, crisscrossed with large fields of corn, soybeans, sorghum and milo. Hedgerows—also called "living fences"—provide excellent cover, as do small woodlots and abandoned homesites.

Much of this country is still open to the hunter willing to scout out productive areas and knock on some farm doors. The style of hunting involves locating several coveys within reasonable driving distance of each other since the farms are less than 500 acres each.

Midwest hunters tend to put more emphasis on chasing singles than do hunters in other parts of the country. An average day of hunting in most years will produce about six separate covey rises. However, in Missouri and Kansas, moving as many as 12 wild coveys in a good day is not unusual.

Great Lakes

The lower Great Lake's region, covers 174,000 square miles and includes Illinois, Indiana, Ohio and Kentucky. With a combined annual bag of less than $2^1/_2$ million birds, this region has a quail quotient of 14. The hunting techniques are similar, but winters in this area tend to be harsher than Kansas or Missouri and agriculture is not such a dominant industry.

As a result, there are fewer birds to hunt. The hotspot in this region is southern Illinois which accounts for almost one-third of the region's total bag. As in other Midwest states, bobwhite hunting is not looked upon as a commercial endeavor by landowners and most hunting is free for the asking.

Northeast

The third region is made up from those states in the northeast that comprise the northern limit of the bobwhite. Covering 130,000 square miles, the region includes West Virginia, Virginia, New Jersey, Delaware, Maryland and parts of Pennsylvania and New York. Understand-

Dogs are almost essential to productive quail hunting, both for local coveys and downed birds. Two or three hunters with a pair of dogs is generally considered ideal.

ably, the northeast has experienced more than its share of habitat loss during the past 50 years. A relatively light annual bag allows this region a rather low comparative quail quotient of six. Again, most of the hunting here is free for the asking.

Finding farms to hunt on is basic salesmanship and common sense. Present yourself well, you have to convince the landowner that you can be trusted to take care of his property. Believe it or not, some of my most memorable moments quail hunting have not been in the actual hunting and shooting, but in getting the permission to hunt. You can have the best dogs in the world, the most expensive double made and all the tailored hunting britches that money can buy, but if you can't get on a farm to hunt, then you'll have to resign yourself to hunting expensive leases or shooting preserves.

My buddy Curt Roseland is better at getting permission to hunt than anyone I have ever seen. The first time I really studied his technique, I was amazed, but it works. His whole manner of asking revolves around just being himself and it's advice we can all take to heart. I remember one door-knocking weekend in particular. In the bobwhite-rich corner of southeast Kansas, Curt racked up an incredible 80 percent success ratio. He put every farmer at ease and he overcame almost every objection. Obtaining permission to hunt is, in many ways, similar to selling vacuum cleaners door to door.

Lesson number one is to always get out of the vehicle and walk up to the house door. Farmers aren't overjoyed at the prospect of strangers driving around their back lots. Always offer your handshake and your name. Curt also looks at the mailbox so he can address the farmer by his proper name. Tell the farmer where you're from, how many are in your party and what you intend to hunt. If permission is granted make sure his fields, fences and gates are treated with respect. Stopping by after the hunt and thanking the landowner for permission to hunt is a good idea and helps to insure permission for future trips.

In these three northern regions, wintertime is one of the best times for locating birds and securing permission. Harvest chores are complete and farmers aren't worrying about muddy fields or hard-to-find combine parts, and they're much more receptive to hunters looking for a place to scare up a few birds.

Brush patches, grassy draws and other covey areas once hidden by early season standing crops are much more visible and should be remembered for future trips. Abandoned railroad right-of-ways often provide another type of desirable bobwhite cover. Keep in mind that in most places railroad tracks are private property, whether in use or not. Permis-

Finding farms to hunt is basic common sense. Present yourself well and convince the landowner that you can be trusted with his property. Those that don't must resign themselves to hunting expensive leases or shooting preserves.

sion from the farmer or rail line owning the land must be granted before hunting, so ask first.

Bobwhites seem to conform to covey habits and hold better during the colder part of the season. November, December and January can also mean snow in most of the bobwhite's northern range, stacking the odds in the hunter's favor.

Though there is no substitute for a good dog, quail tracks in the snow are unmistakable and those fortunate enough to be out when the flakes have just fallen can be in for a trip they will long remember. For dogless hunters, fresh tracks can actually be walked up, building excitement with each step to the final flush. Also, snow can help in finding crippled birds that would otherwise be lost in the heavy cover.

Though snow is a rarity in the regions south of the Mason-Dixon line, the majority of bobwhites call Dixie home. The south can be broken into three separate regions—the mid-South, the deep South and the southeast.

Mid-South

Texas, Oklahoma and Arkansas comprise the mid-South region covering 390,000 square miles. Good years in these three states see a total combined bag of more than six million birds. Disregard a large portion of Texas where there is little quail hunting, and the quail quotient comes out at about 23. In areas of south Texas and western Oklahoma, no doubt, this quotient is above 50.

This region requires a different type of landowner arrangement than the agricultural regions. Quail, like white-tailed deer, are a highly recognized source of income in Texas. Ranchers in western Texas and Oklahoma usually lease their hunting rights to groups of sportsmen, corporations or individual hunters. South Texas ranchers often lease rights for entire seasons as well, but for hunters looking for just a couple of days of fantastic shooting, package hunts for wild birds can be found at affordable prices.

As an example, on the Kennedy Ranch in south Texas, Sarita Safaris runs hunts for wild birds where two dozen covey rises a day are not uncommon. These are not liberated birds, but strong-flying, wild quail, the ultimate in upland hunting. Oklahoma has many excellent commercial wild bird operations in the western part of the state and some good hunting in the eastern section for hunters willing to get out and knock on some doors. Arkansas, with a fairly high, stable bag each season, has relatively few commercial operations and most of the birds are taken by local hunters.

In the northeast, bobwhites often conform to covey habits and hold better during the colder part of the season.

Deep South

The deep South spans about 200,000 square miles and includes the states of Louisiana, Mississippi, Alabama and Tennessee. The total annual bag for all four states runs close to 4 million birds, rating a strong 20 on the quail quotient.

The deep South is one of the traditional bobwhite hot spots. Mississippi and Alabama have several plantation-style operations. While they primarily depend on planted or liberated birds, these hunts provide a delightful insight into what quail hunting must have been like a hundred years ago. Wild birds typically inhabit agricultural areas.

Southeast

The southeast region is much like the deep South, four states totaling 300,000 square miles. North Carolina, South Carolina, Georgia and Florida hunters take four million birds a season, for another 20 on the quail quotient. Many former plantations are now commercial quail hunting operations offering the best in pointers, food and historic accommodations, and a mix of wild and liberated birds.

These hunts usually include a daily limit, with more birds available at an additional cost. The hunts can be from foot, horseback or mule-drawn wagon. The southeast is known as well for its excellent wild bird hunting.

While the midwestern region is often dependent on mild winters for a good carryover and the mid-South needs ample spring rain for chick production, the quail populations in the deep South and southeast are more constant from year to year. But regardless of where they are found, the habits of wild bobwhites are pretty much the same wherever they are found.

From the time they are a month old, little bobs can sustain short bursts of fast flight. Come hunting season, wild coveys pop out of the thick stuff and quickly reach 50 miles an hour on their short cupped wings. Though a fast initial flyer, bobwhites are sprinters, not marathoners, and coveys will usually fly under a thousand yards before gliding back into cover. Heavily hunted birds may fly up to a mile before going down. Opening day coveys will often break and drop back in the same patch, flying only 10 or 20 yards. Birds completely unassociated with dogs or hunters sometimes just jump up into trees above the point, requiring a shake of the limbs to get them to fly. But most often, bobwhites literally explode from cover.

Volumes have been written about how the bobwhite is no longer a point-holding pushover. Writers have described contemporary birds as prone to running ahead of points and flushing out of gun range. They go

Quail, like white-tailed deer, are a highly recognized source of income in Texas. Although south Texas ranchers often lease hunting rights for an entire season, two- or three-day package hunts for wild birds can be found at affordable prices.

on to explain this new found phenomenon with theories of inherited survival traits and learned pressure response.

Most of these articles are kin to what you might find on your bird shootin' boots after a warm fall day of cutting through Grandpa Jack's cow pastures.

I still get the opportunity to hunt the same coveys I first found 20 years ago. Some of these birds have not moved one yard from where they were when I was a teenager. Most didn't hold for a point back then, and they don't hold now.

The wild bobwhite puts a great deal of confidence in his natural ability to remain motionless and hidden while on the ground. From birth this trait keeps him safe from hawks, owls and other airborne menaces. Introduce the popularity of the pointing dog at the turn of the century and during the hunting season adult birds were faced with a new danger. All the camo in the world can't hide a quail from the nose of even a marginally good dog. While birds may be wilder now from increased survival tactics, most don't get spooky until they're hunted for the first time in a season.

After their initial scrape with the strange-looking dogs and the kicking, yelling and shooting that follows, hunted bobwhites no longer associate remaining motionless with being safe. So the next time the big dog comes, the little birds run. On many different occasions I have hunted two or three times on one side of the road where the birds were spooky and consistently ran ahead of the points. On the other side of the road the birds had yet to be hunted that season and they held well and flew only short distances after flushing.

Genetically, the birds were all the same, the difference had to do with being hunted and not being hunted.

The wild bobwhite that is a veteran of two or three flushes is indeed a formidable opponent. He breaks fast, flies hard and does not hesitate to get through the thickest cover available. Like so many satin sheets snapping in a crisp December wind, covey rises end as quickly as they start. Because the action is close in and fast, bobwhite guns should match the bird.

Quail guns should always be open choked. Improved cylinder is about right, and most skeet guns work dandy. Short barreled guns handle better in the thick stuff and are lighter to carry. My old friend Lawton Smith bent two 26-inch barrels in one season, he swings so fast that if there is a tree in the way, the gun and the tree suffer the consequences.

Most good covey shots invariably carry autos. I know several who have fine expensive doubles in their gun racks, but prefer to hunt with something that has the ability to shoot more than twice on a covey rise.

Quail populations in the deep South and southeast are fairly constant from year to year. Many former plantations are now commercial quail hunting operations offering the best in pointers, food and historic accommodations.

Bobwhites are easy birds to kill, an ounce of 7$^1/_2$s or 8s work well. In the early season, 9s can be deadly and pattern quite well in most open choked guns.

Bobwhites, known for their fast burst on the rise, can be tough to hit. Covey rises are both breathtaking and confusing. Concentration is the key to shooting well. All the other quail along with Huns, chukars and sharptails covey, but bobwhites are the only birds that seem to come up all at once and hardly spread out until 20 or 30 yards out in the air.

With such a big ball of targets to shoot at, shooting should be simple. Wrong.

Shooting into the middle of a covey rise will usually result in blowing holes in cold, thin air. Consistently shooting doubles or better on a fast rise separates great wingshooting from good. There are few tricks, you just have to take all the basics of wingshooting and practice all of them three or four times in five seconds!

Good gun fit is imperative to good covey shooting. Shooting covey birds is largely instinctive. The gun's stock should fit so the gun comes up quickly and easily. Even behind pointing dogs where the hunter has ample warning, the gun is not actually mounted until the birds come up. A good fitting gun makes mounting and getting on a bird easier to master.

If you are right-handed, your left hand should be well forward on the forend. Grip with the left lightly. Be at ease. When the covey busts, concentrate. Pick out one bird and one only. Stay on that bird and shoot until you kill him. Once he is down, move on to the next and go on until your gun is empty or no more shots present themselves.

Snap shooters, rather than pointers, do better on covey rises. Snap shooting is a system where the shooter picks out a spot in front of his target and shoots where he thinks the bird will be. Pointing and trying to calculate speed and distance is fine for incoming or crossing birds like doves and ducks but it's too slow for erratic covey rises.

After the covey breaks there is often good opportunity for hunting up the singles. In many parts of the South, where the cover is continuous and singles are hard to pinpoint, hunters often hunt one covey after another, with no breaks in between. In the Midwest where crop fields are crisscrossed by lightly timbered ditches and hedgerows, hunters can often watch the singles and pinpoint their exact location.

Birds that have been hunted a few times will sometimes run, but most will be fairly close to where they light. Singles by themselves often hold better than when they are together in a covey. Singles caught in short, open cover can often be completely shot out. It's good insurance to always leave at least half of the original birds to insure a healthy car-

Quail guns should be short barreled and open choked. Improved cylinder is about right, and most skeet guns work dandy.

The wild bobwhite that is a veteran of two or three flushes is a formidable opponent. He breaks fast and flies hard. Snap shooters, rather than pointers, do better on covey rises.

ryover. The protection that the covey affords is essential to winter survival.

Bobwhites are excellent tablefare. The breasts and legs provide almost all of the meal. They can be prepared a variety of ways and are savored wherever they are found.

7

Western Quail

E ven without bobwhites, the western United States offers excellent quail hunting. Western species include valley, Gambel's, mountain, scaled and Mearns. Not as plentiful as bobs, the total national bag of western quail is only about seven million birds in a good year, compared to 30 or 40 million bobwhites. Still, even with their limited range and tough hunting conditions, cowboy country quail are wonderful game birds.

Actually, habits and habitat are quite diverse for western quail. Scaled and Gambel's quail have an annoying habit of running out of gun range before flushing. Mearns sit so tight, more often than not you walk right past them, and valley and mountain quail take a decathlon champion's legs and lungs to comfortably hunt.

Though the distribution of the five species often overlap, they are all so different that each must be covered separately. Because they are my favorite, let's start with the scaled quail.

Scaled Quail
Scaled quail are partial to the arid grasslands and semi-deserts of the southwest. There are two subspecies. The larger and more common, *C.s. pallida*, is found in Kansas, Colorado, Texas, New Mexico and Arizona. The smaller subspecies, *Castonagastris*, is a southern cousin native to the lower Rio Grande valley of south Texas and Old Mexico.

Scaled quail derive their name from the scaled appearance of their breast feathers. The slate blue feathers edged in black also lend well to another name, the blue quail. The birds sport a fluffy white crest that has earned them yet another popular nickname, "cottontop."

Every scaled quail hunter that I have known has simply called them "blues." Male and female birds are difficult to tell apart except that the hens have colors that are slightly more subdued than males.

A common misconception is that scaled quail are smaller than bobwhites. Personal experience finds both birds about 10 inches long and weighing the same. With the help of Kansas bird hunter Lawrence Smith, the U.S. Forest Service conducted a study of Cimmaron Grassland birds in western Kansas and found the bobs weighed in at seven ounces each, the blues just slightly more. Though not scientific, a similar comparison I did in southwest Texas found the same to be true.

The total U.S. bag of scaled quail is less than one million. New Mexico offers the greatest distribution and hunting opportunities, though I suspect as well that a surprisingly large number of blues are shot in south and west Texas each fall.

Like all western quail, management is based primarily on rainfall. Drought is known to have some short-term effects on populations, but the extent and consequences remain largely unknown and unfounded. Land use practices are a concern in some agricultural and cattle areas, but the majority of birds are found on government land where there is little or no farming.

Hunting pressure appears to have only minor effects on year to year populations. Friendly devils, blues sometimes build up coveys numbering more than 50 birds and hens may raise two broods of chicks each year.

My first introduction to hunting scaled quail came by way of a pair of men named Smith. Two of the finest hunters who have ever flushed a covey, Lawrence Smith and Thayne Smith look like they might be brothers, or at the least cousins.

As it is, they are not even distantly related, but in addition to the same last name they both share a love of quail and quail hunting. Thayne Smith is a highly respected scribe of hunting and fishing tales and Kansas native. Lawrence Smith is a Kansas conservationist with a sixth sense for scaled quail.

Because other writers often ask Thayne where they might find a few blues and because Thayne often refers them on to Lawrence, the latter Smith has been touted in many outdoor journals and books. My introduction was no different and on a cold and snowy day many years ago, Thayne and I rolled out of Tulsa and up to the Cimmaron Grasslands in

*Scaled quail, or "blues," sport slate blue feathers edged in black and a fluffy white crest.
These birds inhabit the arid grasslands and semi-deserts of the southwest, including
Kansas, Colorado, Texas, Arizona and New Mexico.*

southwest Kansas. On the way to Elkhart, we picked up two more hunting companions, Charlie Carroll and Bud Coons.

The first covey was pretty indicative of scaled quail hunting. We found the birds near a "guzzler." Guzzlers are water traps designed to catch and hold water for wildlife and there are 85 of them in the Cimmaron Grasslands. Under contract with the U.S. Forest Service, Lawrence Smith built most of them and as far as I know, he is the only person who knows where they all are.

After running out about 50 yards ahead of my shorthair's point, the first covey busted and flew in just about every direction including straight back at us.

Next followed some hasty shooting, after which we gathered our wits and began to pin down some singles. Then it happened. My weirdest experience in 20 years of quail hunting.

First was the dog. She danced, circled and barked around a 20-foot tall oil storage tank until her tongue lolled out. Though she claimed to be strictly a quail dog, the little pointer was not adverse to running a raccoon or house cat now and then, so I decided to satisfy both her curiosity and mine by climbing the ladder to the top of the tank. When I peeked over the top, I found nary a coon or cat but seven nervous scaled quail! So I decided to do the proper thing, flush 'em and shoot.

Climbing over the top, I reloaded my Model 12, and inched my way towards the birds. They ran to the far side of the tank's roof and waited. Now I had to think, if I kick into them, I might fall off the tank, and besides, cornering cowering quail on a rooftop is not the epitome of sportsman-like quail hunting. So I did the next best thing.

I threw shotgun shells at them to make them fly.

Finally, after the third expertly placed lob of high based $7\frac{1}{2}$s, the birds flew. I ran to the edge and got off two hurried missed shots. When I climbed down the tank, even my dog was laughing. But I learned an important scaled quail hunting lesson. Blues will run rather than fly even when the escape cover is the steel cap of a Kansas oil tank.

Veteran blues' hunters often just watch coveys flush and then concentrate on working the singles with a pointing dog. I have found this to be a worthwhile tactic in most types of cover where blues are found. Though they are noted for their running characteristics and abilities, once the birds are broken up, the singles hold exceptionally well. Fresh snow makes locating both coveys and singles much easier.

In Kansas, Texas and Oklahoma, the range of bobwhites and blues often overlap. When this is the case, both birds can be taken, sometimes from the same covey rise. It is doubtful that the two species mingle within one covey, but the birds do scatter out to share the same feeding

The brightly marked and colored Gambel's quail inhabits the desert regions of the Southwest. Hunters in Arizona take the majority of Gambel's quail, where the annual bag can exceed two million birds in a good year.

areas. In the areas where both are found, blues seem to be the dominant species.

Good pheasant and bobwhite dogs adapt to blues in short order. Hold a dog tight while hunting a covey, let him range wide when trying to locate singles. Some hunters don't even put dogs down until the covey is busted and the singles have scattered.

Because the gregarious blues are so dependent on covey support for survival, it's a good idea to quit hunting at mid-afternoon during the shorter winter days so the birds have a chance to regroup before dark.

When you find the all-around sporting clays gun, (if there is an all-around sporting clays gun) you've found the ideal blue quail gun. Close flushing singles require the old standby open choke, while fast breaking coveys sometimes demand modified or full. A day of hunting can bring situations that call for just about every shotgun variation ever produced.

Then again, it's this same variety that makes hunting blues so much fun.

Gambel's Quail

Gambel's quail are to quail what wood ducks are to waterfowl. The brightly marked and colored birds are striking. Male Gambel's are about 10 inches in length and built a little blockier than a blue or bobwhite. They are found in the desert regions of Arizona, New Mexico, Nevada, southern California and Old Mexico.

Their black topknot plume sets off a white-bordered, rust skullcap and the males have a distinctive black breast spot and a black throat patch. Again, as is the case with most quail species, the female has similar but less distinct markings.

When winter rainfall is plentiful, the Gambel's quail is a prolific bird with clutches of more than 12 birds common. Hens can raise two broods per season. But when the desert receives less than its fair ration of precious water, populations suffer.

The rain lets biologists pretty much determine the success of a quail season six months before it starts. Five inches between October and March is about minimum. Anything less and the hunting is usually poor.

Winter rains spawn green desert plants that are full of vitamin A. Vitamin A allows a hen Gambel's quail to produce more eggs. A wet winter means more quail.

But the rains have to come at the right time. If it comes while the birds are nesting, the nests can wash away. Rain also helps propagate the chick's food supplies of small insects.

Management practices of the desert quail revolve around the rain. Hunting groups police themselves as well and back off the birds earlier

Gambel's quail are also known as desert quail—note the sand and cactus surrounding the female Gambel's above.

in dry years. Habitat loss is not yet a big concern as most of the birds live in areas where the climate is too cruel for cattle or crops. Some sportsman groups have enhanced desert cover with protective thicket piles and thousands of birds benefit from water entrapments originally built for desert bighorn sheep.

Arizona hunters take the majority of Gambel's quail where the annual bag can exceed two million birds in a good year. The hot spots stay the same year to year providing that the birds have a constant source of water. If a tank or water hole should dry up, the covey may move to a new area, but for the most part they are fairly predictable. Most of their food supply consists of the seeds from desert plants, such as mesquite, Russian thistle and alfalfa. A smaller portion is made up of small bugs like grasshoppers and crickets.

Tying the birds to particular patches of food, water and cover, is about the only way to hunt Gambel's quail. My most successful hunts into new areas have resulted from variations of two tactics.

Serious Gambel's quail hunters are reluctant to reveal pet territories so I rely on big game hunting friends to keep me posted about areas where they have noticed lots of birds or tracks. Method number two is to drive desert roads during the early and late hours when the birds are most active and locate a covey. During the spring I'll often ride horseback through favorite areas to see how the hatch has turned out. If by May the hens are only trailed by two or three youngsters, I lay off those birds the next year. If the survival rate jumps up to 10 birds or so per family, the hunting can be expected to be good. Five or six chicks per family means average hunting.

I doubt if the Arizona Game & Fish Department takes much stock in my survey methods, but all and all it works fairly well. Once birds are located, hunting them is fairly simple.

Some coveys run like blues but the majority hold better. Once they flush, they usually don't fly far. The wings of a Gambel's quail are designed for fast take offs, not sustained flight. When the singles land, they can easily be marked. However, they do run when they hit the ground.

Pointing breeds work Gambel's quite well; the German shorthair seems to be the favored breed among Arizona hunters. Unlike their eastern counterparts, western quail dogs have to contend with such hazards as snakes, rocks and painful cactus. Many experienced hunters only go out during the colder months after the snakes have gone underground. It's a good practice that I now personally subscribe to after sitting on a western diamondback one sunny November afternoon.

Guns for Gambel's quail should be light, fast and open choked. The country they are hunted in is often rough, hilly and distant. Days are long

The largest of all quail species, the mountain quail inhabits the brushy hill and mountain cover of the western coastal states and parts of Idaho and Nevada.

and water for the dogs sometimes needs to be carried, the extra weight of a heavy shotgun is a tiresome burden. One point to be taken seriously: towns in good desert quail country are few and the proverbial far between. Take an extra gun and plenty of shells just in case.

The birds are a real challenge. For me, they are one of the toughest of all quail to hit and that makes a trip to the desert even more rewarding.

Mountain Quail

Mountain quail are the largest of all the quail species and the most difficult to hunt. They have a jet black plume like the Gambel's and their most distinguishing marks are seven or eight white bars on each flank. The female's coloration is identical to the male. Adult birds are about 12 inches long and can weigh up to three-quarters of a pound.

Mountain quail seek out the brushy hill and mountain cover of the western coastal states and parts of Idaho and Nevada. Altitudes where the birds are found range from 2,000 to 10,000 feet and the hunting is tough.

The birds need water and lush vegetation and their diet is primarily made up of the seeds and grains of mountain plants and grasses. Where burned off areas have started the regrowth process the birds thrive. Coveys usually consist only of small family groups and large concentrations of birds are only found in extreme cold periods.

The annual bag across the western states is quite low, less than 150,000 birds, making them the second rarest quail next to the Mearns. Most birds are killed by hunters seeking other upland game in California and Oregon. There really are no clear-cut hunting techniques. You start walking in an area known to hold birds and hope that you stumble into a few. The walking is tough and the hunting is frustrating as evidenced by low annual bag.

Mountain quail hold well for pointing dogs because even wild birds are calm by quail standards. The birds are reluctant to fly and often sit tight in their preferred thick mountain cover. When they do bust, they come up fast on short wings designed for speed.

It goes without saying that guns for mountain quail should be lightweight. A sling helps as distances between cover can be long and climbing sometimes takes both hands.

More like chukar hunting than quail hunting, I doubt if mountain quail hunting will ever be a popular hunting sport.

Valley Quail

Next to the mourning dove, the valley quail is the most sought after upland bird in the populous state of California. Like Mountain quail,

Valley quail are the most popular quail species in Idaho, Nevada, Oregon, California and Washington. Coveys have been known to number up to 200 birds, and hold well for pointing dogs.

they have a black topknot, but being hip West Coasters, the valley quail's headgear curves forward.

Besides California, valley quail are the most popular quail in Idaho, Nevada, Oregon and Washington. The annual bag runs more than two million, with the majority shot in California. Valley quail are often referred to as California quail.

Birds feed almost exclusively on plant seeds and leaves. Coveys have been known to number up to 200 birds and reside over several acres. Like most western quail, valley varieties would rather run than fly when flushed. When they do break into the air, they fly strongly for moderate distances, set their wings and glide into the next patch of vegetation. Then they run again.

Because the coveys are so large and the birds inhabit the more accessible valleys and foothills, California quail are easier to find and hunt than their mountain-dwelling kinfolk. Government land supports good numbers of birds, but by far the best hunting occurs on private land in farming areas.

Hunting tactics are about the same as those for Gambel's quail. Coveys can be located by driving farm roads or on tips from farmers, ranchers and other hunting friends. Valley quail don't move far from the thick cover plots where they are raised. When you locate a covey, chances are they'll be in the same general area the next time you're out.

The birds hold well for pointing dogs and are hard to kick out of thick cover. They are probably the toughest of all quail to hit. Since they do sit so tight, a fast, lightweight, open choked gun is needed. Though my taste buds aren't sophisticated enough to tell, valley quail are said to be the most flavorful of all the upland birds. All I know is that I like them all equally, broiled, baked or pan fried!

Mearns Quail

The shyest of all the quail, Mearns are found only on limited ranges in Arizona, New Mexico, Texas and Old Mexico. Texas has no open season and the birds have been legal targets in Arizona and New Mexico only since the early 1960s.

It is quite apparent that not much is known about Mearns quail from the large amount of contradicting information found in the biology books. Numerous reference materials list the weight of a Mearns anywhere from three to seven ounces. Most birds I've seen seem to be about the size of an average bobwhite.

Males have a unique pattern of coloration with pronounced white dots over dark gray flanks. Females are more subdued. The birds are found in wooded grasslands at elevations form 4,000 to 9,000 feet. They

Mearns quail are almost impossible to hunt without a good pointer. The birds hold tight, then fly a fast straight line much like a deceptive bobwhite.

feed on a variety of plant and insect matter including lily bulbs, seeds, berries, crickets and grasshoppers.

Though not tame, Mearns seldom fly when approached by man. Their wild coloration provides excellent camouflage and the birds prefer to sit it out and hope they go unnoticed. For this reason it is almost impossible to hunt Mearns quail without good pointing dogs.

When flushed, they fly a fast straight line and offer about the same type of target as that of a deceptive bobwhite. Initial flights are short and the birds fly into dense cover where the singles hold well and can be effectively hunted.

Thorough, close-working dogs such as German shorthairs and Brittanies have the edge over the wider-ranging pointers and setters that often run right over tight sitting coveys. Open choked guns work best as the flushes are apt to be close to the hunter.

The birds do well on their established ranges but there is little hunting outside those traditional areas. The majority of hunting in the U.S. occurs on the Coronado National Grasslands in southeastern Arizona. The annual bag in this area runs between 30,000 and 80,000 birds. Widespread in Old Mexico, there appears to be only limited hunting at this time.

Mearns quail populations are closely tied to carryover from one year to the next and an adequate growth of grass. Overgrazing and habitat destruction has documented effects on Mearns' numbers and the birds are now closely monitored and managed.

To me, though extremely limited, these are the ultimate game birds. They hold great for dogs, burst from cover and are tough to hit. And like all quail, they make for an excellent Sunday dinner.

8

Pheasants

S treets in Dodge City, Kansas never really quiet down on the eve of the pheasant season opener. There is always some group of enthusiastic bird hunters about preparing in their own way for the equivalent of a religious holiday.

Every hotel room has been booked for months. Restaurants stock up on extra provisions. Taverns and nightclubs double or triple the beer deliveries.

Hunters hit town by every conceivable conveyance. They drive into town in Suburbans and Broncos towing six- and eight-dog trailers. They fly in private planes into Dodge City's small airport. They take commercial flights into Wichita and rent cars to drive across the state in the gathering dusk.

The Kansas pheasant season opens on the morn, and quite conceivably hunters from all 50 states have gathered to salute this American rite of autumn. Such is the powerful allure of a brash and brassy bird called the ringneck pheasant.

In the next 48 hours about one third of the total pheasant harvest for the season will be gathered. That's despite the fact that the season will run for more than two months!

And it's not just a phenomenon unique to the Sunflower State. The scenes are the same whether the town's name is Creston, Iowa; Pierre, South Dakota; or Lincoln, Nebraska. The pheasant season is a huge economic boon to these and countless big and small communities in the

Midwest and Plains States. Everyone, from the hotel owner who hosts the same hunting guests year after year to the housewife who sets up a bird plucking service in her garage, counts on the pheasants and the pheasant hunters. For them, there is much more at stake than "sport." For them the quality of life depends to some degree upon the pheasants.

But there is another kind of pheasant opener, too. One in which a boy and his dad load a springer into a pickup, drive a mile or two and hunt. No fancy preparation. No huge outlay of dollars. No long drive or airline flight through the night. But they appreciate the hunt just as much, and opening day is just as much of a holiday—it's just celebrated in a different tradition.

No other upland bird offers such diverse hunting opportunities in as many parts of North America. Between hunting in large groups, to hunting on your own. Between hunting in the wild, on put-and-take public lands and on licensed shooting preserves. Between hunting driven birds or flushed birds. Between hunting with a pointer, with a flushing dog or dogless. Between hunting grasslands, cornfields, hardwoods or pine belts. The pheasant provides just about any kind of hunting for which you could ask.

Upland purists will laud the civilized attributes of hunting "Gentleman Bob" and the trickiness of the wingshooting afforded by the ruffed grouse, but for the take-it-as-it-comes upland bird hunter, the loud garb and raucous cackle of the rooster pheasant is what autumn and upland hunting are all about.

The Ringneck Pheasant In North America

Though the traditions of ringneck pheasant hunting in America's heartland are as truly red, white and blue as Mom and apple pie, the bird itself is not. The ringneck pheasant is not native to North America. He's a foreigner. Wildlife biologists call him an exotic.

For most folks alive today, it's difficult to remember a time when pheasants weren't part of the countryside in states like North and South Dakota, Kansas, Iowa, Nebraska, Minnesota, Wisconsin and Illinois. But it wasn't until the early 1880's that the first successful stocking of pheasants was made in the United States. Those birds were released in the Wilamette Valley of Oregon by a gentleman named Judge Denny.

It's a sobering thought for the pheasant devotee to imagine this marvelous game bird never coming to American shores. And it's not that far-fetched to think that if the exotic laws back in the late 1800s were as strict as they are today, we wouldn't have a wild pheasant population in this country.

The ringneck pheasant, a foreigner to North America, is today an important financial boon to many Midwestern communities.

The ringneck pheasant's original homelands are the grassy steppe regions of Asia, particularly Mongolia.

Upland bird populations are incredibly dynamic, fluctuating in huge swings depending on habitat loss or gain, weather and predation. As Chapter 16 on upland bird management discusses, it is an exceedingly difficult task to pinpoint populations. But in considering the history of the ringneck pheasant in North America most veteran hunters and farmers agree that the real heyday of the pheasant in North America was the 1940s through the early '50s.

Use Wisconsin for example. The first planting of pheasants in Wisconsin took place in 1916 when Colonel Gustav Pabst made releases in the fields of Waukesha and Jefferson Counties in southeastern Wisconsin. The birds took, and 11 years later Wisconsin held its first open season on pheasants in those two counties.

Encouraged by the success of Pabst's stockings, the old Wisconsin Conservation Department (the predecessor of the Wisconsin Department of Natural Resources) decided to get in on the act. It opened a state game farm at Peninsula State Park, expressly for rearing pheasants. In 1934, the operation was moved to larger facilities in Poynette.

During the '20s and '30s Wisconsin's primary reason for stocking pheasants was expansion of their range, and by 1942 the birds were present in all but 11 of the state's northernmost counties where habitat is not suitable.

Even though 1942 was a war year, Wisconsin hunters harvested an estimated 801,000 birds. Never before or since have Wisconsin pheasant hunters done as well!

At present, Wisconsin is a marginal pheasant hunting state at best. More recent goals in Wisconsin have been to maintain a statewide population of about 385,000 roosters. That's a total *population* figure, not a harvest figure!

Other states like the Dakotas, Iowa and Kansas have fared much better and offer more pheasants to the modern upland bird hunter. But even in these premier pheasant states you'll seldom hunt a whole weekend of the season without running into a lifelong farmer who will regale you with tales of flushing hundreds of pheasants from a single weedy draw! To some extent these may be embellished tales of a lost youth—hunting stories. But to inspire such a plethora of common stories, these scenes must have been witnessed at least a few times in "the good ol' days."

Wherever pheasants have fallen on hard times, temporarily or over the long haul, the primary culprit is loss of habitat. Fence row to fence row farming, the early mowing of hayfields and the pesticides which sweep corn rows completely weedfree, all steal valuable nesting and wintering habitat from pheasants. As farmers have sought to squeeze every bushel of production from the land in tough economic times, these pheasant-killing practices become more and more common.

Thankfully, game departments and folks who love pheasant hunting aren't languishing in remembrances of the past halcyon of the pheasant. They are out trying to make good new days.

Game departments have wisely seen fit to require hunters to purchase "pheasant stamps" with the revenue from their sale earmarked specifically for pheasant habitat recovery. Organizations like Pheasants Forever (Dept. NAH, P. O. Box 75473, St. Paul, MN 55175) are in the forefront of the private sector to support pheasants and pheasant hunting. It's their efforts, with our support, that we must bank on. It's through them that we'll keep the all-American tradition of pheasant hunting alive.

Opening Day Pheasants

There are all kinds of opening day pheasants. Despite what others may say, you can't pin them down and say, "All opening day pheasants always do this," or "All opening day pheasants always do that." The birds are as individual as hunters and can react to opening day hunting tactics in an infinite variety of ways. On opening day, and throughout the hunting season for that matter, pheasants will react based on any number of criteria. Some include the amount and type of cover; weather conditions; hunting pressure and previous experiences, if any, with hunters.

All successful upland bird hunting keys on two components. Number One is locating the birds. Number Two is getting them to behave the way you want them to.

This holds true from the first time you uncase your shotgun on opening day, until you case it after the final hour of the season.

For the upland bird hunter, especially the guy who will be hunting on opening day, locating the birds is usually not a problem. The out-of-state hunter most likely will be hunting with a local contact whether that's a friendly farmer, a guide or a long distance friend. You can rely on them to help you find birds. If you'll be relying on your own reconnaissance, then a bit of preseason scouting is in order.

Scouting for pheasants is really no different than scouting for big game. You can use maps and game department reports to get you going, but the best way to find birds is to get out there and look for them. Drive back roads in the area you hope to hunt and look for pheasants.

Don't make the mistakes of looking only in the road ditches. Take along a pair of binoculars to glass open grain fields and distant fence lines. It's best to do your scouting at the times birds feed or gravel. They are most active then, and easiest to spot.

An increasingly important part of preseason scouting for pheasants is to secure landowner contacts. Who owns that piece of land where you saw eight roosters perched in the hedge apple bushes along the roadside one foggy morning? Will he let you hunt it? These are questions to answer two or three weeks before the season opens—not in the last hour before opening!

Scouting well before the season opens gives you time to check out all your sources thoroughly. A friendly mailman who carries over a large rural route can be a tremendous resource of bird population information. In fact, many states rely on the counts made by postal carriers to determine game bird populations. Since he delivers mail, he may also be able to point out the landowners of specific parcels.

Sheriff's deputies who patrol rural roads, milk truck drivers who pick up at even the most remote farms, fuel oil delivery men—all are potential gold mines of information on pheasant populations and locations. Use your imagination and you can probably come up with several people you know who have the opportunity to travel country roads a lot.

And when someone provides you a hot tip, don't forget to thank them. A sausage, some cheese and a smoked pheasant or two go a long way toward showing your appreciation, and to securing their future hot tips.

Using all the resources available and some serious reconnaissance on your own makes scouting the easier of the two components for a successful hunt. Even in lean years when pheasant populations are down, you'll find birds to hunt if you get out there ahead of time and look for them.

Component Number Two—getting the birds to act the way you want them to—is far more difficult. That's the component that makes hunting hunting.

What kind of birds are you dealing with on opening day?

More than any other time during the season, you'll be working young, inexperienced pheasants. Not dumb pheasants—young and inexperienced pheasants. By the time hunting season rolls around, there really aren't any dumb pheasants. Mortality on first year birds caused by predation and the vagaries of weather is so high that dumb birds do not survive very long.

If pheasants could pass their hunter-wariness from generation to generation, very few would be taken by nimrods who ply the fields! Actually, it's not too farfetched to believe that this could be happening genetically. If a pheasant has in his genes a tendency toward running in-

To the devout pheasant hunter, nothing compares to the traditions of opening day. Scenes like this are what keep us going through the rest of the year.

stead of flying, he is likely to live longer and breed more than his flying kin. That means he'll be passing his traits on to more descendants than the flying bird. Theoretically, over the lifetimes of many hunters, we could be left with a race of running pheasants that seldom take to the air!

That aside, your best bet for encountering inexperienced pheasants is on opening weekend and during the first week of the season. It's at this time that what have become "traditional" pheasant hunting methods work the best.

Even so, careful attention to detail in your hunting strategy will produce faster action and more birds brought to bag.

The Opening Day Drive

For many upland bird hunters, the opening of pheasant season means getting together with a large group of friends to work together to bag some birds—and more importantly have a good time. Like any other convening of a hunting fraternity, there is a great deal to be said for the camaraderie of this kind of hunting. Friends and relatives in a pheasant hunting gang may see each other only once a year, barring weddings and funerals, but they'll list those seldom seen cohorts among their very best friends.

And there's more to be said for opening weekend drives. Properly executed, they can produce outstanding hunts with lots of shooting for everyone.

The most important key to success in any driven hunt, whether for pheasants or deer or any other type of game is a good leader. An effective hunt leader must be a hunter who is familiar with the birds and the land to be hunted, and who is persuasive enough to get everyone in a large, diverse group of excited, anxious hunters to strive for the same goal—that being a *safe* and enjoyable hunt for all. The best hunt leader is often the landowner who is hosting the hunt or the individual who organizes the group in the first place.

Safety is of paramount importance on any hunt—especially a large group hunt. You can never be quite sure of what you're getting into in a large group. There are always newcomers from whom you don't know what to expect and there are some hunters who tend to become lax about safety precautions as they become comfortable with a group. Keep out a watchful eye for both.

The first and most important job for the drive hunt leader is to lay down some basic, inflexible safety rules for the hunters in the group. Rules should include, but are not limited to:

    1)   All hunters must wear a blaze orange hat and at least a blaze orange vest above the waist.

As land access becomes more difficult, thorough preseason scouting becomes more critical.

2) All shots taken by drivers or standers must be above the horizon. That means that sky must show below the barrel when swinging on a bird.
3) Drivers must stay aware of the positions of the hunters on both sides and should not walk ahead or fall behind the line.
4) Standers must stay in their positions until the drive is absolutely finished, meaning that the drivers have passed the line of standers.
5) When a walker drops a bird, the rest of the drive line should stop while the two or three hunters closest to the mark move in quickly to retrieve the bird.
6) Standers should carefully mark fallen birds, but use caution about retrieving them immediately as the drive line approaches the end of the field. It's best to have two or three hunters designated on each drive to assist standers in marking and retrieving fallen birds.

A short "meeting" after breakfast on opening morning is often the best forum in which to present these laws of the day. And it's not "too much" to have a chalkboard handy to draw out what you're talking about. Make sure that there is an opportunity to get the safety points across before guns are uncased and the hunters are shuffling their feet in impatience to hunt.

These rules may seem like common sense, but they must be reiterated several times before the group goes afield. Opening day pheasant drives can be big, really big, with 50 hunters or more joining forces to hunt large fields. Safety can't be emphasized enough.

Besides, some of the same rules that will make a hunt safe will also make it more successful.

For example, keeping drivers in a straight row shortens the distance between drivers, making it less inviting for crafty pheasants to run back between the walkers and hide or flush behind the line. Having blockers refrain from searching for fallen birds until the drive is over will keep them alert for more birds coming by.

Attention to detail can make the difference to the success of an opening day pheasant drive. The same field, carefully pushed by a group of diligent, concentrating hunters, might produce twice as many birds as if it were pushed by hunters moving too fast in a ragged line who are not really thinking about what they are doing.

A successful pheasant drive is slow. The birds are more reluctant to run back through a slow moving line of hunters than a fast one.

The distance between drivers is best dictated by the type of cover. In standing corn, as in Iowa and Nebraska, a walker in every fourth or fifth

A large group of hunters lines up to push a cut milo field toward blockers waiting a ¹/₂-mile away. For some hunters, these large drives and the group camaraderie are what pheasant hunting is all about.

row may not be enough. Hunting cut milo fields in western Kansas, hunters could be spaced as much as 20 to 25 yards apart. Especially when drivers are sparse, flushing dogs like labs and spaniels do well to fill in the gaps. When drive hunting, it is of the utmost importance to have a well mannered dog which obeys commands immediately and which will walk contentedly at heel when called upon to do so. Bringing an unruly dog along on a drive hunt is a very fast way to lose an invitation to hunt with the group again.

Next to running back through gaps in the line of drivers, the favorite evasive technique of the pheasant is to run ahead and around the end of the line. There are two good ways to combat this tactic.

If plenty of hunters are available, position some "standers" along the sides of the field being driven as well as on the end of it. As the drive moves down the field, the standers along the sides of the field join the line when it reaches them. The distance between drivers along the line compresses as more standers become walkers. This results in a tighter and tighter line of drivers as it approaches the blocked end of the field where the birds are most likely to try to sneak back through the line.

If the size of the group doesn't allow enough bodies to block the sides of the field, then the end walkers on the line should swing ahead of the line about 25 or 30 yards, and the drivers second from the ends should be ahead about 15 or 20 yards from the line to the inside of them. This presents to pheasants running to the sides of the main line the illusion that they are surrounded and that they can't circle to the outside of the drive without being detected.

Let the size of the group dictate the size of the fields to be hunted. A group of 50 or 60 hunters can band together and effectively cover half-mile square milo fields in two swings. That means each field would be driven one half at a time. The driving line would be a quarter mile wide and push a half mile of stubble field toward the posted blockers.

Smaller groups naturally must seek out smaller patches of cover to hunt efficiently. A narrow weedy ditch, swale or fence line could be driven effectively by as few as four hunters, or less with a good dog.

Opening Day On Your Own

For some hunters the joy of the hunt is lost in a large group. To them, the tradition of opening day is hunting alone, with a single friend or a small, carefully chosen cadre of hunting soul mates. Often these are hunters with canine companions who get as much pleasure from watching the dogs work as in any aspect of the hunt.

Individuals and small groups of hunters can be very successful on opening day pheasants if they avoid the temptation of the huge fields of standing or recently harvested crops. It is even more important for the lone or small-group hunter to gear himself to the appropriate sized patches of cover. For anyone with doubts, imagine looking down from an airplane on a five-acre patch of standing corn. Just think how little ground is covered at any one time by three hunters and two dogs in that patch. There is no reason that any pheasant in that patch would ever be *forced* to fly as an escape. (Some might do it anyway, but they're the ones that don't get to pass the genes to the next generation of roosters.)

Hunters who seek pheasants on their own or in small groups must take an analytical approach to large patches of cover. Within those large patches are smaller isolated segments of cover that can be effectively hunted. Some of the most obvious are weedy ditches and fence rows. Tiny sloughs are good, too. In states where it is legal to hunt them, road ditches are popular, too. Railroad right-of-ways offer some good opportunities if you can get permission to hunt them.

The small group hunter should think small and think narrow. It's surprising how many birds will flock in a small patch of cover if it provides the right elements to hold them.

The hunter on his own must also work to get birds to flush within range of *his* gun. The drive hunter doesn't have to contend with this problem as much, because if the group is large enough and well organ-

The distance between hunters in a drive is dictated by the cover. In standing crop fields it's best to have a hunter every few rows to keep the birds from sneaking back through the line.

ized, somebody is going to get shooting at every rooster which exits the field in the air.

To hold the birds closer, the individual or small group hunter does better to concentrate on thick cover. Pheasants tend to hold better in thick grass or weeds than in the sanitary rows of a chemically treated cornfield. Look for cover like cattails, plum thickets and dense grass and weeds.

One of the neatest tricks a lone hunter or a small group of hunters can pull is to pick up birds that the drive hunters missed; birds that were right under their noses. For example, in western Kansas a great deal of milo (sorghum) is grown in fields watered by a center pivot irrigation system. These systems usually consist of a one-quarter mile long irrigation pipe mounted on wheels. Water is pumped from the center out to sprinkler heads spaced along the length of the pipe. They call these fields "milo rings" because the system irrigates a half-mile diameter circle around the center of the field.

However, just like anywhere else, the roads in the Kansas countryside are laid out in squares around the fields. That means each milo ring has four corners which are often left fallow. Now, that's perfect pheasant cover, but it's often pushed too fast or not at all by drive hunters who have developed tunnel vision for row crops. A hunter or two with a good dog or two can have a "field" day cleaning up these corners that weren't pushed properly.

For the best success, the individual hunter needs to know the intricacies of the terrain he is hunting. He can make great use of the land to get the birds to behave the way he wants them to.

A stretch of open ground and the end of some dense cover is as effective for the lone hunter as a row of blockers is for a drive hunter. Pheasants will tend to run ahead of hunters and dogs until they come to an open patch of ground. They know that if they cross the patch on foot they'll be as vulnerable as if they flew. Their first alternate plan would be to cut back past the approaching hunter if at all possible. With that alternative eliminated by a slow but steadily approaching hunter who is weaving his way back and forth through a narrow strip of cover, the next choice is to wait it out and hope the hunter doesn't come too close.

When a pheasant makes that decision he's as good as yours if your aim is true. *That is, if you walk out the whole cover!* Never stop short of the end of a strip of dense cover. Always pause for a few moments just inside the edge of the cover, and then for good measure walk out into the open. Very rare is the opening day cock pheasant with nerves steely enough to stay hidden when you've stopped and he's sandwiched be-

Small groups or even individual hunters can enjoy opening day success if the hunt is well thought-out and executed.

tween you and the wide open spaces. Chances are he's gonna fly, and you're gonna get him!

A New Approach For Mid-Season Pheasants

Ten days into the season, the rules change. Except on the most diligently guarded private property there are no inexperienced pheasants left. More of the crop fields may have been taken in but, if the weather hasn't cooperated, the farmers will have little more out of the fields than they did on opening day. Cold weather and snow probably have not arrived either to concentrate the birds and force them into winter cover.

The conditions from this point until winter really sets in present some of the most difficult hunting the upland bird hunter is likely to encounter. He's dealing with hunter-wise birds that have huge tracts of cover in which to maneuver.

The way to score on pheasants during mid-season is to hunt with care and to become as unpredictable as the quarry. That means taking a new approach.

In analyzing a patch of mid-season pheasant cover, try to figure out how other hunters would normally approach the area, then do the opposite.

Consider the following scenario as an example.

You know of a farmer who has granted you permission to hunt his property in the past, so you stop to say "hello" and see if he'll oblige you again. After handshakes and friendly small talk, he tells you you're welcome to hunt, but most of his good areas have already been hunted that morning by his brother and nephews. However, you learn that he bought a new farm during the summer. It's about six miles away and hasn't been hunted since Sunday. It's Friday, so it sounds like it might be worth a try.

With another handshake you take the crude map he drew on a scrap of paper torn from a paper feed bag, and you're off to go hunting. The dogs whine in the crates; they're as anxious as you.

As you drive to this new hunting ground, you think of the other things your farmer friend told you. The place has been hunted about half a dozen times since opening day three weeks ago. The landowner said the guys who hunted it didn't get many birds after opening day, but they have been doing a lot of shooting. In fact, he asked them not to come back because when he was over there picking corn, he found some fenceposts shot up pretty bad.

From what he showed you, your contact owns half the section. A paved road runs the mile along the south end that's his. Just off of that road, about centered in that mile, are the abandoned buildings of the original farmstead. The grass that's grown up where the driveway once was is well matted down from use by farm machinery and by the previous hunters who parked in the yard.

To the east of the buildings is a picked cornfield, which is bordered by a dirt road that runs north-south. To the west is a large plowed field. Directly behind the buildings is a small pond surrounded by head high weeds. It sits at the foot of a long, weed-choked ditch which winds north from the pond toward the far side of the property. The ditch and the grassy lane next to it are about 20 yards wide in total. They separate the plowed field and picked corn, but grassy swales occasionally swing away from the ditch out into the cornfield.

About a quarter mile to the north of the pond the ditch widens into a large fallow area. It includes some timbered swales running north onto adjoining property which is heavily posted, but is mostly fallow crop land enrolled in the Conservation Reserve Program (CRP). (In other words, the farmer is receiving benefits from the government not to grow anything on that land.) It is 60-70 acres of prime mid-season pheasant cover. This unfarmed plot is sort of a U-shape separated from the dirt

Always walk a patch of cover to the very end. Birds will hold tight and never flush if you come up short. Shots are common at the end of cover.

road on the east by part of the cornfield and on the west by the plowed field and a dense fenceline of hedge apples.

Shifting into low, you pull your truck into the abandoned farm lot and reconnoiter. From the condition of the "parking area" in the farm yard, it's quite evident that every group of hunters to date have probably started and ended their hunts here. That means other than the gang which drove the cornfield on opening day (then unpicked), everyone else who hunted this farm probably worked it the same way. They all hunted the ditch back to the CRP land, made some circles out there, then walked the edge of the cornfield back to the vehicles, occasionally pushing the grassy fingers back to the ditch. Depending on the size of the groups, someone may have been blocking at the ditch, maybe not.

If that's true, then the pheasants on this farm have been hunted at least five times in a row pretty much the same way. Imagine what those birds in that ditch will be doing the second they hear the tailgate of your pickup slam shut and the action of your shotgun close. They'll be running north and won't stop until they are on the safe side of the posted fenceline. Those that don't will flush way ahead at the first tinkling of the dog bells.

Though you're dealing with experienced birds, you have an advantage in that they only have experience with hunters doing things the same way over and over. You have the opportunity to add a new twist, and add some of those experienced pheasants to your bag.

You back the truck on to the highway and drive down to the dirt road along the edge of the cornfield. You turn left and follow the dirt road to the fence line on the north side of the cornfield which marks the edge of your friend's property. You pull into the field on a service drive and park well out of the way of any machinery that might come in or out of the field.

Keeping the dogs on leashes, you and your two hunting pals ease the doors and tailgate shut and then walk quietly west on the south side of the fenceline. When you get to the eastern edge of the fallow land one hunter stays near that edge and waits. You walk to about the center of the patch and stop. Hunter number three proceeds over to the western edge of the CRP ground.

At a pre-determined time you all begin a slow, meandering hunt south. You give the dogs plenty of time to work out all the cover thoroughly. By the time you all meet at the top of the ditch, the total bag is four roosters with a couple more missed. The dogs got to work on a bunch of hens, too. Some cold soda pop is in order for the human hunters and the dogs get a well-deserved ration from the canteens.

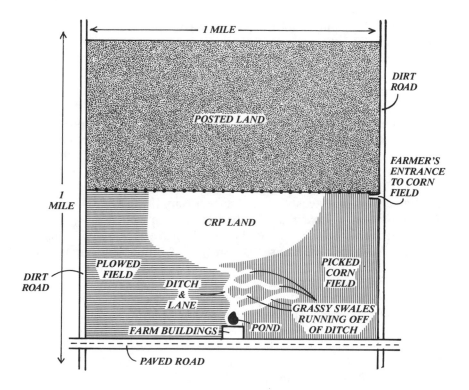

How would you approach the heavily hunted area described in the text?

Before break is over, the guy with the youngest legs finds the dead-furrow in the plowed field and hot foots it for the farm yard. He leaves his dog with you and the senior member of the group.

When you can see the kid's orange coat against the oak tree at the far side of the pond, you and the other hunter set out in that direction. Again, slowly. Your companion takes the ditch and lane with two dogs while you and your pooch walk far out into the cornfield. At the top of the first grassy swale you encounter, you work it back to the ditch where the ditch walker is waiting. As you move within 15 feet of him, two hens take wing.

"Gees, I almost stepped...", a rooster cackles and takes out behind you. You swing through and dump him. Your dog makes a great retrieve over the crest of the hill in the corn stubble.

You head back off to the southeast through the corn and work the next swale back to your buddy in the ditch just the same way. You do this for each swale leading to the ditch. Finally at the pond, you work around the east side and the older gent works to the west. The kid shows you both up when he dumps a double on the two long-spurred roosters that boil out because they've got no way left to turn.

The bag—seven big, beautiful, *experienced* rooster pheasants. The method—a new approach.

Almost any piece of cover can be hunted with a new approach. It may not be the most convenient way to cover a patch of ground (in the example you ended the most productive hunting more than a half mile from your truck), but the results will usually be worth the extra effort.

Careful attention to details can make or break any approach to a hunting area in mid-season. Avoid unnecessary noise or talking. Keep dogs at heel until you are absolutely ready to hunt and shoot. Take the time to hunt every piece of cover thoroughly. Take every opportunity to use a blocker and to use natural barriers that prevent birds from running ahead.

The lone hunter can try new approaches, too. For example, the lone hunter's chances of flushing an experienced pheasant from a long, heavy-cover ditch without the help of a blocker are slim. However, he can become his own blocker. After he has steadily pushed the ditch a 100 yards or so he should watch ahead for a bend. A good distance before he gets to the corner, he should climb out of the swale on the inside of the bend. Doing double time across the open field, he should loop ahead to the next bend, then climb back into the swale and work back in the direction from which he had been approaching.

Any pheasants which rounded the bend ahead of the hunter will still believe they are being pursued from behind, then suddenly run into what they think is a second hunter approaching from the front! They are fooled into feeling surrounded, and that's when pheasants opt for the last resort—flight. And again, with a new approach you've made experienced, mid-season pheasants behave the way you want them to.

In Late Season The Tough Get Going

It takes a tough hunter to hunt tough birds. Hunters after late season pheasants have to be among the toughest.

In most parts of pheasant country, late season is cold. And late season pheasant hunting often means wading through snow, sometimes lots of it.

The birds are at their fewest and wariest. On top of that, they are concentrated. Most of the crops are out, and all of the birds are seeking thick

At any part of the season, the lone hunter will benefit from the assistance of a good dog.

protective cover adjacent to some kind of food source. The cover must offer shelter from wind and storms. The food must be close at hand so that the energy it provides isn't wasted in traveling great distances to and from feeding.

At this time of the season, though, the birds are the easiest to find, they are most difficult to hunt. The hunter after late season birds often has to deal with large numbers of sharp eyes and ears all on alert for danger. Because lesser cover is beaten down and/or covered with snow the birds can see further. And when they are in the preferred, dense cover, an undetected approach is almost impossible.

Hunting late season pheasants can be plain hard work. But the hunter willing to put in the time and excursion can score consistently if he'll use the sound, basic techniques of early and mid-season hunt and combine them with some special late-season know-how:

1) In late season, seek out and hunt the thickest cover you can find. Two favorites are cattail sloughs and evergreen shelter belts. Even small patches of these thick cover types can hold unbelievable numbers of late-season roosters.

Hunting a December cattail slough for pheasants can be a strange experience. You may actually be hunting on the surface of a frozen marsh where you shot ducks over decoys just a few weeks before.

In shelter belts of dense spruce or pine, shooting late season pheasants can be very much akin to hunting ruffed grouse. You take snapshots or you don't shoot.

2) Weather that's not fit for man nor beast is fit for hunting late season pheasants. During late season snowstorms, pheasants will stay in dense cover later into the day and they will hold tighter. Likewise, on extremely cold mornings they will tend to stay on their roosts longer.

Naturally, special precautions for hunters and dogs are necessary in this kind of weather. Check often for frostbite on humans and canines. Keep as little flesh as possible exposed to the wind. Check dog's paws often to keep snow from balling up between the pads. Keep chains and other emergency gear in the truck. Be sure to have plenty of blankets and hot drinks close-at-hand, too. Dogs require more energy to stay warm, too, so keep them well fed.

3) If you can gather enough hardy souls at this season, large drives can still be a successful technique in late season. A large cattail slough is a prime drive target in December or January.

Birds will flush much farther ahead of the drivers than they did on opening weekend. That means less shooting for the walkers and longer range shooting for the blockers. Tighter chokes, larger shot and magnum loads are the order of the late season drive.

Late season pheasants favor heavy cover, and they'll often flush well out of range.

For safety all drivers must still wear blaze orange, but if the group is trustworthy enough and the blockers can be positioned in the open, consider asking the standers to deck themselves out in marshgrass camo or a snow pattern. The pheasants that will be flying their way may have survived earlier drives and they know what that stationary orange blob is all about.

4) Ambush comes into play in late season, if a hunter can determine a route that is regularly used by pheasants moving from protective roosting cover to feed areas. Depending on the weather and their inclinations, pheasants may walk or fly between these areas. So while hunting out the route's ground cover, try to keep one eye on the sky for birds taking an aerial path.

Tail Feathers

Wherever and whenever the pheasant is hunted, it is a bird worthy of tremendous respect. He offers such a diverse range of hunting opportunities for so many hunters that the loss of this game bird would be a tragedy. The effects of that loss would not only be felt by the hunting community, but by the citizens of countless rural communities that rely on an annual influx of revenue from pheasant hunters.

Though the pheasant is making tremendous comebacks in many parts of their range, two factors contribute most greatly to the loss of pheasant hunting opportunities. One is the decimation of nesting and wintering habitat; the other is the closing of private land to hunters. In a single season, either or both can wipeout pheasant hunting in a large area.

Thankfully, the hunter has some control over the first and almost complete control over the second. For the sake of those who cherish the grand old tradition of pheasant hunting and those who have yet to try it, pheasant hunters need to strongly support habitat restoration projects. And they must take it upon themselves to present shining examples of ethical and respectful behavior in the field and out of it.

9

Prairie Birds

North America's Central Plains has the best pheasant hunting in the world and the wildest bobwhites that have ever filled the nose of a pointing dog. As it is, these two species get most of the attention and attract the majority of hunters from out of state. Local bird shooters, however, know that some of the most exciting hunting times can be found in chasing the prairie birds that thrive in the natural grasslands and wide agricultural expanses.

Prairie birds such as sharptails, lesser and greater prairie chickens and sage hens have been popular as food and sport birds since the days of the first covered wagons. Hungarian partridge were imported and released at the turn of the century and have adapted exceedingly well.

The range of these birds often overlaps and it is not uncommon to take a limit of sharptails and chickens on the same hunt and even a few Huns. Though the habitat may be close to the same for all species, they each have distinct habits and must be hunted accordingly.

Sharptails

The first sharptails I ever encountered cost me the chance at a record book antelope. We had covered about 50 square miles of prime southeastern Montana big buck country for four days and I had passed up several good heads. When we finally located a keeper, everything looked perfect. The day was cold and still and there wasn't a hint of wind. A grassy draw led within 200 yards of the small herd over which the buck presided and the cover was more than adequate to hide two men inching along on their bellies.

As we neared the end of the draw after an hour crawl, sharptails began busting out around us like mortar fire. The antelope threw up their heads and punched in the afterburners pronto. I still hold it against the birds every chance I get.

Sharptails, or more properly sharp-tailed grouse, are about 15 inches head to tail with a wingspan of 20 inches. They can weigh up to two pounds and have brown-gray plumage that resembles a hen pheasant. They have white underwings, tail and belly with white breast feathers marked with brown Vs. They get their name from their short pointed tails. Not especially tough targets, sharptails alternately flap and glide in flight, rocking from side to side. Sharptails frequent both prairies and brushland (what scientists call shrub-steppe).

Sharptails nest and forage in grassy meadows and prairies in summer and fall. The young especially depend on insects like grasshoppers for protein and moisture for rapid growth. They also eat a variety of plants and leaves like alfalfa, dandelions and various native forbs (vascular plants). In agricultural areas they'll fly to grain stubble fields like wheat, milo or cane to feed on seeds in the fall. In winter they depend on buds and berries from shrubs and trees like chokecherry, serviceberry, hawthorn, aspen and water birch. The loss of these essential shrubs to agriculture, livestock and housing developments has eliminated sharptails in many areas. In Alaska and Yukon, sharptails live in low elevation shrub fields and wet meadows.

Sharptails are currently found in parts of Wisconsin, Minnesota, upper Michigan, Ontario, Quebec, Manitoba, Saskatchewan, Alberta, British Columbia, Yukon, Alaska, North Dakota, South Dakota, Nebraska, Kansas, Colorado, Wyoming, Montana, Idaho, Utah and Washington. They've been extirpated from California, Oregon and Nevada. Prime hunting states include North Dakota, South Dakota, Nebraska, Montana, Idaho, Colorado, Saskatchewan and Manitoba.

The most beneficial sharptail management consists of protecting native habitats. Michigan cuts and burns aspen stands to create prairie openings for sharptails. Kansas recently reintroduced sharptails to the state. Oregon is investigating options for reintroduction. Montana has brought in birds from British Columbia to augment declining populations of the Columbia subspecies west of Kalispell (there are six subspecies). Idaho has reintroduced the same subspecies to the Hells Canyon area. Eliminating cattle from brushy riparian zones would benefit the species in many states. The conversion of western prairie to wheat fields

From September to mid-October, sharptails hold well and flush at close range; pointing dogs work beautifully at this time. By November, they form big flocks that are spooky, and pass shooting near grain fields is the most practical technique.

during the 1970s/Earl Butz era caused the destruction of millions of sharptails through habitat loss.

During the early season (September to mid-October) sharptails are still in family groups that hold well and flush at close range. Pointing dogs work beautifully at this time. On the prairies a big running pointing breed is a real asset in locating coveys. On hot, calm days, the birds hold extra tight. The cooler and windier it gets, the wilder the birds get.

Frequently the only way to get in range on a windy day is by surprising the birds from behind a ridge. They like to sit just over the leeward edge of ridges on windy days.

By November, sharptails form big flocks (called packs in the Dakotas) that are spooky and almost impossible to approach. These packs fly up to three miles to feeding sites such as grain fields. Pass shooting at these field edges is the only practical hunting technique.

Locating early season coveys can be frustrating. If conditions are dry, alfalfa fields, roadside ditches or any other fields with green vegetation lure the birds. Brush swales and heads of draws bordering grain fields are also good. Binoculars and good ears can locate birds from great distances at sunrise. When sharptails fly out to feed, they frequently cackle and chuckle from hillsides before flying. Scan fields with binoculars and watch for small flocks in flight, flashing their white underwings and bellies. Also, watch for heads sticking above wheat stubble.

Sharptails frequently run from approaching hunters or dogs. Coveys may flush ragged. Expect one to hang around after the bulk of the birds flush.

Lightweight shotguns are best for long carries across prairies. Improved cylinder and modified chokes are best for early season; modified and full are best for late. Full chokes come in handy on windy days when birds flush wild. During the early season 7 $\frac{1}{2}$ or 6 shot is preferred; 6 or 4 shot is preferred during the late season. Steel shot, during any season, is deadly.

Hungarian Partridge

In the parts of Iowa where I grew up, Huns were a common sight. The season was closed south of Interstate 80 and the unharassed birds flourished. About the time the Conservation Commission (as it was then called) decided to open it up, I had a couple of good dogs and pretty much knew where the majority of birds were in the areas I hunted.

The first Hun season in Southern Iowa opened at 8:00 a.m. on a morning in November of 1979. About 8:05 my little female shorthair went on point less than 100 yards from the truck. Fully expecting a big

Sharptails nest and forage in grassy meadows and prairies in summer and fall. That's where this South Dakota hunter bagged these sharptails.

rooster pheasant to come cackling out of the fencerow, I quickly moved up. Then, right out of prime pheasant habitat, two Huns burst out. I didn't shoot, first thinking they were hen pheasants, only they were much too small. At any rate the birds had dipped back into the fencerow before it clicked that they were partridge and now legal game.

I walked down to where they lit, flushed them and bagged both birds. As far as I know, those were the first legal Huns ever shot in southern Iowa. I thought I'd found a new pushover upland bird, then I learned just how tough the little imports could be.

They prefer open fields, shortgrass and grain stubble. Huns frequent the most barren habitat of any game bird. I often used to find them loafing in plowed fields. Many times they will only venture into tall cover, like corn stalks, if the understory is open for running.

Huns have been introduced in many places, but first successfully in Oregon's Willamette Valley in 1909. Now they are found in Alberta, Saskatchewan, Manitoba, North Dakota, South Dakota, Montana, Wyoming, Idaho, Washington, California, British Columbia, Nebraska, Iowa, Minnesota, Illinois, Indiana, Ontario, Wisconsin, Michigan and Ohio. Other states harbor scattered birds, but not in huntable numbers.

These birds are so hardy, little needs to be done except provide basic cover. They'll prosper where other species fail. A few grassy spots, a fencerow or two, a bit of grain stubble for winter food is all they need. Pesticides seem to be limiting population in some areas, although the full effect has not been determined.

As I said, Huns can be tough birds to successfully hunt. After the mating and brood rearing, which is shared by hen and cock, the family group stays together through fall and winter, breaking up in late February or March to establish nesting territories. As a result, along with the species' penchant for open terrain, coveys can be hard to locate. One square yard of ground looks as good as the next. So, even though a covey may spend most of its time in a one-quarter mile diameter area, locating it isn't easy. Wide ranging pointing dogs really help. Otherwise, be prepared for lots of walking, hitting the grassy areas at midday and feed fields morning and evening.

In canyon country where native grass grows on the slopes and wheat grass on the top flats, Huns feed in the fields, hang around the edges and dive into the canyons when disturbed. They also like the edges of benches from which they can catch the wind or dive down for quick escapes.

Huns like to run. In row crops like corn, they'll hotfoot a quarter mile to the end of the field before flushing. Often this flush will be wild and

Bagging sharptails and prairie chickens is not uncommon. Native tall-grass prairie and associated agricultural fields are popular habitat for both species.

beyond shotgun range, especially when windy. If you know Huns are running ahead, one hunter should circle to get ahead of them.

It's important to keep track of a covey's landing spot and follow up. After three or four flushes the birds usually hold well as a group or as singles. I've had to step on singles to get them up.

Huns move fast and are tough for many shooters to handle. Snap shooters do well on them.

Coveys are predictable, seen from year to year if habitat remains constant, so once you find them at one spot at a certain time of year, you'll likely find them there or close by at the same time later. Pay attention and pattern them.

A lightweight gun, with modified or full choke, helps ease the load when doing lots of walking. Screw-in chokes can be used effectively by switching to cylinder or improved cylinder after busting up a covey and getting into singles. Winged birds run like pheasants, so get right on them. A hun is not a bird with heavy bones, so number 6s or $7^1/_2$s work just fine.

Prairie Chicken

Prairie chickens, or just plain "chickens" as the birds are known where they are hunted, have the most limited range of all the prairie upland birds. Once found in seemingly unlimited numbers, prairie chickens can now be hunted on only a fraction of their original habitat. The heath hen, or eastern prairie chicken, became extinct early in this century. The greater and lesser prairie chickens, while not found in their original vast numbers, still offer the opportunity for a fun, change-of-pace hunt.

The greater prairie chicken is, as the name implies, the largest of the two species. Weighing 2 to $2^1/_2$ pounds the birds are only about 14-inches long but have an ample wing span of 27 inches. They have an overall appearance as a short, plump, dark bird. Plumage is a fairly constant brown-gray with dark horizontal barring across the breast and belly. The prairie chicken has a short black tail with a squared-off end lending well to a regional nickname of squaretail. Like all grouse, the feathers cover legs down to the toes.

Chickens favor native tall-grass prairie and associated agricultural fields. Extensive stands of big bluestem, Indian grass, switchgrass and associated species are required by chickens for mating, nesting and brood production.

Once common in the prairies from Ohio and Illinois, west to central Kansas, there are now only remnant populations in their eastern range. There are large, huntable populations in Kansas' Flint Hills, the Ne-

Once found throughout North America, prairie chicken populations have suffered from habitat loss. The highest concentrations of chickens can be found in Kansas' Flint Hills, the Nebraska Sandhills and the South Dakota Missouri River Breaks.

braska Sandhills and the South Dakokta Missouri River Breaks. Less wide-spread populations of birds are found in Michigan, Wisconsin, Indiana, Minnesota, Iowa, Missouri, Oklahoma, Texas, North Dakota, Manitoba and Alberta. The birds find it difficult to survive where farm fields dominate more than half of available prairie. Remnant prairie habitats in eastern states are maintained to preserve these remaining small populations, but at the time of this writing, South Dakota, Nebraska and Kansas habitats get no special management. As long as land remains in native grass, chickens thrive and they also will take advantage of crop fields for feeding in fall and winter.

Chicken hunting is similar to hunting sharptails in South Dakota and Nebraska. In fact, the two species often mix in the same flocks. Early season broods hold well to hunter and dog, especially when the weather is hot and calm. The birds grow wilder as the season progresses, forming large flocks that rise at dawn and fly to feed in fields. In fact, in Kansas, where the season begins in November, almost all hunting is done under passes as the flocks fly into feeding areas. Blinds of grass and wire or hay bales are often built in the centers of fields. It's a hope and prayer that chickens will fly within range, and somehow they usually do. After a morning of feeding, the birds fly to grasslands for a siesta. Dedicated dog men who have tried their sport in Kansas report good success at finding birds at midday for close flush shooting, especially when it's hot. This takes lots of walking and most hunters are too lazy to try it. In the evening flocks return to feed in the fields.

Duck guns are perfect for pass shooting. Modified to full chokes are a good choice with number 6, 5 or 4 shot. Binoculars are useful for watching flocks until they land. Flocks fly considerable distances for upland birds, often staying airborne and circling feed fields several times like ducks. Long-winded and winged, they may fly three miles or more when flushed.

Lesser prairie chickens are about 13 inches overall with a wingspan of 23 inches. They weigh $1^3/_4$ pounds and are almost identical in appearance to the greater prairie chicken, only paler and slightly smaller. Their habits and hunting techniques are similar. Preferring sand-sage prairie and shortgrass prairie, they call home the grasslands of southwest Kansas, western Oklahoma, southeast Colorado, northeast New Mexico and northwest Texas.

Sage Grouse

Sage grouse, the largest of all the prairie upland birds, are the least sporting. Also the largest of all the North American grouse, they flush

Sage grouse sport a three-foot wingspan and weigh up to seven pounds. Some upland hunters liken the flush of a sage grouse to that of an anemic elephant, but the birds can be tough to locate. Put dogs down at waterholes early to find their scent.

like an anemic elephant. They can weigh up to seven pounds and sport a three-foot wingspan.

As the name implies, sage grouse favor sagebrush. They have a vestigial gizzard only and must depend on soft, easily-digested vegetation and insects for diet. Sage grouse survive on sage leaves in the winter and various other plants and insects in the summer. No sage, no sage hens. During the early season, hens with broods can often be found in lowland irrigated alfalfa fields or along green irrigation canals and creeks.

Though they are found in most of the western agricultural states, the majority of the hunting takes place in Wyoming, Montana, Idaho, Colorado and Nevada. Conversion of sagebrush to grass or cropfields is reducing birds in many areas. Pesticides sprayed on alfalfa and potatoes has been documented to have killed birds in Idaho during recent summers.

Retention of sage habitat is about all that is necessary for proper management. Pesticide monitoring is currently underway in many states. Grasshopper spraying of public lands destroys many broods which depend on these insects for protein and moisture.

Sage grouse can be damned tough for a novice to find. Miles and miles of identical-looking habitat make it hard to find a starting point. During early season, look in small alfalfa and hay fields near extensive sage lands. In vast stretches of sage, start looking near water of some form as water is essential. Birds will walk to it early, then wander outward, foraging as they go. Put dogs down at waterholes early to find scent. Sage grouse usually hold well. They will try to run or sneak away, especially when jumped a few times.

They are often dedicated to a special site, returning day after day until conditions change in late fall, when they migrate significant distances to preferred winter range. As with all open country grouse, large concentrations can be found near spring strutting grounds in the early seasons. Typically, hens raise their broods within a mile of the lek, and males visit it for fall displaying. Knowing spring lek locations can lead to fall birds.

Any gauge shotgun will suffice. These big birds are not hard to bring down. As flushes are usually close, improved to full choke is preferred, depending on conditions.

10

The Woodland Birds: Grouse And Woodcock

U pland bird hunting is a sport unmatched by any other. When every-thing is right, a "bird hunting kind of tired" is the closest thing to heavenly bliss that a sportsman is likely to experience in this lifetime.

The hunter who has been there knows it. The one who hasn't yearns for it.

A good day of upland bird hunting heartens thirsting lungs with fresh air, the scent of spruce and the odor of dew-soaked dog. Brisk October sunshine flushes the face with warmth, energy and excitement. A riot of autumn colors, strong in yellow and red, scintilates the eyes. Rolling hills and spongy bottomlands combine to tire legs—just enough, but not too much. Indeed, the tired at the end of a day of upland bird hunting is a very, very good tired.

It could be that this particular kind of tired is why modern men hunt upland birds. It's an after-dinner, warm-all-over, sitting-by-a-fire, it's-only-eight-in-the-evening kind of tired with which every lucky bird hunter is rewarded at the close of a good day afield.

To some extent every species of North American upland bird worth chasing, each in their own way, leaves its hunter with this welcome kind of fatigue. But, without question, the ruffed grouse and the woodcock are the birds that first inspired it. And perhaps that alone is enough to make them the ultimate upland game birds.

Particularly to bird hunters in the northern tier states, ruffed grouse offer the greatest opportunity to be afield under the "perfect" hunting conditions. Seasons are generally long and center around the month of October. In places like Maine, Vermont, New Hampshire, upstate New York, Pennsylvania, Michigan, Wisconsin, Minnesota, Ontario, Quebec and the Maritime Provinces, October is the time to be in the woods. It is autumn. And it is grouse and woodcock season.

Ruffed Grouse—The All-American Gamebird

Travel around North America a bit, and you'll hear the ruffed grouse called a lot of names. New, unprintable ones are coined each season by frustrated hunters who experience the bird's unbelievable talent for avoiding shot patterns, but others are more civil and more standard. In New England and the Northeast you'll hear them called "partridge" or "pats," in some locales farther south they are known as "ruffs." Out West some folks call them "native pheasants." To still other hunters they are simply "grouse" or, simpler yet, "birds."

Ruffed grouse range begins in Northern Canada. They are found, to some extent, in all of the Canadian provinces. Prime range extends through most of the northern United States anywhere there are large, natural woodlands.

Though often thought of only as a northern species, the range of the ruffed grouse today extends into the central and southern United States. Huntable populations are found as far south as Missouri, Kentucky, Tennessee and parts of North Carolina. In these southeastern areas and in the Western states like Washington, Oregon, Idaho, Montana, Wyoming and Utah, grouse are found in the more mountainous, forested terrain.

In this large range, biologists delineate about a dozen subspecies, but all are basically the same size, exhibit similar behavior and inhabit like cover types. Colors can vary to some degree even within subspecies. The most common color phase is gray, but can run through brown to a reddish chestnut.

The "ruffed" part of the grouse's name comes from the black feathers on each side at the base of the bird's neck. In the mating display, the male erects these feathers so they flare out as part of his hormonal theatrics. Likewise, the feathers of the tail form a fan which the cock grouse shows off as part of the courtship display. Just in from the tips of the tail is a half-inch wide black band on each feather. It is outlined by two narrow, cream-colored stripes. These tail markings are somewhat useful in sexing the birds brought to bag. The black band on the center two feath-

Ruffed grouse offer the greatest opportunity to be afield under the "perfect" hunting conditions, especially for bird hunters in the northern tier of the U.S. The "ruffed" part of the grouse's name comes from the black feathers on each side at the base of the bird's neck.

ers of a hen grouse's tail is burred and indistinct. However, young cock birds also sometimes exhibit this kind of marking. It is a safe bet to say that any bird with a solid band across the tail and substantial heft to the body is a cock bird. Mature cock grouse average about 20 to 25 percent larger than hens. There is no way for the hunter to distinguish between hens and cocks on the wing.

The male ruffed grouse is famous for his springtime courtship display which involves "drumming," or beating his wings to produce a booming sound to attract females. This drumming is usually done from a elevated sight such as a log or rock. Because the male grouse often returns to the same site many times to drum, the log he uses over and over is called a "drumming log," but the bird is not beating his wings against the log. The sound results from the disturbance of the air.

Grouse most often drum in April, May or June, depending on the breeding season, but male grouse have been known to drum infrequently at any time of the year. More than one cock has betrayed his presence by drumming during the hunting season.

The drumming vibration sounds for all the world like a stubborn lawn mower which refuses to start. Casual listeners can be fooled until they perhaps remember that they are walking miles from the nearest manicured lawn!

Ruffed grouse are often thought of as birds of the deep woods, but that certainly is not the case. True, they are always found in relation to timber, but population densities are usually sparse in mature stands of forest. Hunters after grouse will do much better to concentrate on the bird's prime habitat.

Like all species of wild animals, the grouse's two main habitat requirements are feed and protective cover. The birds find the greatest abundance of both in fringe areas of forests. That often means regrowth areas from two to twenty years old. Favorites are clear cuts and burned areas a few seasons after the devastation. Even in mature forest areas, the birds gravitate toward openings created by logging roads, beaver cuttings, flood plains, etc.

The first trees to grow back in these areas are aspen. Heavy underbrush of many types is also common in these new growth/regrowth areas. Common ground cover includes berry bushes, grapevines, thorn thickets and other perfectly miserable stuff through which to hunt.

From season to season, grouse populations are extremely dynamic. Mortality can run very high if weather conditions are not hospitable as the young hatch in the spring. A dearth of insects, the young birds' primary source of protein, can adversely affect chick survival. Predators,

Ruffed grouse favor new growth areas from two to twenty years old, like the area pictured above. Even in mature forest areas, the birds gravitate toward openings created by logging roads, beaver cuttings and flood plains.

especially hawks and owls, can take a heavy toll of young birds through the summer.

In addition to these usual population checks encountered by upland birds, the ruffed grouse seems to be on its own seven- to ten-year cycle of population highs and lows. In Minnesota for example, grouse populations tend to peak on a 10-year cycle which happens to coincide with the end of each decade. Minnesota Department of Natural Resources records seem to indicate a "super cycle" as well which occurs every 20 years. Hunters lucky enough to hunt a super cycle can expect to see a 30 to 50 percent higher than average numbers of birds.

To count grouse, biologists do drumming counts in the spring. This method and its related calculations appears to give surprisingly accurate numbers for a bird living in such dense cover. Hunters can do their own counts by keeping track of flushes per man hour of hunting from season to season.

No one is quite sure why grouse experience the bust and boom cycle. Research has been done on everything from cyclic changes in the cock to hen ratio to infestations of parasites. Even so, none of the studies have proven conclusive. However, according to Bill Berg, a DNR wildlife research specialist based in Grand Rapids, Minnesota the effects of the bust portion of the cycle can be softened if the birds have enough appropriate cover available.

Early Season Grouse Hunting

North American Hunting Club Shooting Advisory Council Coordinator Dr. John Woods was after a bear. He came from Mississippi to the woods of east central Minnesota to try to bag a bruin with his .41 Magnum pistol. But not much cooperated to make his trip a success.

The weather didn't cooperate; it was so windy a big guy like John had to wonder about his own sanity for sitting high in a tree stand overlooking a bear bait.

Because of the wind, the bear didn't cooperate. They only worked up enough nerve to forage for delicacies under the cover of total darkness.

Even the trees didn't cooperate. No matter how hard the wind blew the leaves weren't ready to fall, visibility was limited to the immediate bait area, not much more.

Though he didn't take home a black bear rug for his family room floor, John did bag one heck of a trophy. He supplemented the bruin hunting with some early season ruffed grouse hunting and managed to bag his first!

"*Just* a grouse?" the uninitiated might say.

Yes, one grouse...an early-season grouse. And John went back to Mississippi mighty happy. Despite hunting with a good dog and a fellow NAHC member who has hunted grouse since he was old enough to walk, John's bird came tough! In two days of hunting, the team put more than 30 birds to wing. They got shooting at five. They got one!

That's a pretty typical average for birds in the early season. Many areas open up for grouse hunting in early September. That means green leaves. Lots of 'em. Still on the trees. That also means tough hunting.

Early season grouse hunting is a hit or miss proposition, mostly miss. The birds take to the air from dense cover with no warning. Their explosive flush thundering on your ear drums is the only reward you'll get nine times out of ten. That tenth time you'll get a glimpse. If you get a glimpse, take the shot.

There are a couple of ways the early-season hunter can combat the grouse's tendency to flush without being seen. One is to survey a piece of cover to determine the best way to hunt it. In early season it is especially

More than one hunter has found a downed bird that he couldn't even see when he pulled the trigger, like this grouse that Gunner found. After every shot, mark the spot where the bird might have dropped. If you have a dog, let him work the area. If you're without a dog, search a tight spiral radiating from the spot.

important to position hunters in such a way that a flushing bird is likely to cross some kind of opening to escape. So instead of the lone hunter walking a logging road or forest trail to flush birds, he should walk off in the brush to the side of the road. This way birds pinned between the hunter and the road may flush across the road offering an open shot.

Two hunters can do the same thing, one walking on each side of the trail. The best option would be to have three hunters working together; one on each side of the road and one on it who is in the best position to shoot.

As always, it's critically important for hunters to keep track of each other and blaze orange helps tremendously. In such dense cover don't be afraid to communicate. Holler when a bird gets up to let your companions know one is coming and to tell them where you are.

Early in the hunting season, you may find young grouse bunched up in fairly large groups. They spend the entire summer together as a family unit, then begin to disperse just about the time hunting season begins. Grouse will seldom all take to flight at once, so when you hear one flush, move in that direction and be prepared for more. If you get off a shot, stop and reload quickly before moving on to look for the bird you shot at.

In any part of the season, following up every shot at ruffed grouse is extremely important. Grouse are masters at putting cover between you and them. More than one tree has squarely absorbed a full load of 7 $1/_2$s as a grouse has swung behind it. Likewise, more than one hunter has found a stone dead bird that he couldn't even see when he pulled the trigger!

Follow up every shot! Mark carefully where the bird would have landed had it dropped when you shot. Walk to that spot and place your hat or glove or handkerchief on a nearby limb. If you have a dog, call him over and let him work the area thoroughly. If you're without a dog, cover the ground carefully. Slowly walk a tight spiral radiating from your visible marker. Give it some time. It's the least we owe the ultimate upland game bird.

Darn few *sportsmen* take limits of grouse during the early season. Limits are bagged for sure, especially by slobs driving backroads and shooting birds on the ground. Doing so is not ethical, it's not sporting and it's not hunting. The ultimate upland game bird deserves far better than that.

Prime-Time Grouse Hunting

Mid-season grouse hunting is glamour and pageantry. It is the golden days of which bird hunters dream. It is the burning yellow of aspen and tamarack. It is the flaming red of maple and sumac. In good

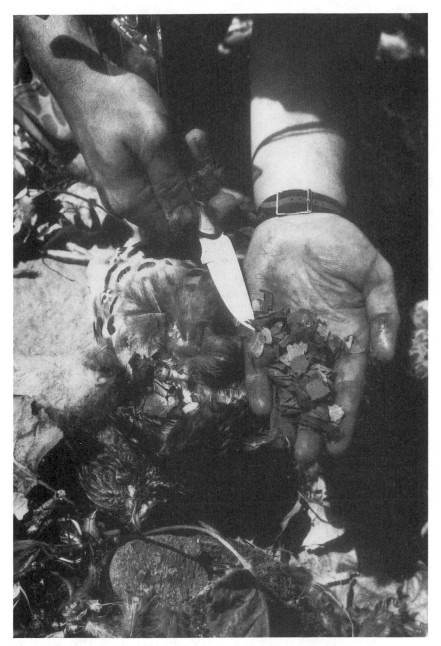

To determine which food source is of primary importance at a specific time, open the crop of the first grouse taken. Then concentrate your hunting efforts in cover containing that food source.

years and good covers, it's fast action. In bad years or poor covers, it's time to relax and contemplate.

And if you're ever going to take a limit of grouse, this is the time to do it!

Successful grouse hunting is more than just a walk in the woods. As always, a planned hunt will be a more productive hunt.

Mid-season is the best time of the year to hunt birds by their daily routine. In other words, try to determine what the birds will be doing at certain parts of the day, figure out where they'll be doing it, then hunt there.

Early morning, sun-up, will find the birds on the roost where they spent the night. This will often be in the branches of a large tree surrounded by dense, shorter cover. Depending on the terrain, it may be a deciduous tree of some kind, but just as likely a conifer. As the frost or dew leaves the ground cover, grouse will move to their feeding areas. They may fly to feed, they may move through the tree tops to a feeding sight or they may walk to feed; whatever mood strikes them that particular day.

Food will vary greatly with terrain but, in many areas, preferred mid-season foods for grouse are fruits, berries and nuts. Grouse are extremely fond of apples, grapes, dogwood berries, wintergreen berries and leaves, elderberries, sumac berries (both ordinary and poisonous varieties) and the leaves of many plants.

With such a varied diet, it can be difficult to determine which food source is of primary importance at a specific time. One trick that some grouse hunters use is to open the crop of the first bird taken to determine what it has been eating. Using this information, they concentrate their hunting efforts in cover containing that food source. This works well if the first taken bird was not a gourmet with unusual tastes.

If you try this trick remember that it is a good source of hunting strategy only as long as you don't let it override all else. Don't forget that a grouse doesn't feed all day, or even every day for that matter.

The next stop on the typical routine of a grouse might be a gravel road or some other area where it can pick up grit for digestion. As the clock ticks on toward noon hour, grouse often tend to move back into thick, protective cover to wile away the midday hours, doing whatever grouse do on crisp October days.

Late afternoon, about three or so, may find the birds looking for a dust bath, so it's back to the dirt roads. A few more bites to fight hunger in the long night ahead and birds will work their way back to roost for the night.

You'll find more grouse, those that hold tighter, if you get back in away from the main thoroughfares.

Grouse certainly are hunted successfully throughout the day in all these types of cover. To best utilize often limited hunting time, it's best to plan an all-day hunt route that will keep you in high percentage areas as much as possible.

Seriously mapping out a hunting route will reveal the most efficient way to hunt a particular area and keep you in action all day long. In planning your route, try to avoid long treks through mature stands of forest. If you have to, don't be afraid to hoof it through these sterile areas to get back in prime cover. Instead, develop a plan which keeps you moving along some type of fringe as much as possible. You'll run into a few birds in the big woods, but the higher densities and better shooting will be in those thick, new growth areas.

In mapping out a mid-season hunt, also look for opportunities to get away from the beaten path. Between road hunters and those neophytes who are too timid to penetrate more than a stone's throw from the nearest road, birds on these outside edges are wont to be spooky. You'll find more grouse, those that hold tighter, if you get back in away from the main thoroughfares.

At any season, grouse hunters quickly learn that the birds have an uncanny knack of flushing at the most inopportune times. They always seem to take wing when you've unloaded your gun to cross a fence, while you're stooped over to remove a burr from your dog's coat or while you're answering nature's call.

Mystic as the grouse may seem, he can't be credited with omnipotence. There is no way that a bird which has probably encountered very few humans can reason out that a good time to escape is while a hunter is reaching for his fly!

The smart hunter quickly determines the common denominator in all of these flush impetuses—his forward progress has stopped. The smarter hunter uses that knowledge to improve his hunting success.

Attuned to the ways of natural threats, grouse know that when a predator freezes stock still, it has probably seen or smelled them. Under such circumstances, the grouse takes to the air to avoid danger. So when the hunter stops, for whatever reason, the grouse figures the jig is up and takes off for safer parts.

Because of this common behavior a slow, stop-and-start hunting strategy often results in more birds flushed, especially for the dogless hunter.

Late Season Grouse Hunting

Imagine a feathered quarry that could suddenly materialize from nowhere. One split second there's nothing ahead of you but the bright sun of a clear, cold December morning glinting off a new cover of snow. The next, the game you seek suddenly erupts from the nothingness to leave you slack-jawed with your shotgun halfway to your shoulder.

A bird with such a talent would have to be the undisputed ultimate upland game bird!

He might add another twist, too. On the same hunt, on the same morning, in the same cover, he would be just as likely to take flight from a hidden perch high in the tops of the evergreens.

The ultimate upland bird provides that kind of late season excitement. Such is late season grouse hunting!

Ruffed grouse use deep snow as protection from predators and inclement weather. If a grouse is hotly pursued by a hawk or an owl, it can dive into a soft snow drift to elude the predator. Grouse will also often sit motionless during a heavy snow to allow themselves to be covered completely by the falling flakes. With their feathers puffed against the cold, they utilize the inherent insulating qualities of the snow to survive the storm.

Contrary to the benefit of most other woodland inhabitants, deep powdery snow is an important aid to ruffed grouse in their struggle through winter. Even their feet have a built-in snowshoe design to help navigate the unstable drifts. Grouse so rely on the snow in northern areas of their range that winter mortality among the birds is at its highest when snow is covered by a hard crust of ice and the birds can not burrow or dive into it!

The hunter out for a brisk hunt early in the morning following a good, powdery snowfall had better house a strong heart behind his ribs. Unexpected grouse flushing within inches of his boots will certainly test it!

A fresh snow also provides another unusual advantage for the upland bird hunter—the opportunity to track his quarry. Once birds are out and about after a snowstorm, the hunter can keep a sharp eye out for the delicate strings of tracks which betray a grouse's recent activity and whereabouts.

The hunter who dogs the tracks long enough will be gratified with a flush, or at least the marks in the fresh snow will show where the bird got out earlier. If you find wing prints in the snow, look up and around quickly. Grouse often flush only to light on a nearby limb and wait to see who or what is following them. But remember, as soon as you stop you start tightening the tension spring under any nearby bird who thinks he has been spotted!

The motto of the grouse hunter: "Be prepared...every second!"

Grouse also exhibit the tendency to roost in dense pine cover once snow covers the ground and the bottom drops out of the thermometer. If you were to build the "perfect late season grouse gunner" from scratch, the plans would call for two sets of eyes. One normal pair on the front of the head would be for looking forward. The second pair would be situated on top of the hunter's head to pick up faster on tree-top flushes.

Dense pine cover brings grouse hunting technique full circle. Late season shooting in thick pine stands is like early-season hunting when the leaves are still on the deciduous trees. You've got to scheme to make the birds fly across open areas, or you won't bag very many!

Woodcock Hunting

By upland bird species standards, the woodcock is a strange bird. For one, the woodcock is migratory. They nest in the North and winter in the South.

Also unique among upland game birds, the woodcock's diet consists almost exclusively of earthworms! To some extent, that explains the migration. He can't stay where his long beak can't penetrate the frozen soil to probe for nourishment.

That diet is also why woodcock relate to one particular cover-type more than any other species of upland bird. Woodcock have to live in or near areas where the soil is damp and easily probed, and where earthworms live within six inches of the soil surface.

In North America, the woodcock's range is primarily east of the line running from the western border of Minnesota south to the western border of Louisiana. Breeding and nesting take place primarily in southern Canada, northern New England and the northern reaches of the Great Lakes states.

With his long bill, stubby wings and delicate legs and feet, the woodcock is really a shorebird gone upland. Because of the bird's migratory traits, hunting seasons and limits are in part regulated by the federal government just as they are for waterfowl. Seasons are generally long, but in most areas the hunting is really hot only for a few weeks while the birds are passing through. They seem to be on some sort of calendar because they tend to show up in the same areas about the same time each season.

Woodcock migration is in part timed by the advancing frostline. Just before the ground freezes the birds move on. Some research also indicates that the birds are most likely to move on with a brisk north wind at their tails. Though they are masters of aerial acrobatics, their ballish bodies are not of the most efficient aerodynamic design for long-distance flight. Even so, these robin-sized game birds travel thousands of miles each year.

With his long bill, stubby wings and delicate legs and feet, the woodcock is really a shorebird gone upland. Woodcock nest in the North and migrate south for the winter. Although seasons are long, the hunting is really hot only a few weeks while the birds are passing through.

In the north country, woodcock are often thought of as bonus birds for the grouse hunter, but a large number of hunters in Louisiana and other southern states have long recognized the sporting attributes of this little game bird. As pressure on other species increases elsewhere, more northern hunters are seeking them out, too.

The places where woodcock are found are called coverts for a good reason. The experienced woodcock hunter is extremely covert in his efforts to keep the location of these sporting goldmines a secret. If you can find a veteran hunter willing to share his coverts with you, you are indeed lucky. If not, you'll just have to go out and find them yourself.

In searching for woodcock country, keep in mind the necessity of wet ground. Favorite haunts are lowlands with many small alders and other eight- to ten-feet-tall brush. Areas along creeks and around beaver ponds are often good bets. Look for brush, but not a lot of ground cover. Woodcock don't like to sit in dense grass.

Also keep in mind the woodcock's wanderlust. If a piece of cover looks prime, visit as often as you can during the season. The birds will probably show up there sooner or later, and you have to hunt it when they do. Even if you don't actually flush a bird, you can detect their presence by locating bore holes where they probed the soft soil with their long beaks. These areas will also be marked with "chalk"—white woodcock droppings.

When flushed, the classic maneuver of the woodcock is to tower straight up into the air to brush-top height, then bore straight away from the hunter. That's the classic maneuver, but the woodcock's bag of tricks contains a lot of unclassic maneuvers, too; enough that the beginning woodcock hunter shouldn't over-anticipate that kind of shot.

Normally, a flushed woodcock does not fly very far before landing again. You can often mark one down and flush the same bird again. Often, they'll begin to land just as you pull the trigger. This is deceiving, because in thick cover it is difficult to tell if the bird went down because it was hit or because it was going to land anyway. Always approach a bird like this with a loaded gun in the ready position. The bird may be down, but he may have pulled the old fakeroo and jump again as you approach. Just as recommended for grouse, *always follow up your shots in thick cover*!

Woodcock hold notoriously tight. That makes them a prime species for hunting with pointing dogs. Hunting timberdoodles over a close working Brittany, Gordon setter or English setter is civilized upland sport at its finest. A well-trained springer or cocker spaniel will give some exciting performances too.

In the North Country woodcock are often thought of as bonus birds for grouse hunters. NAHC Associate Editor Dan Dietrich bagged these grouse and woodcock in Minnesota.

Because the birds hold so tight, they can be very frustrating game for the dogless hunter. When the flights are heavy, the dogless hunter has the best chance of bumping out enough birds to make for an interesting shoot. The best strategy is a slow, meandering stroll through prime cover. Like grouse, woodcock are susceptible to a start-and-stop hunting strategy, but for timberdoodle the stops will have to be even longer and more frequent. Trying to keep that important concentration edge through a long stretch of this type of woodcock hunting can be difficult, especially if the time between flushes is great. To avoid mental fatigue that will cause misses, take breaks frequently.

Besides, stopping to smell the roses is what upland bird hunting is really about anyway.

The Importance Of A Hunting Journal

It can be said, of ruffed grouse in particular, that birds are both surprisingly reliable and reliably surprising. Woodcock, though legal quarry for hunters through a lengthy season, offer prime gunning only for a week or two each year in any given locale. For both species, a record of past events can lead to exciting new discoveries that boost hunting success and enjoyment.

The astute upland bird hunter records his takes in the form of a hunting journal. With an eye toward improving the flushes per hour ratio, the upland bird hunter's log should record things like weather information, locations hunted, number of birds seen, number of shots fired, number of birds bagged, and new discoveries about hunting areas.

A well-kept hunting journal can add nearly as many grouse to a hunter's bag as a well-trained dog. Grouse very often frequent specific areas of cover under certain conditions. For example, if you find grouse in a particular abandoned apple orchard on a foggy morning at about 9:30 a.m., chances are extremely good that you'll find them there at that same time on the next hunting day that offers similar conditions. If you found them in a particular section of 30-year-old pine plantings on a clear December morning after a blizzard, you'll likely find birds there the next time those conditions are repeated.

A good hunting journal will also tell you if the approach you took the last time you hunted a particular piece of cover was successful. If it was, you can repeat it. If it was not, you can try something new that might offer more shooting.

It's even more critical for the woodcock hunter to maintain a journal if he wishes to keep himself in the action. Because woodcock are a migratory bird, during the hunting season they reside in certain areas only for short periods of time. With often surprising punctuality, they show

NOVEMBER 18, 1989

GROUSE HUNTING
BRUNO PROPERTY

COMPANIONS: DAN DIETRICH & DEAN PETERS
DOG: GUNNER
GUN: RUGER RED LABEL 20 GAUGE
SHELLS: ACTIV TARGET LOADS # 8's
WEATHER: DOWN RIGHT COOL, ABOUT FIVE DEGREES WHEN WE LEFT THE
TRUCK AT 8:00 A.M.. WARMED TO ABOUT 20 DEGREES BY NOON.
ABOUT TWO INCHES OF SNOW ON THE GROUND.

DEER HUNTERS REPORTED SEEING LOTS OF GROUSE PREVIOUS TWO WEEKENDS.
ANTICIPATION FOR GOOD LATE SEASON HUNT WAS HIGH. DIDN'T PAN OUT AS
FAR AS BIRDS WERE CONCERNED. ONLY SIX FLUSHES HUNTING FROM 8:00
A.M. TO 1:00 P.M.. NO BIRDS BAGGED. DEAN CONNECTED ON A SNOWSHOE
HARE — ONLY THE THIRD I'VE EVER SEEN ON PROPERTY. GUNNER WORKED
BETTER THAN USUAL AHEAD OF A GROUP OF HUNTERS. DON'T JUST HUNT FOR
ME.

HUNTED DOWN ROAD AND TRAIL TO BEAVER POND. CUT ACROSS TO ISLAND
ON NEW DAM. SWAMP FROZEN ON BACKSIDE OF ISLAND, SO WE CROSSED TO
FAR SHORE OF POND. HUNTED ALL THE WAY BACK TO POINT. SAW THREE OF
THE SIX BIRDS ON FAR SIDE OF ISLAND. FOUND HIDDEN PARTS OF THE POND
THAT I DIDN'T EVEN KNOW WERE THERE. GREAT PROSPECT FOR EARLY TO MID
SEASON DUCK STALK WITH THREE OR FOUR PEOPLE. (REMEMBER TO HUNT THIS
AREA WITH STEEL SHOT NEXT YEAR.)

HUNTED BACK TO TRUCK. FLUSHED ONE BIRD JUST PAST END OF TRAIL. DAN
AND I HAD GOOD OPPORTUNITY, BIRD WENT DOWN. GUNNER FOUND HIM AND

This is an excerpt from co-author Miller's hunting journal. Upland bird hunting memories are too hard won to let them slip casually into blurred recollection. It took too many stolen hours to collect them. The hunting journal is the answer.

up in particular coverts within a few days of a specific date year after year. Even coverts within a few miles of each other may be traditionally hottest during different weeks of the season. For the serious woodcock hunter to stay in the birds, he must go where they are, and remembering precise "hot" dates for each covert can be tough.

The hunting journal makes it easy for him. As it builds over the seasons, it becomes more and more valuable. Comparing and compiling the information can reveal important population and behavior trends that the upland bird hunter can use to improve his efficiency.

But a good hunting diary is much more than simply a tool to improve hunting efficiency. It's a memory book to spark nostalgia of great guns, great dogs and great hunting companions.

Each fall a new hunting season arrives. And like the freshly honed edge on a favorite hunting knife, the memories we make in the days and weeks ahead will be shaving sharp. Through the season, we aren't calling on year-old memories. Instead, we experience what sardines tasted like eaten in a September tamarack swamp. Sunday muscles are achingly reacquainted with Saturday's hot and heavy dove shoot.

But what about eight months down the road? Two years down the road? A decade down the road? How fresh can the memories remain?

Certainly, fine hunting memories never leave us, especially the glory days of full bags and sunshine. But as the years pass and the cumulative hours afield swell, memories can blur together. You took that double on grouse in 1970, but were you hunting Tailor's Ridge or 3R Saddle? Your setter ran into her first porcupine at The Crossing, but was it opening day or the second day of the season? What was the name of that old timer you ran into who kept telling you that he hunted quail with a collie?

Upland bird hunting memories are too hard won to let them slip casually into blurred recollection. It took too many stolen hours to collect them.

The hunting journal is the answer.

To many hunters who are less than fond of writing, keeping a formal hunting journal seems like a lot of work that could otherwise taint fine memories. But a good journal doesn't have to be formal, nor does it have to be a lot of work.

For example, a collection of hunting licenses from seasons past and a few notes scribbled on the back of each can be a great repository of memories and valuable information. Photographs with brief captions are another great way to keep hunting memories fresh. And don't forget to take some photos of camp, too. They'll record for posterity those wonderful times that will never be duplicated. On the back of the photos be

A good hunting diary is more than a tool to improve hunting efficiency. It's a memory to spark nostalgia of great guns, great dogs and great hunting companions.

sure to jot down names, dates, weather conditions and the like. They'll make those treasured shots even more valuable.

The advent of video camcorders is rife with possibilities for hunting journals. A brief pictorial and narrative following a hunt could eliminate the tedium of writing altogether.

NAHC Member and longtime outdoor writer Don Johnson uses maps to record his hunting experiences. Whenever he hunts a new area, he makes it a point to obtain a map of that place. Then as special events occur, as they always do while hunting, Don simply puts a point on the map and scribbles details in the margin. And extensive collection of these maps built through the years not only improves hunting skills, but keeps fresh the days before condos were built in the cornfield where you took your first cock pheasant.

If you can muster the energy to tear yourself away from that great bird-hunting tired and faithfully record the day's events in your journal, you'll soon find yourself referring to this log to plan your next hunt as well as to taste those tamarack swamp sardines in February.

11

Hunting Mountain Birds: Chukars, Ptarmigan, Blue Grouse

U pland hunting in the alpine is, by nature, a limited sport. Hunters are usually in for a long trip by car and then some rough walking and climbing. The reward, however, is often 60 to 80 ptarmigan per square mile or a chukar covey that's home to 50 or more birds!

Just the same, while most of us know men who pride themselves in being called expert quail or grouse hunters, there are few who want to be known as ace blue grouse or willow ptarmigan hunters. Truth be known, most mountain birds are taken by big game hunters who happen to have shotguns with them.

When the sheep ranges of Alaska and Canada were opened up, more than one pack horse carried an extra scabbard stuffed with a little Model 42, .410 pump that was used for potting camp meat and filling the void between hunting areas. Likewise, mule deer hunters in the Northwest learned long ago that packing a shotgun for chukars was a great idea, just in case their buck should be tagged on the first day or two. And we've all heard the story of the downed bush pilot who survived on blue grouse for five weeks by popping them off tree limbs with a .22 pistol.

Incidental to big game or not, for those with the desire, legs and lungs, the mountain upland birds provide great opportunity for a quality, uncrowded hunt. Ptarmigan come in three varieties, chukars are plentiful in the wild and make popular, hardy game farm birds while blue grouse offer some of the most underutilized hunting in the nation.

Chukars

By far the most popular of the high country mountain birds, the chukar is an import from Asia. A stocky bird, big chukars measure 15 inches from head to tail and top $1^1/_2$ pounds. Though strikingly marked, chukars often appear dull gray during the hunting season when plumage is not fully developed. Introduced in the 1930s from Nepal, chukars prospered with another Asian import, cheat grass.

The stout, red-legged birds prefer steep, dry rocky slopes and, of course, cheat grass. In fact, cheat grass is almost an essential. Steep slopes definitely are. The birds will move down to grainfields to feed, but seldom more than a quick flight from steep slopes and canyons.

Chukars seek out shade under bushes and shrubs during hot days and, though residents of the high dry country, they like hanging out close to creeks, springs and rivers. Chukars are hunted in Nevada, Wyoming, Idaho, Colorado, Oregon, Washington and California. They have been introduced in other places and may persist, but not in huntable numbers. The big, dry desert canyons like the Snake and Columbia Rivers are ideal habitats. Hardy birds, chukars require no special management. Chukar habitat is so steep, rocky and dry that the only thing effecting chukar populations are overgrazing and cold, wet spring weather. They are widely released as training birds and game farm targets.

One of the most effective hunting techniques revolves around detecting chukars by their distinctive "chukar, chukar, chukar, chuduck, duck, duck, duck" calls during the morning and evening. Hunt for them from above on their level. An approach from the bottom merely pushes them uphill a lot faster than you can climb. Once they get to the top they fly back down and start over again.

A favorite technique is to leave one vehicle at the bottom of a canyon and ride another to the top. Hunt down and drive back up. That saves time and energy so you can hunt longer.

During the hot early season, look for springs, creeks and green patches indicating watering areas on dry slopes. Hunt around these watering areas and listen for calling birds at dawn, then maneuver above them. North facing slopes are often cooler, wetter and more likely to hold birds. Chukars hold well for pointing dogs, so use them, and make sure they like to retrieve. It's a long fall down some of those slopes.

During early season, chukars often form huge flocks around waterholes. Between 50 and 100 might flush ragged from a clump of shady brush.

Chukars were introduced into North America during the 1930s. Originally from Nepal, these stout birds favor big, dry desert canyons like the Snake and Columbia Rivers. The birds are also successfully taken on hunting preserves.

When fall rains begin, chukars scatter. When snow falls on north slopes, they gather on south slopes, usually near the top to get at grain-fields. River floating can be an easy, productive technique in early season when chukars are staying near the water. Float to them, park, sneak above and flush them back toward the water. Floating is a wonderful, change-of-pace upland trip. Fall weather is usually comfortable in chukar country and chukar rivers often hold good populations of trout and other game fish. Even when getting to the general area by boat or raft, the actual hunting is physically demanding and not for the weak of heart or legs.

For the hunter who wants to shoot a chukar but doesn't care to conquer Mt. Everest, many shooting preserves offer released chukars. The birds adapt readily to controlled shooting situations and fly strong when released.

Though the double may be the queen of the upland guns, consider a lightweight pump or auto for chukars. Sometimes you'll climb and sweat all day for one incredible flush of 50 birds. It's nice to have more than two shots at them. Veteran hunters prefer $7^1/_2$ or 6 shot. Sturdy, hard-soled boots are essential on the often loose, rocky terrain that the birds so love to hang out around.

Ptarmigan

Ptarmigan are unusual for several reasons. First off is their name: The "P" is silent, they're really pronounced "tarmigan." Second, the birds change colors from one season to another and back again. Most people lump all ptarmigan together, when really there are three distinct species.

The willow ptarmigan is the most widespread, found from one end of Canada to the other, as well as Alaska. The rock ptarmigan is found across the northern reaches of Canada and all of Alaska. The white-tailed ptarmigan is not only the smallest of the three but also has the most limited range, found only in western Canada, parts of Alaska, and a few of the lower 48 states.

Back when the outdoor magazines were filled with stories of the far north's sheep, caribou and bears, the hunting public was exposed on a regular basis to these fascinating north country birds. In recent years, a few gypsy-footed bird hunters have trekked north with dog trailers in tow to hunt them exclusively. The results are usually quite rewarding.

White-tailed ptarmigan are found closer to hunting populations and are a good eating bird that holds well for pointing dogs. Whitetails are a bit smaller than a chukar and weigh about a pound.

Ptarmigan (pronounced tarmigan) inhabit the Rockies and High Sierras. Commonly grouped as one species, there are actually three distinct ptarmigan species, including the white-tailed, rock and willow ptarmigan (above).

White-tailed ptarmigan favor the mountainous terrain above timberline in the alpine and sub-alpine zones. Barren country, the only trees in this cold, windy habitat are dwarf birch, dwarf willow, sub-alpine fire and Engleman spruce of the stunted size.

The birds are found in the Rockies and High Sierras of New Mexico, Colorado, Wyoming, Montana, Washington, Oregon, California, Alberta, British Columbia, Yukon, Alaska and Northwest Territories. Colorado is probably the most popular hunting state for this species since several highways lead to alpine habitats above 11,000 feet.

Game departments put little emphasis on white-tailed ptarmigan management. The species was introduced to the High Sierras, where they have done well. As long as alpine habitat persists, whitetails will prosper.

Hunting can be a hit-or-miss situation. Walk the high alpine zone until you stumble onto birds. A wide-ranging pointing dog really helps. Whitetails will often remain motionless, trusting natural camouflage for protection, holding well for a dog. They are white in winter, mottled brown with white bellies and wings in spring through August. By October they are mostly white again. If snow hasn't fallen, they are easy to spot. Listen for them calling and chattering at dawn, as they can be quite noisy, cackling and whining. Binoculars are particularly effective on the wide-open alpine slopes. Just glass for brown or white birds standing in the open. It's as simple as that. When flushed, whitetails usually fly low and around a shoulder of the mountain or drop quickly downslope and out of sight. They will also fly across big canyons or valleys.

Willow ptarmigan are slightly larger than whitetails, weighing about one-fourth of a pound more. Like all ptarmigan, they can fly up to 35 miles per hour. The males are noticeably redder in plumage during summer months than their white-tailed and rock cousins. They turn white in late fall except for their black tail feathers. Most birds found during the hunting season are a mottled brown and white.

As the name implies, they prefer the willow thickets of the tundra, feeding on buds. More often than the other two species, willow ptarmigan can be found in deciduous thickets and riparian habitats.

Rock ptarmigan are the largest of the three species at about 18 ounces. They prefer a rockier habitat than the other two, hence their name. They are found across North America above the 55th parallel and will often mix in with flocks of willow ptarmigan. Since the birds live in areas where hunting pressure is light and habitat is almost changeless, little is done in the way of management.

Except a lightweight shotgun and sturdy boots, no special equipment is needed to hunt rock ptarmigan. In the late fall, ptarmigan will form

Much like ruffed grouse, blue grouse flush strong, providing quick shooting opportunities as they slip behind cover. Blue grouse inhabit the Rocky Mountains, Sierras and Cascade Range.

large flocks and often flush raggedly. Once a flock is located, it is not extremely difficult or unusual to take a limit from one flush. Rock ptarmigan are noisy and listening for them in the early hours is often one of the best locating methods.

In the frying pan, the birds are excellent. No wonder to this day they're still a staple menu item on north country big game hunts.

Blue Grouse

Blue grouse can reach speeds of 35 miles per hour. But hunters seldom see this as they disappear in short order after a flush into the trees. During the hunting season their plumage is mostly a mottled brownish-gray with a dark tail. The dusky blue plumage of the male is not as pronounced in the fall as in the spring.

Blue grouse favor deciduous woods and grassy meadows in the summer and fall, moving to fir and pine ridges in winter. In September they can often be found on grass or sage ridges just below treeline in dry western mountain slopes. Grassy parks at high elevations are another favored hangout.

Blue grouse are found in the Rocky Mountains, Sierras and Cascade Range in Arizona, New Mexico, Colorado, Utah, Wyoming, Nevada, Oregon, California, Idaho, Montana, Alberta, British Columbia and the Yukon. Extensive western forests retain consistent populations. South Dakota reintroduced the species to the Black Hills during the 1970s.

Most blue grouse are taken from tree perches with rifles by elk and deer hunters. Shotgunners in the know have learned to walk the ridges where trees and grasslands meet. Berry thickets are particularly productive in late summer and early fall. An effective technique is to drive logging roads to find birds, then get out to hunt. Dogs can be used, but birds will frequently fly into trees at the sight of one. They generally flush strong and fly well, providing quick shooting opportunities as they slip behind trees—much like a ruffed grouse. On slopes it works well to place one shooter below birds while another gets above and flushes. They provide tricky shooting through the trees as they zoom by.

Many consider the blue grouse to be the best eating of all the grouse, especially during the early season when they are feeding heavily on berries and green plants.

12

Doves

P aloma. The word somehow seems more romantic than just plain
dove. And fittingly so, for a good part of the year the little banditos
spend most of their time conversing in Spanish south of the border.
Every fall on the way down, they drive a couple of million gringo
wingshooters crazy. No game captures the magic and romance of flight
like the common mourning dove and his white-winged cousin. And no
game bird gets shot at as much, cussed at as much and missed as much.

There is really not much wisdom, tradition or lore to dove hunting.
Least ways, not in the same sense lavished upon plantation quail hunting
or shooting driven pheasants in England. Fact is, dove hunting isn't really dove hunting, it's dove shooting. A basic Saturday morning of dove
shooting starts out by loading up the truck with a cooler of cold drinks
and number 8s while dressed like Rambo at a tropical Club Med. Then
you drive to a cut grain field where birds are known to be feeding, post
yourself at a likely vantage point and wait until one zips over your head.
Of course there are variations to the game plan. I've shot them over stock
tanks in west Texas, goat weeds in east Texas and feed lots in north
Texas.

Not to mention irrigation ditches and fig fields in Arizona and various other cut crop fields in other southern states and Sonora. Though the
hunting may vary from location to location, the physical characteristics
of the birds are pretty much the same.

Mourning doves are extremely handsome birds weighing four to five ounces each and averaging a little over a foot from beak to tail. The males sport softly blended blues and bluish-grays on the head, running down the back into olives and browns. Female mourning doves are a bit smaller and their colors are not as vivid, though not so much so that most hunters notice.

White-wing doves are larger, often outweighing comparative mourning doves by one or two ounces. The white-wing's head and neck are more purple but the tell-tale distinction is broad white stripes over the tops of the wings and secondary feathers. Like mourning doves, female white-wings are smaller and more muted.

While mourning doves are found in all the lower 48 states and much of Canada, white-wing doves have an aversion to cold weather. Their principle breeding and hunting range is southern Arizona, New Mexico, and extreme southern areas of Texas and Mexico.

During the early hunting season in Arizona, there is usually a fair number of white-wings, but the native population heads south quick. In Sonora, I have shot mourning doves and white-wings in ratios as great as three-to-one as late as March, though usually they move south earlier. Texas has a highly regulated early season for white-wings depending on native nesting populations. The eastern birds found in Texas are a subspecies of the white-wings in the western U.S. and Mexico.

But regardless of species, dove hunting is a fast-paced shooting sport. Indeed, to those unaccustomed to the incoming shots and sharp angles, a first-time dove hunt can be a humiliating experience. To be sure, many more doves pass on from old age than fall to a well-directed ounce of number 8 shot.

In fact, statistics show that hunting has little effect on dove populations. Studies conducted by game biologists have shown the natural mortality rate for first-year birds to run as high as 60 to 70 percent. Weather, habitat loss and disease have played much larger roles in the decline of dove numbers, and while the hunting is not what it used to be, it's still pretty good.

Doves generally feed twice a day, morning and evening. The fields they feed in are often the best places to hunt. Doves feed almost entirely on seeds, grain and plant food, and their feeding habits are the key to hunting success.

Coming into water or grain, it is generally accepted that white-wings aren't the top gun pilots that mourning doves are. Personally, I cuss and miss them at about the same pace. Those who study such things tell me that white-wings top out at 55 miles an hour while their sleeker cousins can punch the after burners up to about 60. That's fast. No matter how

Fast-paced shooting, plenty of empty shells and a delectable bag are typical of dove hunting. Despite an annual harvest of 50 million birds, studies show that the natural *mortality for first-year birds runs from 60 to 70 percent.*

much I study the science of shotgun swing and lead, I'm not going to be able to calculate the difference when they come screaming 30 or 40 feet over my head.

For some peculiar reason, the little speedsters love to buzz by a high mark in their feeding fields like a power pole or tree. Those power poles and trees are good places to be positioned while dove hunting. Hide yourself far enough away so the tree doesn't block your view or hinder your shooting. Anything in the field that gives the doves a line of flight is also a good place to set up, as doves tend to fly the length of fencerows or ditches on their way in to feed. Water in or around the field brings the birds in, too. In places like Arizona and southern California, irrigation ditches around grain fields often provide a busy shooting lane.

To the uninitiated in an upper Midwestern state, a lone dove on a telephone wire seems hardly a sporting target. Take the same dove, plus a couple of hundred friends and relatives that he has picked up along his migration route, and you have the most challenging wingshooting game around. A typical hunt scenario plays something like this:

The first cool nights of August find several family groups in South Dakota forming into a flock of 25. Heading south they meet other loosely knit groups and decide to enjoy some warm Oklahoma sunshine and a fresh-cut maize field. Some of the individual birds have been to the same maize in seasons past. Mechanical harvesters leave plenty for dinner, year after year.

A sportsman and his two sons know the birds will be there as well and, after a short walk from the gravel road, the three take up positions around the field 150 yards apart. Though the temperature is above 90 degrees, a cool afternoon breeze makes the waiting tolerable. Each hunter is dressed the same, in a camo T-shirt and a baseball hat. That's more for insurance than anything; it's hard to keep the doves out. About 3 p.m., they start winging over the tree-lined creek that borders the southern half of the field. The youngest hunter races back and forth down the grove, searching for the ultimate spot.

No matter, in the next couple of hours each gets to shoot almost a box of shells. The match is over long before dark and the doves have pretty much won. Nonetheless, the trio returns to the road with 15 birds.

Nothing fancy. No duck boats, decoys or almost-human Labs. No far-ranging pointers and horse-drawn wagons. Just a fresh cut grainfield, a couple of eager boys and plenty of shells. Find where the birds feed or water and you'll have dove shooting. The same play is staged much the same in several states every September. A pretty casual affair compared to other types of upland hunting but, south of the border, dove shooting is serious business.

About three days of dove shooting in Mexico is all the average shooter can take. The practical aftermath of a Mexican dove hunt is a bruised shoulder, the impractical is a waning desire to sample such shooting more than once a year. Nothing urgent; maybe next season, maybe next month. Sometimes just knowing that such a "Birdshoot in Wonderland" exists is gratification enough.

The logistics are fairly simple. Catch a commercial jet to a place such as Hermillsilio or Guymas or even drive across Laredo or Brownsville, it doesn't really matter where.

Unless you're extremely partial to your personal scattergun, leave it at home. The Mexican paperwork and money required isn't worth the government gun permit. Rental guns, for the most part, are quality American-made 20 gauge pumps and the shells, though Mexican-made, are hard to distinguish from their U.S. counterparts. Accommodations range from slick city hotels to traditional haciendas and lake-side lodges.

Reputable operations rotate fields for low pressure shooting and limit the number of shooters to no more than two or three in a 20-acre patch. About two hours in the morning and a few more in the evening is all anyone can take when the shooting is really hot.

Evening dinners consist of lots of fresh seafood, good beef and south-of-the border specialties. In fact, I'm still not convinced that I don't go more for the food than for the doves.

Some of the best of both is found in Sonora in bird camps that have yet to be discovered by American shooters, where a sunny afternoon may find only two or three hunters in a field as busy with doves as O'Hare is with planes during rush hour.

Starting with the sun, the birds stream over the treetops and into the cut fields of sorghum. For two or three hours in the morning and another couple in the evening, you shoot your rental gun until your shoulder or shell pocketbook can't stand it any longer. But there is no mercy. Push yourself and enjoy it, the package usually lasts only two or three days. On more than one occasion I have looked down at my right shoulder and discovered a bright patch of crimson from flesh pounded raw with ten boxes a morning, the pain not noticed until later. For those who enjoy shooting in general and dove shooting in particular, Mexico must be experienced at least once.

Regardless of where you hunt, you have to be able to hit doves, and that requires the appropriate scattergun. Personally, it takes me a couple of shots at the start of each year to semi-perfect leads and angles. I like to think that my poor shooting is the gun manufacturer's fault for never building a specialty dove gun. I know it's a lame excuse, but any excuse is better than saying "I missed him clean, simple and fair." Oh sure, the big three ammo companies have stocked our shelves high and full with "dove and quail" loads, but no fool has yet to stake his job on the ideal dove gun. Choosing the ideal dove gun can be a pretty intellectual experience. Conditions vary greatly from field to field and sometimes from day to day in the same field.

Most dove hunts are a short walk from the car, so reducing a pound or two on the gun isn't a big deal. I like a relatively heavy gun with at least a 28-inch barrel. Long barreled guns serve two masters. They help compensate for underleading a bird, which is much more common than shooting ahead of one, and in dove hunting situations where a hunter may go through a box of shells every hour or so, heavier guns help reduce recoil.

Another must on a dove gun is a ventilated rib. Since many times the opening of dove season coincides with 90 degree temperatures, barrels heat up fast. Vent ribs help dissipate the heat and reduce bothersome heat waves. Modified chokes are generally preferred, but the hunter with a screw-in choke gun is smart to bring every tube that he owns so he can match the pattern size to the shooting conditions.

Doves are easy birds to kill. With small bones and light feathers, an ounce of shot is all that is needed to kill one, so just about any gauge is adequate. I personally love to shoot doves with my little Model 42, .410 pump. Pay particular attention to the fact that I said "shoot at." Most shooters will find that their average really goes down when they move to the smaller gauges.

One note of caution: As mentioned before, doves are a warm weather game bird. Perspiration from hands and face can quickly ruin the blue and wood finish on finely crafted older guns. Many serious hunters are switching to "special purpose" type guns with tough, non-reflective wood and metal finishes.

The most common mistake in shooting doves is not giving the birds enough lead. Shooters that swing, follow through and get out ahead of the birds hit more than the shooters who shoot at the bird. "Pointers" rather than snap shooters usually make better dove shots. Seasoned dove hunters average about eight birds from a box of shells. A 50 percent shooting average is fantastic. To put this in perspective, in Mexico, where it is common to shoot a case of shells on a two-day hunt, a shooter with that kind of average could easily kill 250 birds!

My good friend Alberto Noriega who, with his partner Leon Hoeffer, runs one of the most personalized dove hunts in Mexico through Sonora Outfitters, has the opportunity to watch several hunters shoot at several thousand birds each winter. He claims that the biggest fault of most American shooters is that they're always in a hurry. They don't

There's nothing fancy about dove hunting. No duck boats, decoys or almost-hunter Labs. No far-ranging pointers or horse-drawn wagons. Just a fresh cut grainfield, a box or two of number 8s and a lot of incoming shots. Find where the birds feed or water and you'll have a great shoot.

pick their shots and they shoot without swinging. Noriega's best advice is to take your time, pick only the better shots and follow through on the swing.

Of course, in any sport there is always one technique that separates the pros from the armchair quarterbacks. Lawton Smith is one of those pros. Hunting over stock tanks in west Texas, he averages almost one bird per shell but, what's even more amazing, is that he shoots incoming birds from the right off of his right shoulder and incoming birds from the left off of his left shoulder.

Field care of doves when the shooting is over is critical. Due to the almost certain hot weather that the birds are hunted in, they should be picked or breasted quickly and placed on ice. A vest with a mesh game bag is nice for hunters who move around, as is a bird belt. Don't pile doves in a bucket where the air can't circulate, as the meat can quickly spoil.

Though only the breasts are used in most recipes, doves are a rich, flavorful game bird. Dark-meated dove tastes more like duck than other upland birds. Quick field care is imperative to what the birds will ultimately taste like at the dinner table.

With more than three million hunters taking an estimated 50 million birds each year, dove hunting is a popular sport. In terms of harvest, more doves are shot each year than all the quail, ruffed grouse and pheasants put together.

And even with so many ending up in the game bag, many millions more are shot at and missed, but that's what makes them so much fun.

13

Other Upland Species

S nipe hunting is among the oldest practical jokes in the world. More than one neophyte to the great outdoors has been left in woods "holding the bag" by his compadres. His lonely flashlight beam diligently waving to lure the mythical creatures into a gunny sack, the poor snipe hunter's voice shortly turns to a croak as he continues his call of "snipe, snipe, snipe" through the long, cold night.

Snipe hunting is also one of the longest standing upland sports in North America. *Real* snipe hunting, that is. Why, there were snipe in North America long before anyone even thought of bringing pheasants here. Today, the glamour and allure of other, more well-known species has eclipsed the popularity of the snipe, but this bird can offer excellent, uncrowded hunting for the upland bird hunter willing to seek it out.

This is likewise true of a handful of other upland or semi-upland species in North America. In some locales, hunting them is very popular, but in other areas, even in the same state, few hunters have heard of, much less hunted, these species.

The Common Snipe

There is a game bird called the snipe. Like the woodcock, it is a shorebird gone upland, though not to the extent of the woodcock. Its appearance is also similar to the woodcock, though it is more elongated and less chunky than the timberdoodle. The snipe's wings are also longer and each forms a distinctive "V" when the bird is in flight.

The hunter will find snipe frequenting wet meadows, particularly low-lying hay or crop fields, and marshes. The birds migrate with the season, staying well ahead of freeze-up. Though the snipe seeks his prey in more open terrain, he has the same requirements as the woodcock. He needs soft soil and earthworms within six inches of the surface so he can use his long, flexible bill to feed.

Snipe are solitary while breeding, but the hunter is likely to find them migrating in small flocks called "wisps." Where hunters know about them, snipe are often hunted incidentally to other species. In Texas, for example, Pat Johnson's Wild Goose Hunting Club offers afternoon snipe hunting to round out the day after a morning waterfowl hunt. More than once, co-author Miller has forsaken an early-season bear stand or bowhunting stand for whitetail when he flushed snipe while walking through a wet field on the way to his post.

When the birds are in, the common snipe offers tremendous sport, especially for the small gauge hunter. Even the renowned waterfowl and quail hunter Nash Buckingham wrote of snipe hunts where barrels became too hot to touch.

When snipe flush from cover, they usually squawk to unnerve the hunter. They fly a twisted, sometimes cork-screwing path, then drop quickly back into cover. Because of their coloration and the thick grass into which they often seem to fall, the tiny snipe is one of the most difficult birds to retrieve if a good mark is not made. They even seem to give off little scent for a dog to work.

Rails

Technically rails are not upland birds. They are birds of the marsh. Their haunts include both freshwater marshes and, more importantly, the brackish and salty tidal marshes of the East Coast. The rails are also migratory birds which provided untapped sport over a large area of the eastern United States. Where they are hunted regularly, like the tidal marshes of New Jersey, they are pursued with a passion.

Even though they are members of the same family as the coot and can swim darn near as well, there is good reason for including a passage on rails in an upland bird hunting book. Because of the method by which they are most commonly hunted, they are more like upland birds than waterfowl.

Three species of rails are commonly pursued by wingshooters in North America. The largest of these is the clapper rail. It is about 14 to 16 inches long with a medium length, slightly curved bill. Its body shape is somewhat chicken-like.

Like woodcock, snipe are shorebirds gone upland. More elongated and less chunky than timberdoodle, snipe frequent wet meadows and marshes. Hunters often locate snipe migrating in small flocks.

The Virginia rail is smaller, but similar in build to the clapper. Its coloration is different and it has a slightly longer, more slender bill.

The sora rail is much smaller, only eight to ten inches in length and it has a short yellow beak.

In coastal marshes, rails are hunted on the high tide when birds are forced to seek cover on small grass patches sticking above the water. A light, flat-bottomed boat is poled into these patches with the gunner sitting or standing in the front. Rails flush as the boat approaches. Shots can range from very close to very long, depending on the cover and the wariness of the birds. Dogs are extremely useful in retrieving downed rails from cover and open water; however, a good mark by the hunter and the poler are a tremendous help.

Limits on rails are high, and they offer the small gauge shooter some remarkably sporty and unpressured wingshooting.

Band-Tailed Pigeon

As its name implies, the band-tailed pigeon has a light-colored band across the end of its tail. Also known as the blue pigeon, it is native to the western and southwestern regions of the United States and on south to northern and central Mexico.

With the passing of the passenger pigeon, the band-tailed pigeon has the distinction of being the only remaining wild, native pigeon in North America. In size and appearance it is similar to the common pigeon, or rock dove, which was introduced from Europe.

The home of the band-tailed pigeon is the oak-conifer forests of western North America. They are migratory and remain in flocks during the winter.

Like mourning doves, the band-tailed pigeon is monogamous. The females lay one or two eggs in a clutch, but may lay and hatch several clutches a season. The adults feed the young, or "squab," on pigeon milk. The adult's diet consists of seeds, berries and other woodland forage.

Though larger than mourning doves (band-tailed pigeons are approximately 14 to 15 inches in length), pigeons have similar flight characteristics, making them a favorite of ammunition manufacturers and a welcome frustration for wingshooters. The birds are hunted much like mourning doves; that is, by ambush at feeding areas, etc. However, because of the woodland cover in which the birds thrive, the added challenge of overhead cover offers a whole new wingshooting twist.

Hunters will find the greatest opportunities for band-tailed pigeon hunting in Colorado, New Mexico, Arizona and Mexico.

The chachalaca, or Mexican pheasant, inhabits the smallest range of any North American gamebird. It is hunted in the Lower Rio Grande Valley in Texas, and in Mexico.

Whatinthehellisachachalaca?

If your hunting partner ever said, "Let's load up the dog and go chachalaca hunting," you would have every right to wonder if he was taking you on a "snipe hunt" or a wild goose chase. But indeed, there is an upland game bird in North America called the chachalaca (pronounced "cha-cha" like the dance, and "lock-a").

In the United States, the chachalaca has the smallest range of any gamebird. To hunt them, you'll have to go to the Lower Rio Grande Valley in Texas. They can also be hunted to some extent in Mexico.

Also known locally as the Mexican pheasant, the chachalaca is indeed a pheasant-sized member of the curassow family. In Central and South America, curassows are prized as game birds because of their delicious meat and their vibrant coloration, often set against a shiny black plumage.

The chachalaca wears less flamboyant feathering in mostly brown and pale green. Also like a pheasant, the chachalaca has a long tail.

The name chachalaca comes from the bird's loud call.

According to limited sources of information, chachalaca are most commonly hunted on foot. When the birds flush, they stay low to the ground as they fly through the brushy woods, thickets and timber which they inhabit.

14

Practice For The Hunter

P ractice makes perfect. Shotgunners of every stature have been preached that doctrine a million times. Now make that a million and one. They in turn preach it to friends and acquaintances coming into the sport. And the vicious cycle goes on and on and on.

In some cases, it may be closer to the truth to say that practice can be pointless. It can if the practice sessions are without purpose. To walk out into a field and shoot a shotgun at the sky is not practice. Even the addition of targets flying about does not necessarily constitute legitimate practice.

Practice in wingshooting, as in anything else, is only worth the effort if you concentrate on what you are doing—really concentrate. You must critique each shot. Think it through. "Where did I miss that last target? Why did I miss it there? What can I do the next time to hit it?"

But don't just concentrate on the negatives. Do the same things when you hit a target. Again, think it through. "What made that shot 'feel' right? Where was the barrel when I pulled the trigger? What did the swing-through feel like?" Try to imprint those sights and sensations on your brain, and use them to hit other targets—at practice and in the field.

Getting Started

The way to learn to hit birds aflight in the uplands is to learn to hit clay targets aflight on the local trap and skeet ranges. There are a lot of crusty oldsters out there who will try to tell you that formal target shooting can ruin a good field shot. That is a philosophy with a lot of holes in it. About as many as a well-used patterning board.

Traditional trap and skeet offer the best, make that the only, way to develop a wingshooting style. Everything is controlled at the target range, allowing the shooter to concentrate on what he is doing. It makes it easy for the wingshooter to walk before he runs.

For example, in formal trap and skeet the gun is mounted to the shoulder before the bird is called from the house. That isn't the way things happen in the field, but it is the way to learn how a properly mounted gun should feel. Once most of the clays are breaking comes the time to add the more complicated step of starting the gun from a field carry position. Walk before you run.

Getting started really begins even before one heads to the trap and skeet ranges. Start at home in front of a full-length bedroom mirror. Take the gun you want to learn to shoot from the rack. Open the action to check the chamber to make sure it's empty.

Step up to a full-length mirror, but far enough back so the barrel won't hit the glass when you shoulder the gun. Position your feet comfortably apart. For the right-handed shooter, the left foot should be forward with his weight balanced slightly on the lead foot. Southpaws will have their right foot forward and the weight favoring it.

Relax! Bend the knees slightly. Drop the arms loosely. *Just be comfortable.*

Now pick up the shotgun. Shoulder it, bringing the stock to your cheek. *Do not lower your head to the stock*! If the rib or barrel has a center and front bead, the back bead should rest just under the front bead to form a figure eight. If the shotgun only has a front bead, it is all that should appear over the plane of the barrel.

Once this feels comfortable, forget about the bead(s) and look at the reflection in the mirror. Fix the image of how you look pointing a gun in your mind. Lower the gun and mount it again. And again. And again.

Each evening, mount the gun 10 or 15 times, concentrating to make sure it is done the same way in the same position every time. Slowly increase the speed with which you shoulder the shotgun, but don't allow yourself to get sloppy. Force yourself to do it the same way *every single time*!

As simple as this procedure may sound, it is practice with a purpose. And that makes it worthwhile. Even veteran bird hunters who don't often pick up a shotgun in the off season can benefit by beginning this drill several weeks before opening day. It helps tone muscles that have forgotten how to react, and it will make them function more quickly when that first grouse thunders through the early season cover.

Just as in checking gun fit, practice begins in front of the full-length mirror. Try to develop a "feel" for proper, instinctive mounting.

Don't be afraid of gun clubs! You'll meet a lot of great people there who are anxious to help you improve your wingshooting skills.

No Reason For Cold Feet

Perhaps the reason hunters are often timid about improving their basic wingshooting skills at the target range is that they don't understand the games and are embarrassed to admit it. Really, both trap and skeet are very simple.

Trap. In regulation trap, five shooters participate in a round. Each of them stands at one of the five stations which spread evenly 16 yards behind the trap house. Mounted in this house is a mechanical wonder called an "oscillating trap" which throws clay targets in a 90-degree area to the front of the house.

When the trap is operating properly and the wind isn't affecting their flight, the elevation of the targets and the speed at which they leave the trap never changes. The trap swings back and forth at random allowing targets to be released at any point in that 90-degree range.

Targets are released immediately when a shooter calls "pull!"

The shooter on station one calls and shoots the first target. Next, the shooter on station two calls for a target and shoots it. Then the shooter on station three, and so on.

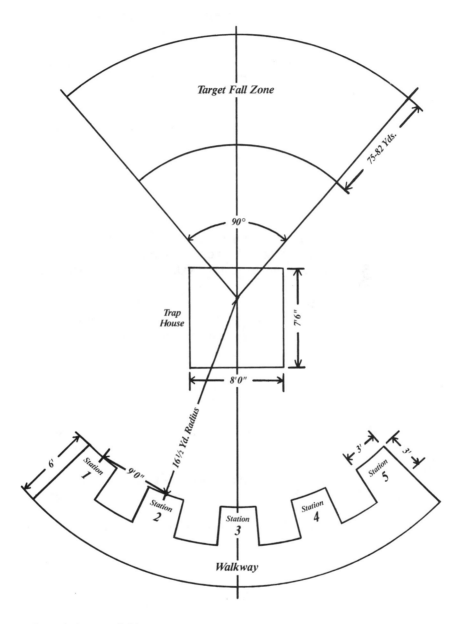

A regulation trap field.

This series is repeated for five shots by each shooter. Then, all shooters move one station to the right, with the shooter who has just finished on station five moving to station one.

When everyone is back on the line and ready, the shooter who started on station one calls for his bird and shoots it. No matter which station he rotates to, the shooter who started on station one always calls the first bird after a switch.

Next the shooter who started on station two (and is now on station three) calls for his bird and shoots it. And so on until each shooter has taken five shots from his new position.

Thisfive-shots-and-switch routine continues until each shooter has taken five consecutive shots from each of the five stations. At this point a round is complete. Each shooter will have shot at 25 targets, a box of shells.

If you are still timid about going out and plunging into a new sport, just go out to the trap range and watch a couple of rounds before you sign up to shoot. You'll quickly understand how the round flows, and you'll be telling yourself, "Aw, that don't look so tough!"

In terms of etiquette, just use common sense when it comes to firearms safety. Rule number one at any trap range is *always keep your shotgun pointed downrange! Never point the gun behind the firing line!*

When shooting trap at a club, never load more than one shell in your gun at a time, unless you're shooting doubles or some special game. Never close the action on your gun until it is actually your turn to call for a bird and shoot. If there is a malfunction with the trap and a range helper has to go check it, unload your gun and keep it pointed at the ground just downrange of your feet until he returns to a safe position behind the firing line. Some clubs will have you leave the line and rack your gun until the malfunction is corrected.

Some clubs have special rules about recovering shells that touch the ground or taking a "coach" to the firing line with you, but they are easily worked around.

You may be nervous the first couple of times you shoot a formal round of trap or skeet, but that will soon subside as you concentrate on improving your shooting and you see it happen with more and more puffs of "smoke" before your barrel.

Skeet. American skeet fields have two houses from which birds are thrown. Each of them houses a fixed trap which throws clay targets on a preset line. Again, barring wind or trap malfunction, the targets from skeet houses never vary in elevation or speed. And, unlike targets in the game of trap, the angle at which they are thrown in relation to the house never varies.

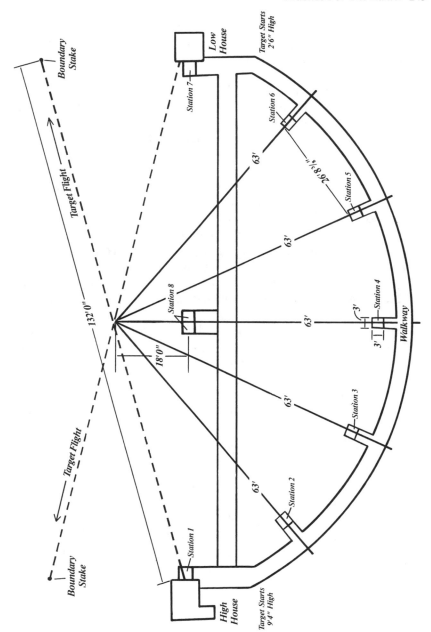

A regulation skeet field.

In fact, when you watch range helpers calibrate a skeet field, you'll see them take a steel ring on a long pole and mount it on a stake which is pounded into the ground just downrange of the center point between the two houses. They will adjust the traps in both houses until the targets from both are consistently flying through that ring.

With the shooter looking downrange, the trap house on his left is the high house. In it, the fixed thrower is mounted on a platform 15 feet off of the ground. The house on the right side of the field is the low house. The trap in it is mounted at ground level. These houses are 40 yards apart. Remember that the traps throw toward each other and are aimed to throw the targets through that ring 15 feet in the air, 18 feet downrange of the centerpoint between the two houses.

The skeet field has eight stations. Station one is located directly underneath the door of the high house. Station seven is next to the door of the low house. Station eight is located at the center point on a straight line running between the two houses. Using that line as the diameter of a circle, stations two through six are evenly spaced on the uprange half of that circle. Station four is halfway around the circle, an equal distance from both houses.

The order of shooting for skeet is a bit more complex because there are two houses from which birds are thrown and because some of the stations involve doubles. Again, if you're a timid soul, watch a few rounds before you shoot or try to find an experienced shooter to coach you the first couple of times through.

Instead of alternating shots as in trap, skeet shooters take all of their shots from a station, then let the next shooter take all of his shots. A station is complete when all five shooters have taken all the shots they are allotted at that position. The squad moves as a group from station to station.

At each station only put enough shells in your gun for each call of "pull." For singles that naturally means one, and for doubles, two. At some clubs you'll see experienced shooters loading for more than one call at a time, but beginners are better off with the minimum number of shells in the gun. There's too many other distractions in learning the game and the club etiquette, so why add the worry of not remembering if the gun is empty? Your new-found friends will appreciate your safety consciousness.

At station one, the first shot is a single from the high house. The second shot is a single from the low house. The third and fourth shots are comprised of a double with a single bird released simultaneously from each house. On all doubles in skeet, the shooter takes the bird moving away first and then concentrates on the incoming bird. So from station

Though the targets on a skeet field fly on a preset path, you can develop your own "game" to challenge your increasing skills.

one, this means that the bird from the high house is taken first, the bird from the low house is taken second. Only one shot is fired at each bird, so even if you miss the first, you must move on to shoot at the second.

This series of four birds completes the shooting at station one. Station two is a repeat of this same shooting series.

At stations three, four and five a single bird is called from each house. The order on singles is always high house first, low house second.

Stations six and seven are repeats of the series at Stations one and two with the exception that on the doubles, the low house bird is taken first, because from this side of the field it is moving away from the gunner.

Station eight is the exception to the shoot-the-whole-station rotation. When station eight is properly shot, all the shooters in the squad rotate through the high house shot, then they all step to the other side of the shooting pad and alternate through the low house shot.

Okay, who has been counting the shots? Four each on stations one, two, six and seven; that's 16. Two each on three, four, five and eight;

that's another eight for a total of 24. So what do you do with the extra shell from the box of 25 you started with?

Regulation skeet has a target called the "option" bird. This target is taken as a repeat of a shooter's first miss during the round. So if you miss the first bird on station one, you immediately repeat that shot as your option. If your first miss is one of the birds in a double, you immediately repeat the bird you missed from the double.

Would-be bird hunters who are using skeet to develop or enhance field shooting skills probably won't have to worry about running 24 straight right away, but in that case the option shot is taken last from any station of the shooter's choice. (You'll most often see it shot as a repeat of low house eight for convenience sake and because the shooter who has taken the first 24 without fail has a pretty good chance of getting that bird. However, the first time you run 'em, don't be embarrassed to ask the puller to move to the station you feel most confident shooting. It's your *option*.)

All of this makes skeet sound more complicated than it really is. Watching a couple of rounds and then shooting with some newly-made friends who take pleasure in helping beginners, teaches the game much more quickly and enjoyably than any text or videotape possibly could.

Though slightly more complicated than trap, the skeet field is an even better place to get down the basics of wingshooting. The element of surprise generated by an oscillating trap is eliminated on the skeet field. In this game you know exactly where the birds are going. That allows you to concentrate on form and on learning what it takes to hit on different kinds of shots. Knowing where the bird is going before it comes out of the house also makes it easier for you or your coach to tell what went wrong on a miss so you can correct it next time.

Start with a mounted gun, concentrate on swinging. Concentrate on what the sight picture looks like when you're pulling the trigger. When that becomes instinctive, then add the complexity of mounting the gun after the bird leaves the house. Walk before you run.

Other Versions Of Trap And Skeet. There are other variations to these games, known as Olympic or International Trap and International Skeet. These are more difficult versions of these games and are not suitable as a practice tool for the hunter developing wingshooting skills. They are fun for the seasoned shooter to really challenge his already fundamentally sound skills, but, unfortunately, facilities offering these games are not widespread in the states.

Even if the upland bird hunter heads to the trap and skeet club without the foggiest notion of what to expect, he's not likely to find anyone who will laugh at his questions. As long as he practices appropriate basic

Informal sessions with a hand-thrower and a few clay targets in the game pouch can simulate hunting situations pretty closely.

safety skills, he will find a whole new bunch of friends more than willing to help him get into these enjoyable games to whatever degree he wishes.

To find a local gun club, any upland bird hunter can contact the National Shooting Sports Foundation at (203) 762-1320. For a complete directory of gun clubs in the U.S., send $2.00 to: NSSF, Dept. NAH, 555 Danbury Road, Wilton, CT 06897.

More Practice At The Trap And Skeet Range

Many wingshots who begin to use formal trap and skeet to learn and enhance wingshooting skills will end up loving the games. They may even join a league, which is a wonderful idea because it promotes regular, concentrated shooting.

But there's more to be learned at the trap and skeet field once the basic skills have become "instinct." At every opportunity, try new things that test your basic skills. During slack periods many clubs will allow shooters to go out onto fields by themselves or alone with a puller. Then you have the freedom to try whatever you'd like. Maybe doubles from station four on the skeet field. Maybe trap targets while you're standing on top of the house or in the bleachers behind the field. Try to duplicate shots that you might expect to take in the field and practice them in reps almost like a weightlifter pumps iron in the gym. Once a shot has been emblazoned in the memory banks it is difficult to wipe out, even if it is practiced only occasionally.

Like always, concentrate when you're practicing. Try to repeat what you're doing right and alter what you're doing wrong. And *use* both to become a better wingshooter.

Do-It-Yourself Target Games

In the absence of convenient facilities to regularly shoot skeet and trap, the hunter can learn a lot and improve his wingshooting skills with nothing more than a hand-thrower, a case of targets and a safe place to shoot. Sessions of this type, in addition to more formal shooting games, can be of great benefit to the wingshooter.

Informal clay target shooting has a lot of advantages. For one, it's inexpensive, which means you can shoot a lot more for the same money. Secondly, there is no pressure; you can just go out and have fun. No matter how hard you try to forget it when you're practicing on a trap or skeet field, you can never completely shake the feeling of competition, of someone keeping score. Finally, there is no embarrassment, even for the most timid wingshooter. If it's just you and your best hunting buddy, there's no crowd around to see your misses.

One pitfall sometimes encountered by the gravel pit gang is complacency. They're having such a good time, they forget to critique each miss and each hit as to what went wrong or right. That's practice without a purpose, which for the serious wingshooter is as good as no practice at all.

Another trap to avoid is making the shots too easy. Once the basics of wingshooting are mastered, the only way to improve is to attempt more and more difficult shots. It's the same in the development of skills for any sport. In tennis, for example, (a great game, by the way, for wingshooters to use in the development of hand-eye coordination) you don't become a better player by playing only those opponents you know you can beat. You learn to be a better player by challenging players who are better than you are...over and over again...until your skills eventually meet, then exceed, theirs. Of course, there are physical limitations which vary for each individual, but few tennis players and far fewer wingshots practice enough against challenging opponents (read targets) to ever come close to reaching their potential.

One device sure to keep hand-thrown targets from becoming too easy is the "stick bird" thrower. Simply, this is a hand-thrower mounted

Sporting clays shooting is as close as you can get to hunting without feathers. Stations are specifically designed to imitate the terrain and flight characteristics of many upland bird species.

on the end of a golf club shaft. The additional leverage increases the speed at which the target can be thrown, and a practiced hand can get exaggerated, dips, twists and wiggles out of a standard clay target.

Of course, there are any number of ways that the wingshooter can prevent hand-thrown targets from becoming too easy. You can use the available cover and terrain to restrict the length of time a target is visible. You can throw more than one target at a time. One could even be of a different color to indicate a hen bird or no-shot. Birds could be thrown without warning to surprise the shooter while walking down a trail in the woods. Targets can be thrown with infinitely more challenge as a shooter's skills improve.

And now you've entered the realm of sporting clays.

Sporting Clays—The Graduate School For Wingshooters

Sit around the clubhouse at your local sporting clays establishment, and chances are that you'll hear three comments from first-timers who have just completed the course. No matter how good of wingshots they thought they were before shooting sporting clays, first-time shooters will always say the same thing.

Still under shock from what they've just experienced, the first-time sporting clays shooter will begin by mumbling something like, "Boy, that was a humbling experience," or "Guess I ate my share of humble pie this morning." Whatever the exact phrase it most assuredly will contain some conjugation of the word "humble." As described by Webster humble is "not proud or haughty; not arrogant or assertive; reflecting a spirit of submission." Humble is the perfect word to describe what a sporting clays course can do for any wingshooter.

With a cold drink to help reinstill some lost bravado, the flow of the conversation will move to something like, "Man, I wish I could go out and shoot that again right now. I know I could do better than that!"

Then, perhaps after an hour or so to reflect on the shoot and compare it to other successes and failures in the field and on the target range, there comes the philosophical stage. With his chair balanced on its rear legs and his head reclined on his hands with fingers laced behind his neck, he'll pop off with something like, "You know, this game really is the closest thing to hunting without feathers!"

Sporting clays is relatively new on this side of the Atlantic. It has only really caught on here in the last decade or so. But it is already the fastest growing inanimate shooting game in this country. Why? Well, it's much like golf. For the wingshot with a competitive streak it is an addicting form of frustration. If you have that kind of personality, once you've shot the game, you'll go back again and again in a struggle to

The trap boy has up to three seconds to launch the bird after the shooter says, "pull!"

shoot one bird better than your buddy and one bird better than your personal best.

"Clays" is also the game for the wingshot who is the equivalent of golf's duffer. It can be a very relaxing game and is far more social than the other clay target games.

Once he has mastered the basics, sporting clays is *the* game for the birdgunner. No other course of fire offers the similarity to hunting as does a well-designed sporting clays course.

The only way to "learn" sporting clays is to go and shoot a round, or two, or three, or four... It's best, but not essential, to find a friend who has shot the course before to go with you. He can give you pointers on what to expect, much the way a hunting buddy or guide could do.

Sporting clays courses, again like golf courses, are as variable as the terrain they are built on. They can be anything from a partially overgrown trail with a trap or two hidden in the weeds, to a million dollar-plus country club course complete with $20,000 bronzes of wild game designating each shooting station. The difficulty and type of shots can be just as varied.

One of the great things about sporting clays is that nobody hits them all! There is plenty of opportunity to rib your buddies...and congratulate them on fine shots.

Even the same station can be changed from shoot to shoot by varying the elevation, angle and speed of the targets—just like moving the hole placement on a golf course green.

As always, common sense safety techniques for gun handling are mandatory at the sporting clays range. Load only enough shells to shoot once at each target released on a single pull. That means one shell for singles and two for doubles. Always keep your gun unloaded, the action open and the safety on between shots.

Depending on the course and the type of shooting station, some sporting stations are shot in trap style in which shooters alternate shots, and some are shot in skeet style, meaning that each shooter takes all his shots from a shooting position before the next shooter steps up and takes his.

The rules for competitive sporting clays shooting are that the bird must be called for without the gun mounted. This means with the complete butt of the gun visible below the shooter's armpit. Unlike trap and skeet in which the puller releases the bird immediately on the command of the shooter, the sporting clays puller can delay a pull up to three sec-

The only way to become a better wingshot is to practice with a purpose.

onds after the call for the bird. The shooter can not shoulder the gun until he actually makes eye contact with the target.

When you're not shooting in competition, these fine points can be adhered to as you see fit. Your first priority should be to practice the part of your technique that needs work. For example, if it's swing you'll be concentrating on during a practice round of clays, then whether the gun is exactly four inches or more from your shoulder when you call for the bird isn't overly important.

When you shoot sporting clays as practice for hunting, think of it as hunting. Try to use the gun, loads and clothing you'll have with you in the field. Try to duplicate hunting conditions as closely as possible.

Without a doubt, sporting clays *is* the shooting game for upland bird hunters. A few serious practice outings of sporting clays prior to the upland seasons will most assuredly up your percentage of success on live birds.

For complete information on course availability near your home and in your favorite hunting areas, write to: National Sporting Clay Association (NSCA), Dept. NAH, P.O. Box 680007, San Antonio, TX 78268. The National Shooting Sports Foundation is also deeply involved in the promotion of recreational sporting clays shooting. They'll help you with info from the address and phone number given earlier in this chapter.

Wingshooting Schools

The ultimate step for the wingshot who wishes to learn and develop shotgunning skills is to attend a formal shooting school. Private lessons are offered by "pros" at some larger trap and skeet clubs and at many sporting clays courses.

Three- to five-day shooting schools are conducted by many firearms and accessories companies. Some of the more famous are run by Orvis, Griffin & Howe, Holland & Holland and Pachmayr. They are by no stretch of the imagination inexpensive. But they also offer an opportunity to improve skills that isn't matched by any other learning method. In such a school, pupils receive personal instruction from the finest wingshots in the world. Many also offer fitting services which will tell you the exact measurements of the stock that best fits your build and wingshooting style.

15

Trophies For The Wall
And The Dinner Table

T he concept of the "trophy" upland bird is not a new one. The nobles and gentry of Europe long ago prized pheasants and partridge to such a degree that it was a hanging offense for a peasant to kill one. Such was the value of the sport.

Culinary geniuses around the globe base some of their most renowned and elegant dishes on the tender, succulent meats of pheasant and partridge. Had the ruffed grouse been native or imported to the Continent, its delicious meat would certainly rank among the most called for in the world.

But today, in North America, the idea of an upland bird's trophy value has taken on a new twist.

The sheer opportunity to hunt "native" birds becomes rarer and more treasured each season. Like the deer hunter who doggedly pursues a record book 10-pointer or the big game hunter who travels to Alaska for a grizzly bear, we begin to hear bird hunters talk more of quality birds instead of quantities of birds. They compare tail feathers on grouse, spurs on rooster pheasants and the bodily bulk of "timber" bobs. They spend more money and travel to more exotic places to take birds they don't have in the fields back home.

Obviously, this phenomenon isn't motivated by a desire to fill the family larder, as was the case in the early years of North American upland bird hunting. There are much, much cheaper ways to put food on the table. Heck, a nonresident hunter could probably eat steak all year on what it costs him to take a possession limit of pheasants on a fully outfitted hunt in South Dakota or Kansas.

So there is obviously something more to it.

Hunters know what it is. It's the birds. It's the guns. It's the dogs. It's the companions. It's the sport. It's the memories.

For years, hunters have savored these memories over fine meals of the season's harvest. But today, it is more and more common to mount a "trophy" bird to keep the memories alive for years to come.

To Mount A Trophy Bird

As in taxidermy work for any kind of fish or game, there are two kinds of upland bird mounts—good ones and bad ones. The good ones are treasured heirlooms that, with care, can be passed from father to son. The bad ones are wastes of money that end up in the back of the shed as moth food.

The quality of a mount is partially determined by the care the trophy receives in the field. Just like doctors, the best taxidermists can only do so much to save an abused patient. If the patient arrives in good shape, the results are usually excellent. If the patient arrives in tough shape, there's little hope he'll ever reach the level of quality that everyone would like.

Actually, the road to a quality upland bird mount begins even before the bird is ever flushed or shot. It starts with research before the season to find a taxidermist whose previous work meets your standards of quality.

A good place to look for superior quality taxidermists during the off-season is at sport shows. Many will have booths displaying their work at these events. Often, taxidermy competitions are run in conjunction with sport shows, and the finest work of artists from a large area will be on display. It's fine to use competitions as a starting point in your research, but keep in mind that taxidermists only enter their best work. Upland bird specimens for these displays were often killed with gas or by some other method that does no damage to the feathers or skin. Before you make a decision, be sure to view some of the artist's samples of birds taken by hunters. There is a lot to be seen in the quality of repairs a taxidermist makes to a shotgun-harvested skin.

When you find a taxidermist whose work interests you, try to find other hunters with mounts he has done. Many taxidermists will have references available for you to call, but you'll need to judge carefully the value of a list of happy customers provided by the taxidermist who's trying to get your business.

All of this may sound like you shouldn't trust taxidermists. That's not the case at all. Taxidermists are, by and large, dedicated artists who can provide you with all kinds of valuable information on hunting upland birds and preserving trophies with high quality taxidermy services. However, you could very easily be spending $200 or more, depending on the upland bird mount you're after. That's a lot of money if the result is only fit for moth food. A conscientious taxidermist won't mind you thoroughly checking him out.

On the flip side of the coin, don't balk at high prices for quality work. Truly artistic mounts don't happen overnight. The best work doesn't come from a taxidermist who cranks the trophies through his shop on a production line. That kind of taxidermist can afford to lower his prices because he is doing volume. The real artists do fewer mounts each year, so they have to charge more to make the same amount of money. Though it may be hard to believe when you plunk down a good piece of change the day you take your trophy home, the years will prove the old adage true: If you try to scrimp and get a lousy mount, you'll remember exactly how much it cost every time you look at it. If you spend a few extra bucks to get a real work of art, you'll always have the memory of the hunt and soon forget the price of the mount.

Once you've selected a taxidermist, *talk to him*! He'll tell you exactly the procedure he wants you to follow in handling and preparing birds for him. He can recommend poses or even action scenes that will best suit the place you'll display your mount. He'll most likely have pictures or previous mounts and of live animals that you can view together to determine the most realistic positioning of your trophy. He's likely to have ideas for mounts you may have overlooked, like a pair of fighting cock pheasants, a drumming grouse or a whistling bobwhite. Some taxidermists have a particular type of mount in which they specialize. If his specialty suits your needs, the results might even be award winning!

Field Care For The Best Mounts

You're ready to go hunting. You've lined up a top-notch taxidermist who is anxious to work on a bird for you and, if the red gods smile, this will be your year to put a trophy upland bird on the wall.

To properly care for an upland bird destined for the taxidermist, you'll need to prepare a kit to carry with you in the field. A quick trip to the medicine cabinet in your bathroom will supply most of what you need. Grab some cotton balls and a half-dozen cotton swabs. Some gauze or absorbent cloth, like an old diaper, could come in handy, too. Get ahold of a pair of run panty hose or nylons that were headed for the garbage. Cut the legs off, put the other items inside the toe and role up the kit. Stretch a rubber band around the whole package and put this tiny, nearly weightless ball in a pocket of your bird hunting coat or vest. Then, forget it...until you shoot that trophy bird.

It's obviously best if the bird is killed with one shot and is dead when it hits the ground. Though it may be poor form not to let a dog work and retrieve a downed bird, try to retrieve a bird for mounting yourself. The damage a hard-mouthed dog can do is irreparable, but even the gentlest-mouthed retriever will still wet the feathers with saliva, perhaps spreading blood where none would have gone had the bird been picked up by hand. The two greatest detriments to good taxidermy work on birds are blood stains and damaged feathers. In handling a trophy bird, you should do everything you can to avoid either.

If the bird is still alive when you pick it up or the dog brings it to you, do not finish it off with a traditional neck-wringing. Try not to let the bird flap or fight and in the process damage or lose feathers. Grasp the bird around its body, holding both wings in so they won't be damaged. With larger species like pheasants, hold the bird with the base of its breast on the ground, then kneel on the middle of the back applying enough pressure to collapse the heart and lungs. With smaller birds like quail, you can apply pressure to the same points with your fingers underneath the bird and your thumbs on its back. In less than 30 seconds the bird will become completely relaxed and motionless. This method of euthanizing wounded birds is humane and causes little damage to feathers if done carefully.

After your hunting buddies pat you on the back for a great shot, or you pat yourself on the back if you're alone, dig out your kit and spread the items out on a convenient log or on the ground. Use the cotton swabs and the gauze or cloth to wipe away any blood on the feathers, beak, legs, etc. Remove any field debris such as leaves, soil or seeds from the feathers at this time as well. Try to keep it as free as possible from such debris at all times.

In all steps of handling the bird try to work with the grain of the feathers; never against it. Always try to smooth the feathers against the bird. Don't ruffle them up.

With wads pulled and rolled from the cotton balls, plug the throat and vent of the bird. This will protect the feathers from draining blood and body fluids. It's also a good idea to push cotton into the nostrils and any shot holes.

With the bird cleaned up as well as can be in the field, tuck it's head back under a wing or against the body. Again, working *with the feathers*, not against them, slide your trophy bird into the nylon stocking. These wonders of modern science stretch snugly around the bird to hold all of

Proper field care of birds headed for the taxidermist include plugging mouth, nostrils and vent with cotton, then sliding the bird into a nylon stocking.

the feathers in place, yet allow any blood you missed to soak out, away from the feathers and dry.

The best thing you could do at this point is quit hunting for the day and take the bird right to the taxidermist's shop. However, hunting situations and other commitments seldom afford that opportunity, so the next best thing is to get the bird back to your vehicle or to camp as soon as possible and place it in a cool, shaded, dry location. A large cooler with a bag of ice is ideal, just be sure to keep the bird well away from moisture.

Avoid carrying the bird in a game bag on your vest or coat. Carrying any bird, whether for mounting or for the table, in this hot, plastic-coated environment for an extended period is not proper field care. If you must carry the bird in your game bag, make sure that it is as free of debris as possible. Even if you've only worn your coat or vest once before, you'll be amazed at the collection of garbage it picks up. Before carrying your trophy bird in it, take a minute to dump it out and pick the old feathers, leaves, twigs and gum wrappers out of the bottom.

Insert the nylon-covered bird into the pouch going with the feathers, meaning head first, and extract it from the other side of the pouch the same way.

Home Care For The Best Mounts

Try to get the bird to the taxidermist the same day it is taken. If that is not possible, you'll get the best results from freezing the bird whole.

If no blood or fluids have leaked out onto the feathers, you can leave the bird right in the stocking and freeze it. If you need to take the bird out of the stocking to do some more cleaning, do so by cutting the toe out of the stocking and pushing the bird on through. *Do not pull it back out of the top of the stocking against the feathers*!

White plumage soiled by blood or body fluids must be carefully rinsed clean with a small amount of cold water. If you've taken the bird out of the stocking, go ahead and wrap its feet in wet paper towels to prevent dehydration in the freezer. Take a clean nylon stocking from the pair and insert the bird as you did in the field.

Gently roll the bird in two or three sheets of newspaper or freezer paper. Seal out air as much as possible, even around the tail of a pheasant, to avoid freezer burn. Place the paper-wrapped bird in a plastic bag and secure the top. Label the bird clearly with your name, address, phone number, hunting license number and the date it was shot.

Lay the bird flat in a chest-type freezer if you have access to one. *Don't pile anything else on top of it, and be sure the lid doesn't crush the package when you close the freezer*!

A lot of variables can effect the freezer life of a properly cared-for and packaged bird. The rule of thumb should be to take your trophy to the taxidermist as soon as possible. When you go, take your hunting license and be prepared to pay a deposit for the work on which you agree.

If you take these steps to care for your bird, you'll experience pride in the accolades of the taxidermist when he describes the beautiful mount he'll be able to produce for you. It is certainly reassuring to hear him say, "I wish everyone would take care of their birds like this!" Instead of, "Well, I'll see what I can do with this one, but I'm not making any promises..."

Trophies On The Table

On the whole, upland birds make exquisite table fare. Sure you'll run into a tough old pheasant or a gamy woodcock now and then, but seldom with more frequency than you'll pick a tough T-bone from the butcher's display case. For centuries, wild upland birds have been the meat around which honest-to-goodness meals fit for kings have been prepared.

Proper field care of upland birds headed for the table is just as important—no, more important—than proper care of birds to be mounted. The quality of the meat you'll eat is in direct relation to how well you care for the birds brought to bag.

To this day you'll hear of gourmands who demand that upland birds be "hung" or "aged" for the table. That means the birds are hung in a cool, dry place for as much as two weeks with the innards still on the inside and the skin and feathers still on the outside!

There's no reason to "age" upland birds in this day and age. The roots of this tradition are based in the days before refrigeration. Those folks didn't have any choice for preserving meat that couldn't be eaten fresh. Besides, most of the recipes that call for hanging birds include so much fancy-shmancy sauce and seasoning that the delicate, delicious flavor of the meat is completely lost. If anyone tells you to hang your birds, tell 'em to go fly a kite.

In handling your upland birds in the field, think of them just as a big game hunter thinks of the animals he harvests. The most pressing concerns are getting out the entrails and cooling the carcass.

Field dressing upland birds is simple and quick. It can be accomplished quickly with only a knife, but a gut hook can be handy, too.

Again, if the bird is not dead when it comes to hand, finish it off as quickly and humanely as possible. Most often this is done by wringing the bird's neck by either twisting the head or grasping the head and swinging the body in a sharp circle. Another method is to insert the point of a knife through a bird's open mouth, up into its brain. Hunting preserve guides who dispatch hundreds of birds in a season often carry a tool that is sort of a specialized pliers/punch which quickly severs the spinal cord from the base of the brain.

When the bird has quieted, pluck the feathers in the area from the base of the breast back around the anus to the base of the tail feathers. Also, pluck the feathers from the base of the neck to the front edge of the breast.

Slit the length of the rear feather-free area with a knife, working around the anus. In the front, cut or pull out the bird's crop. Reach in the rear slit and pull out all the entrails. You may have to scrape your fingernails along the connection of the ribs and the backbone a couple of times to remove as many particles of the lungs as possible. Use caution when inserting your hand in the bird to avoid cutting fingers on sharp, broken bones. Running a fine rib bone under your fingernail makes a less than enjoyable job absolutely miserable!

With all entrails removed, you now have a field dressed bird. If law permits, you can also remove the head at this stage if you wish. Even on the largest pheasant you shouldn't have blood much above your wrist. If you think of it, carry along paper towels to wipe your hands; but if you forget, grass, cornstalks and a handy pond or puddle have worked before and will again. With practice you'll be able to field dress a bird in about 45 seconds or less.

A bird so dressed will cool nicely.

The rubberized game bag is still not the best environment to carry even a dressed bird. Cooling air can't circulate in there, especially as more birds are brought to bag. Go ahead and use the game bag on your coat or vest if the duration of your hunt won't be long. But if you'll be out all day, use a bird carrier that attaches to your belt or slings over your shoulders. These will at least keep the birds out in the open where the air is circulating.

Dove hunters on traditional field shoots have it best when it comes to cooling birds. They generally have a cooler of cold soft drinks close at hand, and they can replace drinks with birds. Even so, the hunter would do his dinner guests well to remove the entrails of the birds during the first lull in the action.

Field-dressed birds can be iced and taken home or to camp for cleaning. If you want, and transport regulations allow, you could finish the cleaning process in the field, too. Whenever you're cleaning your kill, take into consideration the sensitivities of anyone who is liable to come across the viscera. Don't leave a pile of guts and feathers and heads and wings lying near a road or public trail. Ask landowners if they mind you dressing the birds in the field.

Any upland bird can be quickly dressed or cleaned in the field, even without a knife!

Know The Law

Different states enforce different regulations covering the transport of upland birds. Some states require that at least one fully feathered wing remain attached to the carcass for identification purposes. In other places it's a foot that must remain intact. Some states say the fully feathered head has to stay on during transport.

Know the law before you clean your birds. You could be cited if you are checked by a warden or stopped at a game check station, even though you thought you were in the right!

To Pluck Or Skin—That Is The Question

In preparing upland birds for the table or freezer, you really have two options: Either pluck the feathers and leave the skin on the bird or remove the skin entirely. The decision is based on how you will cook the birds and your personal preference. The best way to decide which you prefer is to try a couple each way and see which you like better.

Plucking. Recipes in which the whole bird is roasted are usually better for birds with the skin left on. This is not difficult to do on most upland birds. The most difficult part on soft-skinned species like ruffed grouse is not tearing the delicate skin as the feathers are pulled.

Some hunters find it easier to pluck the birds after they have been scalded in hot water. Simply bring a large pot of water to boil on the stove. Remove it, and quickly dip the bird in the water. Do not hold the bird in the water too long. You're not trying to pre-cook it, just loosen the feathers.

In many cases, dry plucking is just as thorough and is accomplished with a lot less hassle, though the feathers tend to fly around the garage or basement.

Skinning. Skinning an upland bird is faster and, in many ways, more convenient. You don't have to deal with individual feathers flying all over the place; they all stay attached to the skin. The meat, sans skin, is just as delicious prepared many ordinary ways.

Skinning an upland bird is quite simple. To skin a bird which has been field dressed as described, remove the head if that hasn't been done. Insert the knife just under the skin, being careful not to slice into the breast meat. Connect the two openings by slitting the skin from front to back. Put the knife away, and using just your fingers, roll the carcass right out of the skin. You may have to do a little pulling and tugging around the wings and legs, but the final result will be a skin-free, feather-free bird ready for washing and the freezer.

Breasting. The fastest and most convenient of all methods for cleaning upland birds is breasting. It can replace the separate steps of field dressing and skinning with one quick procedure that doesn't even require a knife!

Breasting is appropriate for birds that don't carry much meat anywhere else. Such birds are ruffed grouse, woodcock, bobwhites and doves. It would be a shame to breast a pheasant, for example, and lose all the great dark meat on the legs and thighs.

Also, be aware that the method of breasting described here leaves only the fully-feathered wings attached to the skinned out breast. If you want the skin on the breast or the law requires that other identifiers remain attached, you'll have to modify this method. If you breast birds in the woods, carry along some plastic bags in which to carry the breasts.

To breast an upland bird, pluck away the feathers from the base of the neck to the front of the breast so you can see what you're doing. Pull out the crop. Insert the index and middle finger of each hand through the point where the crop was. With the fingers of your right hand (for a right-handed hunter) on the underside of the breast bone and the fingers of your left hand against the backbone, carefully pull the breast out of the bird. The head, neck, legs, entrails and feathered skin will stay together in one package in your left hand. In your right hand, you'll have the breast with the fully-feathered wings attached.

The result has been described as "looking like a premium fowl breast from the grocery store with two wings attached." This method is very simple. Though it requires some serious grunting on larger birds, once you have the procedure down you can breast birds in 30 seconds or less.

The illustrations in this chapter should set you well on your way to enjoying this method of cleaning chesty upland birds.

Detailing Upland Birds

Using any of these methods will give you a quickly dressed bird, but before cooking or freezing you should work over the bird again. In cold, fresh water rinse away any feathers clinging to the meat. While holding the bird under the running water poke your thumb or a knife blade into any shot holes. Try to release the coagulated blood from any bloodshot areas you locate.

Look the meat over, carefully looking for any black or dark gray areas just under the surface. Cut into such areas and remove the spots. Most often these will be feathers pushed into the meat by the shot. Sometimes you'll find pellets lodged in the meat with a ball of feathers wrapped around it. Remove any shot pellets you can find. This makes eating game birds safer for anyone with expensive dental work.

To quickly breast an upland bird, pluck a small patch of feathers from the base of the neck back to the middle of the breast.

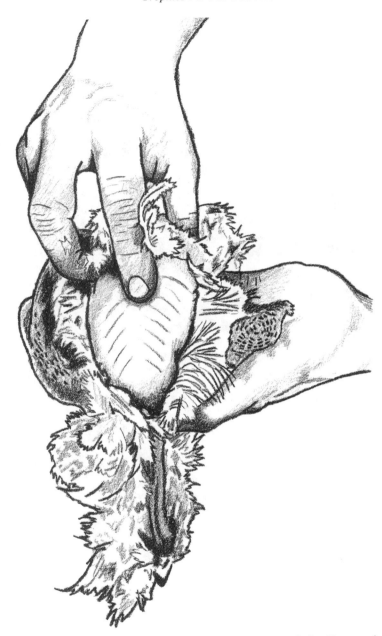

Peel off the skin, tear out the crop and locate the opening between the backbone and the breast.

Insert the index and middle finger of each hand in that opening. Brace one pair against the underside of the breastbone, the other against the backbone. Be careful with the two fingers against the backbone; it's often sharp.

Pull the bird apart. Viscera usually stays with the head, neck and rear body parts.

Continue pulling the bird apart, but take care to leave the wings attached to the breast for identification during transport.

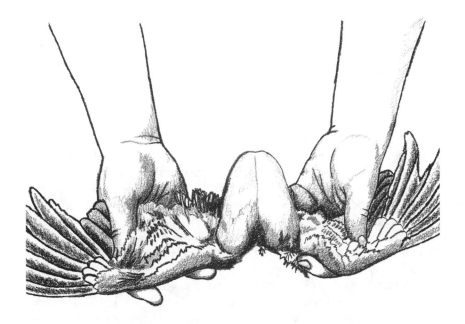

The result is a clean, skinned breast with the wings still attached for identification purposes. Don't use this method if other body parts are required for identification in the state in which you are hunting.

This kind of careful detailing is one of the advantages of skinning the upland birds you bag. You won't see all of these flavor deterrents if the skin is still on the bird.

Freezing Upland Birds

If you'll be eating your harvest within a day or two, simply refrigerating the birds is fine. But if they'll be stored longer, they must be frozen.

Air is the greatest danger to frozen fowl. The more air that can be removed when packaging the birds the longer they will keep without freezer burn. The best method for doing this is to use a kitchen vacuum sealer that sucks all the air out of a package, then heat seals it. With this method, wild game can be stored in the freezer almost indefinitely.

Birds can also be frozen in water. Save and clean milk cartons for this purpose or use plastic containers. Place the bird in the container and add fresh cold water, but don't quite fill it to the top. Freeze the water solid, then add enough water to cover any exposed areas of the bird. Cover, label and freeze. When thawing birds frozen this way, it's best to put the block of ice in a strainer suspended over a bowl or the sink. This will allow the water to immediately drain away from the meat as it thaws. Sitting in water as it thaws will tend to make the naturally firm meat mushy.

If you won't be keeping the birds in the freezer too long before they are prepared, they can simply be frozen in heavy duty freezer bags or freezer wrap. Make every effort to exclude all air by squeezing it out before you seal the package.

Cooking Upland Birds

Considering all the species of upland birds available to North American hunters, recipes for each species are beyond the scope of this book. Great recipes are available in hundreds of wild game cookbooks, but NAHC members know they can count on the best in the North American Hunting Club's annual *Wild Game Cookbook*. For more information on these great references for all types of wild game cookery, contact: North American Hunting Club, Wild Game Cookbook, P.O. Box 3401, Minnetonka, MN 55343.

Whatever recipes you decide to try for your upland bird harvest, don't let anyone tell you that preparing these birds has to involve complicated sauces and marinades. Some very simple recipes can produce marvelous results. With them you'll make meals as memorable as your hunts.

16

Upland Bird Management— The Hunter's Responsibility

U pland bird hunting is enjoyed in one form or another in each of the 50 states. In New England, upland bird hunters laud the grouse and woodcock. In the Southeast, the bobwhite quail is king. In the heartland, "birds" means pheasants. In the West, sportsmen have elusive and exotic critters, such as the chukar partridge and the California quail, to hunt.

At the close of each upland bird hunting season, state game officials tabulate the harvest and make plans for the spring and summer upland bird censuses. But, despite all of the effort and concern, management of most upland bird species is little more than a crapshoot. One of the dice is weather. The other is available habitat.

In pheasant country, for example, one sign of the approaching hunting season is the annual hearings to solicit public comment on proposed hunting regulations. And the wide range of opinion on what's best for the pheasants is sure to produce heated debate every time the subject is broached. Because determining exactly what constitutes upland bird management is such an elusive concept, anyone and everyone can be an expert.

The state department in charge of wildlife will come to the meeting loaded with statistics from spring and summer brood counts which show the pheasants brought off a bumper crop. But sportsmen who had a lousy season the last fall will maintain that populations are in trouble. They'll trot out old-timers who will recount days when pheasants were so thick they kept snowplows on their trucks just to push aside the feeding flocks of cocks. Supported by such scientific testimony, they are likely to push for a reduced bag limit and a shortened or, perhaps, closed season to "bring back the pheasants."

Farmers are likely to be at the meeting as well. They'll be pushing for a shorter season and legal shooting hours which begin daily at noon. At the meeting, they'll say they believe that the birds are too vulnerable to hunters in the morning hours. In reality, they hope that a later start and a short season will reduce the amount of time spent bothering with hunters who want permission to hunt and shagging out trespassers who didn't bother to ask.

Of course, the meeting will also be attended by some hunters who enjoy the give-and-take hunting offered on public lands around the county. They'll be recommending that the state find more dollars to put into propagation and stocking programs. They'll probably want an open season on hens, too, since the state boys told them that few stocked pheasants of either sex make it through their first winter in the wild.

These days, it's more likely there will be anti-hunters there, too. They'll be at the meeting making long speeches, asking each hunter to search deep in his heart and question how he can so thoughtlessly snuff out the life of a pheasant. Just think about all the little chicks at home!

Each faction is entitled to its own point of view. That's what the United States Constitution is talking about when it says that each citizen can pursue happiness. But in the real world, in the cornfield outside of the meeting hall, the pheasants could be having a good cackle.

Upland species face a 70 to 80 percent population loss each year, regardless of whether or not they are hunted. In a year with good weather and nesting conditions, hunters will see and take more birds regardless of the limit or length of the season. In a poor year, the birds will be few and far between. Hunters won't see as many birds to shoot, and they are less likely to spend as many hours afield. No matter which, state upland bird biologists report approximately 20 to 30 percent of brood stock stays intact.

In a recent statement, the Kansas Fish and Game Commission said, "Biologically, season closure or reduction of season length accomplishes little more than to deprive sportsmen of hunting opportunity. It also serves to perpetuate a myth that season length and bag limits are crucial to population maintenance or recovery. Thus, attention is directed away from important habitat considerations. Season length is recognized as a sociological, not a biological, issue."

Given cover and a bit of food, some species of upland birds can hang on almost anywhere. Denied those basics, the birds will disappear.

According to game managers in South Dakota, a state with great success in maintaining and increasing its upland bird populations, there are two disasters that really dent upland bird numbers: a severe blizzard or a late spring. For pheasants, quail, Hungarian partridge and other birds of the north country, couple these natural events with the man-made disaster of inadequate habitat, and the die-off can be almost complete. In the South, the same tragic story can be told, only the players and the scenery are different.

Town hall and bar arguments on upland bird management will never cease. But given an area of good winter cover, a few rows of standing corn, a handy supply of grit and those pheasants will perpetuate themselves for next season. The problem is that good winter cover and a few standing rows of corn are harder and harder to come by.

Upland Bird Management In The '90s And Beyond

Despite the threats of the anti-hunters, despite the economic pressures faced by American farmers, despite America's aging population and the decline in hunting's popularity and despite the increasing costs of land acquisition and game management, the greatest burden of conserving upland bird species will continue to fall on the hunter. Indeed, anti-hunters, non-hunters, farmers and other landowners will play a role, but if upland bird hunting in North America is to survive and improve, it will be the hunters who again foot the bill and provide a lot of the sweat.

The birds will propagate themselves if given half a chance. It's the hunter who has to see that the chance is provided.

The Role Of The Farmer

Hunters must realize that the farmer on whose land upland birds nest and live are in business. They are not in the shooting preserve business. They are producing crops and food products to feed hunters and non-hunters alike. On the most basic level, farmers aren't doing it because, "it's the right thing to do." With the help of Mother Nature, they are trying to make enough money for their families to live. Many aren't interested in making a lot of money; just enough so they can stick with a job they enjoy. In that respect they are no different than most hunters.

And they deserve no less respect.

The land is to a farmer what a diamond in the rough is to a diamond cutter. It is filled with awesome potential if it is handled in just the right way. Land is to a farmer what chisels are to a wood carver. It is a tool that can produce beauty and profit.

Good farmers care for their land in a way that reflects its personal importance to them. Perhaps the best way for an upland bird hunter to

Suburban and rural habitat loss squeeze out upland birds...forever.

understand the farmer's relationship to his land is to think of an heirloom shotgun passed from generation to generation in a family of hunters. If you owned such a gun you would certainly think twice about loaning it out even to a close friend. And you probably would never be convinced that it should be altered in any way.

That's the way a farmer feels when he is approached by a hunter who is seeking permission to hunt on his land or by a conservation group who wants him to participate in an upland bird management program. The land he owns may very well have been passed on from generation to generation in his family.

The economic pressures faced by farmers are tremendous. Those financial stresses are what lie behind the practices known as "clean farming." Clean farming is the removal of fencerows, wetlands and fallow fields. The ultimate clean farm would be solid crops from property line to property line. Some farms today aren't too far from this. Clean farming also relies heavily on pesticides and herbicides to keep crops free of weeds and pests.

Plain and simple, clean farming leaves no room for upland birds. The feed is there, tainted with chemicals, but it's there. What's missing is wintering cover and nesting cover. In the case of the pheasant, clean farming's greatest sin is the early mowing of hayfields. Hayfields are vital nesting habitat for hen pheasants, and thousands of birds die each year defending their clutches against relentless mowers. The broods are wiped out, too.

As intensive or clean farming has become more and more commonplace, it almost makes laughable the advice of long-ago conservationists who struggled to see pheasants take hold and prosper in the United States. Famed conservationist Aldo Leopold wrote his book, *Game Management*, when the majority of farm work was still done with animals, but he recommends a way of saving pheasant nests in hayfields that could still work today if farmers could be convinced to do it.

Leopold suggested that, just prior to mowing, two men walk around at least the edges of the hayfield to be cut dragging a length of rope between them. When a hen pheasant is flushed, the men mark the nest with a stake. Once cutting begins, the farmer leaves an island of grass standing around the nest. The bird will return and with luck bring off a successful hatch.

Difficult to convince a modern farmer to take this precaution for the sake of a few pheasants? Yes, and he can't be blamed, considering the difficulties he faces today just trying to stay in business. But if a local Boy Scout troop or 4-H Club were to offer to spend the time marking nests for him and pay for the few bails of hay lost to the standing alfalfa, maybe he would consider it.

The role of the farmer in upland bird management is a vitally important one. For many upland species, the farmer has the greatest opportunity to maintain and increase populations. It's his feed and his cover that will ensure successful nesting and hunting season after season. Even so, the responsibility still lies with the caring hunter to provide the motivation for the farmer to take measures to improve upland bird habitat on his land.

In some cases that impetus will be monetary. One of the greatest boons to upland birds have been Conservation Reserve Programs, in which farmers are paid to keep land out of production. These fallow fields provide great cover for all types of wildlife, including upland birds. In other areas, sportsmen's clubs pay farmers to leave a field or

Landowners/farmers, like NAHC Life Member Bud Estes of Buckland, Kansas, play a crucial role in the management of upland birds. They deserve all the support hunters can give them.

two of crops standing through the winter, or they buy areas of wetland which farmers had slated for drainage.

In other cases, education is what's called for. There are still many farmers out there who don't realize that some of the best things for upland birds are the same things that, in the long run, are best for the land. Conservation plantings, for example, are intermittent stands of trees meant to break the wind and prevent erosion of bare fields during the time when fields lay plowed and exposed to the wind. Wetlands are nature's sewage treatment facilities and play a vital role in purifying water used to irrigate croplands and water livestock.

The farmer's role is indeed important, but it is in direct relation to the hunter's equally important role of showing how good upland bird management practices can benefit the farm he cherishes and his economic straits.

The Role Of Shooting Preserves

Game farms, shooting preserves, hunting clubs—whatever you prefer to call them—play an important role in the scheme of upland bird management.

Obviously, hunting preserves take some of the pressure off wild bird populations. But, as mentioned earlier, hunting isn't a major factor in the population swings of wild upland bird populations. Instead, shooting preserves are there to satiate some of the desires of hunters which have no place in the wild.

When most upland bird hunters look deep down, they want to experience, at least once in their lifetime, a hunt like their grandfathers had. A hunt where the birds are plentiful and limits non-existent. They want to take a break from the pressures of the wild where good ethics dictate that they put something back for each bird they take. Just for a while, they want to be consumers of a product instead of stewards of a public natural resource.

The place to quench those urges is not in the wild uplands, no matter how good the hunting might be. The limit is the limit, and it doesn't matter how many times you run home to stash birds in the freezer. If you shoot more than your legal limit, you've broken the law and put at great risk the efforts of law-abiding hunters who have genuine concern for the sport.

On licensed shooting preserves, the limit of the day's bag is set only by the thickness of the hunter's wallet. The birds at a shooting preserve are raised to be hunted. Like cattle are raised for beef, like chickens are raised for frying, the upland birds on a shooting preserve are artificially propagated to ultimately provide food for humans, but additionally they

Licensed shooting preserves offer hunters the opportunity to enjoy the great social aspects of bird hunting without the worry of not finding birds. Preserves are a great place to introduce newcomers whose patience might not hold out for finding wild birds on the first trip or two.

provide pleasure along the way for hunters. There is nothing wrong with it!

If there is a place for hunters to vent their competitive traits, it is the shooting preserve. Wild birds deserve better than to be pawns in any kind of game where the prize is not the meaningful experience of simply having hunted. To reward a hunter in the wild uplands for having taken the most birds in the shortest time is demeaning to the birds. On shooting preserves, it may not be desirable, but it is tolerable.

In 1976, the following article appeared in the South Dakota Department of Game, Fish and Parks' newsletter. The author is unknown, but it succinctly addresses the impropriety of competitive hunting in the wild:

> *The power that drives this old world may well be what we generally call "competition". Certainly, the competitive urge makes things happen in work, business and athletics. But just as certainly the introduction of competition has a disastrous effect on the sport of hunting.*
>
> *The man who heads for the game fields and packs along the same competitive drives that motivate him in his working life misses much. He is enslaved to the habit of comparing himself with others. Did he take as many birds as the other guy? Was his buck the biggest in camp? Did he fill his limit? This poor soul*

never knows the pleasure of not having to prove anything, of doing something simply for the sake of doing it.

In extreme cases, competitive hunting becomes not a sport at all, but rather an unprincipled drive to achieve, to win. At that point, the pursuit of game has nothing to do with the ethical hunting.

The sportsman, though he enjoys good companions, is a solitary sort. Even while hunting with friends, he makes his own judgments and evaluates the hunt in very personal terms. He establishes personal standards and lives by them. He knows that hunting is something that happens between him and the game, between him and the natural world.

For the competitor, time, money, and luck are enough—sooner or later he will win if he spends enough and has enough. For the ethical hunter, time, money and luck are good to have, but not essential because he judges himself, and he sets his own rules, within the law, exclusive of what others may think or say.

That's the whole charm of hunting—doing something difficult and demanding for the simple sake of doing it. So that keeping score doesn't matter, and filling a limit doesn't count. The important thing is doing it right. And meeting the requirements that you establish for yourself. Solitary and individual.

Come to think of it, hunting is one of the very few things you can do in this world according to rules you make for yourself.

It is left to each hunter to decide how competitive he wants to be. But, for the sake of hunting's powerful critics, competition should be reserved for the preserves where the birds are a consumable product instead of a public natural resource.

Besides acting as a buffer for wild upland bird populations, shooting preserves have a lot more going for them. They play a vital role in modern upland bird management and the future of upland bird hunting.

For example, preserve seasons are long. In most states they run from early fall well into the spring. This extended season offers great opportunity for the hunter and his canine companion to stay sharp for the real show. Dogs can be worked on preserves in situations which duplicate those they'll encounter in the wild uplands, without the problem of harassing wild birds during the off season. More practice means better hunting skills, more humane kills, and fewer lost cripples.

Likewise for the hunter, shooting preserves offer the opportunity to practice game shots over and over. Hunting clubs and shooting preserves are also leading the way in the development of sporting clays shooting on this side of the Atlantic. Between sporting clays and the copious hunting/shooting opportunities available, hunters can find ample practice to improve their field wingshooting skills.

Finally and perhaps most importantly, shooting preserves are a great place to start out new hunters. Just as in developing wingshooting skills, it's best to start a young hunter's field career with as few worries as possible. Game farms allow you to concentrate on instilling the basics of safety and hunting ethics without worrying if you'll see any birds. Several days of hard hunting in a poor year is a tough way to start out a youngster. With careful guidance, the glories of wild upland bird hunting will come to light for the novice hunter, but only if he or she sticks with the sport. Young people have short attention spans if action is slow and you may have a hard time getting them to go a second or third time if they were bored by the first experiences.

Shooting preserves, even for a tour of the facilities if not a hunt, will keep their attention during those critical early exposures.

"Frank," a quail guide and upland bird manager at the Longleaf Plantation near Purvis, Mississippi, recounts the scary episodes of a group of older, first time hunters. They accounted for a dozen Jeep radiators in a single season. He says they'll never change because they never got an early, basic introduction to hunting. But in the next breath Frank recounts, with equal excitement, the tales of young men and women who took their first quail on a covey rise and are now hooked for life.

Introducing new hunters to the sport and hooking them for good is an important role of shooting preserves. There are so many important responsibilities of upland bird management for the conscientious upland bird hunter to bear, and it sure is great to have some more solid shoulders to help bear the burden.

There is a great organization, called the North American Gamebird Association, Inc., of which hundreds of topnotch shooting preserves are members. They'll happily provide NAHC members with a directory of affiliated hunting resorts across North America. For more information contact: *North American Gamebird Association, Dept. NAH, Wildlife Harvest Publications, Goose Lake, IA 52750.*

The Role Of The Government
When upland bird populations seem low to hunters, who are the first people to catch hell for it?

The answer, without a doubt, is state wildlife managers. Hunters are often quick to point a finger at anyone but themselves. Fact is, game managers can only work with what they are given. Like anyone else, they do not have unlimited funds and they are not omnipotent. They can't snap their fingers to create habitat where there isn't any. They can't reliably predict weather months ahead of time, and they can't change it even if they could. They can't prevent reality from occasionally flying in the face of even the best research data.

The role of the professional upland bird manager is to gather all the information he can about the birds. His sources, if the job is done correctly, will include all of the people who have an interest in the future of upland birds. Most importantly, his information will be provided by the birds themselves. He needs to get a handle on populations, available habitat, winter survival...all the numbers, all the facts.

His next step is to use that information to formulate a plan. Using the information gathered through his own research in his own area, and the collected wisdom of game managers before him, he is charged with the responsibility of making a recommendation to his employers. Through the election system in the United States, that ultimately means the public and, most importantly, the hunters who are part of that public.

So again, hunters are ultimately responsible for how upland birds are managed. If we put enough people in office who are aware of the needs of upland birds, our agenda will carry and the birds will prosper. If we fail and ignore the guidance of state game managers, we have no one to blame but ourselves.

The Role Of The Hunter

By now, you can tell that the greatest role of upland bird management must be borne by the hunter. It's his support, both financial and moral, that motivate the farmer. He's aided by the availability of the licensed shooting preserve. He's guided by the wildlife biologist. But when it's all said and done, the future of the birds and of upland hunting depends almost solely on the hunter.

Through involvement at every level—sponsoring upland bird conservation organizations, sweating on the farm, bringing new hunters to the sport and exhibiting exemplary ethics and behavior every moment we're afield—we're doing our best for the birds. But there's one more thing we must do. We have to defend ourselves. In doing so, we are defending the birds.

Today, more than ever, hunting is under attack. Anti-hunters and their false doctrines are as convincing and alluring to non-hunters as the promises of a cultist are to the weak of mind. In the end, if hunting is

The ultimate responsibility for upland bird management falls upon the concerned, ethical hunter. If he doesn't take action to conserve birds, no one will.

ended so are the birds. It is the hunters, their efforts and their money that drive the conservation machine. If that fuel is eliminated, so are the conservation and habitat restoration programs. When those go, the birds have no chance.

To draw a bead on the anti-hunting menace, it is most important to get this truthful, factual information to the non-hunter—the one who hasn't made up his mind about hunting and the one who sways back and forth. It would be nice if we could make them all hunters, but that won't happen. Instead it is the hunter's responsibility to make them well-informed citizens who understand the basic principles of upland bird management and recognize all the essential roles of the hunter.

If we can succeed at that, the battle of upland bird management is half won.

17

A Look To The Future

Headlines call it a "national emergency." Anti-gun fanatics push for a wide-sweeping federal firearms law that would require the registration of shotguns and rifles!

The year is 1951. Most sportsmen laugh or yawn at this "emergency." Doesn't the Constitution state: "The right of the people to keep and bear arms shall not be infringed."? No need to worry, many people think. As hunters and citizens of the United States, we're protected. Registration of firearms will never happen.

But it did. Less than 20 years later, the anti-gun faction was successful at forcing all law-abiding sportsmen to register their guns at the time of purchase and they ended, for all practical purposes, the buying and selling of firearms through the mail. The gun control people were organized. The hunters and gun owners were not.

The criminals were not affected. The dark back alleys and dimly lit bars where they buy their guns have no need or use for yellow sheets of paper. Then again, the thugs and murderers were not the targets, the sportsman was.

It took them awhile. About the time it takes your youngster to go from diapers to graduation. That's not an incredibly long time for those used to working with the legal system. Yet most hunters and sportsmen sat on the back porch and let it happen. They outnumbered the opposition, but the opposition was organized. And so is the new wave of fanatics—the anti-hunter.

The future of bird hunting in North America may be threatened most by people wearing the disguise of conservationists—the anti-hunters. Can they put an end to upland bird hunting? No, not if we band together and understand our roles and responsibilities in the ensuing confrontations that are sure to come. But first, we have to understand from where we have evolved and what we are facing.

The North American upland hunter, for the most part, has prospered without interference for the past 300 years. Apart from the popular native game birds, sportsmen have enjoyed an abundance of introduced species like the ringneck pheasant, chukar and Hungarian partridge. While we have prospered, grown fat, dumb and happy, so-to-speak, we have also taken our sport for granted. Sure, we have put together impressive conservation organizations and have supported local game departments, but can we honestly say that we have laid down a definite line of defense in the offensive wake of the anti-hunter?

In an era where it appears we are finally coming to grips with our environment, finally understanding what must be done to maintain stable, huntable populations of game birds, we are facing the most threatening force of the century—the anti-hunter.

A responsibility and awareness of our rights is essential. Proper habitat management and modern conservation practices are crucial, but as hunters we must also realize who we are up against and change our style to survive.

Needless to say, it has always been the North American hunter who has played the key role in conservation. He has paid for his pastime by purchasing hunting licenses and equipment. He has paid important excise taxes that have been put directly into state and federal fish and wildlife agency funds to manage wildlife, both game and non-game species. Hunters are, undeniably, the greatest conservationists.

Yet, oddly enough, that's the title that the anti-hunters have also bestowed upon their own letterhead. And those stacks of letterheads are growing taller.

Rough estimates have it that five percent of the American population is against hunting and belong, in some way, to organizations attempting to limit or ban hunting.

On the other hand, there are nearly 20 million hunters, which translates to at least 10 percent of the American public. So far, by standing together and continuing membership in hunting clubs and conservation groups, we have had general success in keeping the anti-hunters at bay.

Unfortunately, the minority anti-hunters are getting better at playing the political games which guide our freedoms. Their onslaught of anti-hunting legislation threatens the future of bird hunting in North America.

Obviously, the objective of animals' rights organizations is to ban the harvest of wild game animals. Some animals' rights groups are against such non-consumptive animal use as rodeos and horse and dog racing. It is not right, they say, to consume milk or eggs. Other anti-hunting groups say that having a pet is a form of slavery. To owners of hunting dogs, this is a real slap in the face, and it is an example of the incomprehensible philosophy of an anti-hunter. It has been documented several times before where animal shelters will not allow a hunter to adopt a dog if it might be used to hunt. Yet, each year these shelters "put to sleep" abandoned and unwanted pets. That's an odd twist of animals' rights reasoning.

While sportsmen in North America find it a ridiculous notion to outlaw a tradition that is deeply rooted in American history, the issue of bird hunting has become a controversial topic in several state legislatures. Bills operating under the guise of "animal cruelty" or "pit bull" legislation have justly failed. But there is the persistent push by animals' rights groups to pass these bills into law at the state and federal level.

Take, for example, the Anti-Live Animal Lure Act. The bill proposed to end "coursing," the use of live animals to train racing dogs, and to prevent the use of tease animals in the training of fighting dogs. The second purpose is quite pointless to begin with, as dog fighting is illegal.

The bill had the support of the Humane Society of the United States, North America's largest and most powerful anti-hunting organization, and 50 U.S. Representatives who co-sponsored it.

The bill contained extremely vague language. For example, it defined coursing as an activity that "involves the pursuit by one or more dogs of another animal used as a visual lure; and is conducted for the purposes related to animal training, sport wagering or entertainment."

Clearly, this definition went beyond the training of dogs for racing. It would have left open the opportunity to ban the use of any live animal (read bird) for dog training or sport and ending any hunting dog competition using live animals. Of course, this would also have put an end to the proven technique of training hunting dogs with pigeons.

The bill also attempted to shift the traditional state regulation of sporting events to the federal government through the Congress' power to regulate interstate commerce. Crossing a state line with a hunting dog could have become illegal. Forget the trips to new places and bird coverts with ol' Duke in the back seat.

Tricky? Yes. Vague language is a common tactic. But thanks to the concerted effort of upland bird hunters, that bill was defeated.

Vague language is a common tactic of the frustrated anti-hunter. A group of bills, spurred by the pit bull scare, were loosely worded so that they would have included any animals "which attack humans or animals." Further, several bills said that any animal declared "vicious" or "dangerous" (needing only to chase or bite a cat to be declared such) must have liability insurance of $50,000 to $100,000! That would have been expensive!

The bills, operating under the guise of dangerous animal containment and riding the pit bull hysteria, could have made it far too expensive to own a hunting dog—at least for the average sportsman, who saves his dollars and forgoes other amenities so he or she can hunt in the fall.

Other clauses in these bills would have required such things as "proper" grooming and "comfortable" housing for dogs. Nothing was specifically defined, so the language was vague enough to leave the door open for anti-hunters to, at a later date, make it very difficult for sportsmen to own a hunting dog.

These bills attack bird hunting in North America in a roundabout fashion. They attempt to make it difficult and expensive to own a dog. The primary goal, it seems, is the same: Make it as difficult as possible for sportsmen to hunt.

Unfortunately, several of these bills have the general but misguided support of some of the non-hunting public, simply because these anti-hunting groups present themselves as opponents of animal cruelty and proponents of human safety laws.

One can only assume that the animals' rights and anti-hunting groups are going to get better and trickier at playing this political game.

There have been other legislative bills that promised to threaten the future of bird hunting. For example:

—In Ohio, a bill was presented to the state's general assembly aimed at prohibiting hunting, in any way, any animal not native to the state. The pheasant and the partridge, both widely hunted game birds that inhabit North America thanks to the efforts of sportsmen who stock these birds, are not native to Ohio.

—In Pennsylvania, a state in which many NAHC members reside, the animals' rights group Trans Species Unlimited was behind a bill to outlaw live pigeon shoots in the state.

It is a complicated situation. A growing concern for the environment is good. With it comes increased involvement, stronger conservation organizations and hunting clubs, and more money for wildlife through license and equipment sales.

Sportsmen are North America's true conservationists. Money from hunting licenses, pheasant stamps and self-imposed taxes on hunting equipment pays for the lion's share of conservation efforts. In 1989, hunters' contributions totalled $1 billion—nearly $3 million per day!

But there are those who would bring down what has been built up and supported by North America's greatest conservationists.

The anti-hunters believe we should leave nature alone, throw huge walls around the parks and let nature take its course. But that would be a step back. We have learned to manage wildlife and maintain stable populations of both game and non-game animals. Hunting has proven to be a successful management tool in that process.

There is grim irony here, however. Despite hunter's substantial role in conservation, despite the continued financial support that has kept fish and game agencies and conservation groups fiscally sound, despite this long history and success, it is the hunter who is threatened.

As upland hunters, there are several ways we can ensure another 300 years of prosperity. With the anti-hunters spending $75 million annually, mostly in propaganda and legislative efforts, the average upland hunter can pitch in by joining one of several organizations that specialize in defending the rights of hunters.

One such organized group is the Wildlife Legislative Fund of America. With the expertise, knowledge and research needed to do battle in the political corridors across the nation, the group has been successful in stopping several bills of legislation which, among other things, would have prevented hunting and trapping on thousands of acres of federal land.

The WLFA has a simple and ultimate goal: "To protect the heritage of American sportsmen to hunt, fish and trap and protect scientific wildlife management practices." The WLFA lobbies legislators, defends outdoor sports in the legal system and assists local sportsmen in public relations efforts across the country.

As such a specialized organization, the WLFA has been the driving force to date in defending our rights as upland hunters. Many of the aforementioned horror stories have been stopped thanks to the group's efforts.

Membership costs about the same as two boxes of shotgun shells and, if just half of the nation's upland hunters joined, the WLFA would have twice as much annually as the anti-hunters to spend in legislative battles.

The non-profit conservation affiliate of the North American Hunting Club is another organization dedicated to keeping the hunting tradition alive. Wildlife Forever has three main purposes. They are to educate the public about wildlife management, to acquire precious habitat and to fund programs and studies which will ensure wildlife for future generations.

For our children to realize the joy of hunting upland birds, we must pledge our support to conservation groups like Wildlife Forever. In addition to educating the public about the role hunters play in wildlife management, Wildlife Forever acquires precious habitat and supports research and restoration efforts.

The Izaak Walton League of America Inc., is yet another organization that has taken up the cause, but in a slightly different manner. For the past several years, the league has been promoting a more ethical approach to hunting.

How we hunt and how we treat our game birds is something that we can all take to heart. If we each start our own private public relations campaign, the threat of anti-hunters is lessened.

Slob hunters will have to be eliminated. They give us all a bad name, to say nothing of adverse landowner-hunter relationships. Shooting signs or cutting loose on pheasants from the car window certainly will do nothing to improve our image. Yet to stop this kind of behavior ourselves is not enough, we must prevent our friends and associates from partaking in it as well.

The care of gamebirds is another area where some hunters have failed. Some people pile their birds in a car trunk, or in a paper sack in the back of the truck. Farmers see this lack of care and disrespect and wonder if they should let the next hunter who knocks on the door hunt. Neighbors see the birds wasted in trash bins and develop a negative opinion about hunters where once there was none.

The responsibility is ours and ours alone. The 85 percent of the population that does not have an opinion one way or another is not going to step in and fight for us.

We can write letters to our representatives as well. There is growing concern that our own government may discriminate against hunters. In the past, there have been actions of the law enforcement division of the U.S. Fish and Wildlife Service, the National Park Service and even some state wildlife agency directors, that indicate that some agency policies may be biased against the sportsman.

Ultimately, it is the sportsman's elected representative that controls the policies of these organizations. A well thought out and organized letter campaign can do wonders when heaped upon the desk of an elected official.

The National Hunting and Fishing Day is a single day of activities focusing on the importance of conserving our nation's resources and another great way to personally get involved. Sportsmen can introduce the general public to the benefits of hunting as a conservation and wildlife management tool, as well as to encourage safe and responsible hunting among sportsmen.

The point is, as upland hunters, we must become organized. The threat is real. If we sit on our porch like those generations before us, our sport will suffer. If we band together and voice our rights, our sport will prosper.

The WLFA has a fitting phrase that they have popularized.

"Nothing for nothing any longer. For every right that you cherish, you have a duty you must fulfill. For every hope that you entertain, you have a task to perform. For every good that you wish to preserve you will have to sacrifice your comfort and ease. There is nothing for nothing any longer."

These words were not written by a modern day sportsman fighting off a horde of anti-hunters. They were written by George Washington 200 years ago, but the verse has never been more timely than it is today. We have enjoyed interference-free hunting for many years, but unfortunately there is, as George said, "nothing for nothing any longer."

Don't sit back. Take an active role in your own future as a North American bird hunter.

Appendix:
Where The Birds Are

Where can you hunt doves in December? How about grouse in September or bobwhite in October? When does the Iowa pheasant season open, in October or November? If you plan to hunt upland birds anywhere in North America, this appendix should be your starting point.

Whether you're planning a five-day hunt for bobwhite or a two-day shoot for doves, "Where The Birds Are" will get you off on the right foot. It shows you which states hold what birds. And during which months the season is open.

This appendix can also be your source for planning your next upland bird hunt. Included are the phone numbers and addresses for state game and fish departments. Contact these agencies for specifics, including exact season dates, license fees, population densities, prospective hunt areas, etc. All 50 states and 10 Canadian provinces are included in this 25-page section.

Every successful bird hunter double checks his source. You should, too. *Do not use this appendix as your only information source.* The season dates included here are generalizations, and huntable species are subject to change. Always consult state regulations before hunting.

State Game & Fish Dept.	Chukar Partridge	Dove	Grouse
Alabama Alabama Dept. of Conserv. Game & Fish Division— Wildlife Section Montgomery, AL 35130 (205) 261-3486		Mourning: mid-Sept. through early Jan.	
Alaska Alaska Dept. of Fish & Game P.O. Box 3-2000 Juneau, AK 99802 (907) 465-4100			Spruce, blue, ruffed, sharp- tailed: early Aug. through mid-May
Arizona Arizona Game & Fish Dept. 2222 W. Greenway Rd. Phoenix, AZ 85023 (602) 942-3000	Mid-Oct. through mid-Feb.	Mourning, white-winged: early Sept. through mid-Jan.	Blue: early Sept. through mid-Nov.
Arkansas Arkansas Game & Fish Comm. #2 Natural Resources Dr. Little Rock, AR 72205 (501) 223-6300		Mourning: early Sept. through early Jan.	
California California Fish & Game Comm. 1416 Ninth Street Sacramento, CA 94244-2090 (916) 445-3531	Late Oct. through late Jan.	Mourning, white-winged, green turtle, Chinese spotted: early Sept. Sept. through mid-Nov.	Blue, sage, ruffed: early Sept. through mid-Oct.
Colorado Colorado Dept. of Natural Res. 1213 Sherman Room #718 Denver, CO 80203 (303) 291-7372	Early Sept. through late Nov.	Mourning: early Sept. through late Oct.	Sage, prairie chicken, sharp-tailed: mid-Sept. through mid-Jan.

Always consult state regulations before hunting.

Hungarian Partridge	Pheasant	Ptarmigan	Quail	Woodcock
			Bobwhite: mid-Nov. through Feb.	Late Nov. through Jan.
		Early Aug. through mid-May		
	Mid-Oct. to mid-Feb. (falconry and archery only)		Gambel's, scaled: mid-Oct. through mid-Feb. Mearns, valley: mid-Nov. through mid-Feb.	
			Bobwhite: mid-Nov. through Feb.	
	Mid-Nov. through mid-Dec.	Early through mid-Sept.	Mountain: mid-Sept. through late Oct. Valley: late Sept. through late Jan.	
		Early Sept. through early Oct.	Gambel's, bob-white, scaled: mid-Nov. through mid-Jan.	

Always consult state regulations before hunting.

State Game & Fish Dept.	Chukar Partridge	Dove	Grouse
Connecticut Connecticut Dept. of Environ. 165 Capital Hill Hartford, CT 06106 (203) 566-5599	Late Oct. through late Dec.		Blue: late Oct. through late Dec.
Delaware Delaware Div. of Fish & Wildlife P.O. Box 1401 Dover, DE 19903 (302) 736-4431	Early Sept. through mid-Jan.		
Florida Florida Game and Freshwater Fish Comm. 620 S. Meridian St. Tallahassee, FL 32399 (904) 488-1960		Mourning: early Oct. through Jan.	
Georgia Georgia Dept. of Natural Res. 205 Butler St. S.E. Suite 1258 Atlanta, GA 30334 (404) 656-3530		Mourning: early Sept. through early Oct.	Ruffed: mid-Oct. through Feb.
Hawaii Hawaii Division of Forestry & Wildlife Dept. of Land and Natural Res. 1151 Punchbowl Street Honolulu, HI 96813 (808) 548-8850 *availability depends upon island hunted	Early Nov. through late Jan.*	Mourning, spotted, barred: early Nov. through late Jan.*	
Idaho Idaho Fish & Game Dept. 600 S. Walnut St. Box 25 Boise, ID 83707 (208) 334-3700	Mid-Sept. through Dec.	Mourning: Sept.	Sharp-tailed, sage: mid-Sept. through early Oct.

Always consult state regulations before hunting.

Hungarian Partridge	Pheasant	Ptarmigan	Quail	Woodcock
Late Oct. through late Dec.			Bobwhite: late Oct. through early Nov.	
	Late Nov. through Feb.		Bobwhite: late Nov. through Feb.	Late Nov. through early Jan.
			Bobwhite: mid-Nov. through early March	Early Dec. to late Jan.
			Bobwhite: mid-Nov. through Feb.	Late Nov. through early Jan.
Nepal: early Nov. through late Jan.*	Ring-necked, green: early Nov. through late Jan.*	Grey, black, Erckel's francolin: early Nov. through late Jan.*	Valley, gambel's, Japanese: early Nov. through late Jan.*	Indian Sangrouse: early Nov. through late Jan.*
Mid-Sept. through Dec.	Mid-Oct. through mid-Dec.		Bobwhite, valley: mid-Sept. through Dec.	

Always consult state regulations before hunting.

State Game & Fish Dept.	Chukar Partridge	Dove	Grouse
Illinois Illinois Dept. of Conserv. Lincoln Tower Plaza 524 So. 2nd St. Springfield, IL 62701-1787 (217) 782-6302		Mourning: early Sept. through late Oct.	
Indiana Indiana Dept. of Natural Res. State Office Bldg. Indianapolis, IN 46204-2267 (317) 232-4050		Mourning: early Sept. through late Nov.	Ruffed: mid-Oct. through Jan.
Iowa Iowa Dept. of Natural Res. Wallace State Office Bldg. East 9th & Grand Ave. Des Moines, IA 50319-0034 (515) 281-5145			Ruffed: early Oct. through Jan.
Kansas Kansas Dept. of Wildlife & Parks R.R. 2, Box 54A Pratt, KS 67124 (316) 672-5911			Prairie Chicken: late Sept. through Jan. Bobwhite, scaled: mid-Nov. through Jan.
Kentucky Kentucky Dept. of Fish & Wildlife Res. #1 Game Farm Road Frankfort, KY 40601 (502) 564-3400		Mourning: Sept. through early Dec.	Ruffed: early Oct. through Feb.
Louisiana Louisiana Dept. of Wildlife & Fisheries P.O. Box 98000 Baton Rouge, LA 70898 (504) 765-2800		Mourning: early Sept. through early Jan.	

Always consult state regulations before hunting.

Hungarian Partridge	Pheasant	Ptarmigan	Quail	Woodcock
Early Nov. through early Jan.	Early Nov. through early Jan.		Bobwhite: early Nov. through early Jan.	Early Nov. through early Jan.
	Early Nov. through late Dec.		Bobwhite: early Nov. through mid-Jan.	Mid-Sept. through late Nov.
Early Oct. through Jan.	Late Oct. through mid-Jan.		Bobwhite: late Oct. through mid-Jan.	Mid-Sept. through mid-Dec.
	Mid-Nov. through Jan.			Early Oct. through mid-Dec.
			Bobwhite: early Nov. through Jan.	Early Oct. through early Dec.
			Bobwhite: late Nov. through Feb.	Early Dec. through mid-Feb.

Always consult state regulations before hunting.

State Game & Fish Dept.	Chukar Partridge	Dove	Grouse
Maine Main Dept. of Inland Fisheries & Wildlife 284 State Street State House Station 41 Augusta, ME 04333 (207) 289-2766			Ruffed: early Oct. through mid-Dec.
Maryland Maryland Dept. of Natural Res. Tawes State Office Bldg. Annapolis, MD 21401 (301) 974-3195		Mourning: mid-Nov. through late Dec.	
Massachusetts Massachusetts Dept. of Fisheries & Wildlife 100 Cambridge St. Boston, MA 02202 (617) 727-3151			Ruffed: mid-Oct. through early Jan.
Michigan Michigan Dept. of Natural Res. Box 30028 Lansing, MI 48909 (517) 373-1220			Ruffed: mid-Sept. through Jan. Sharp-tailed: mid-Sept. through mid-Nov.
Minnesota Minnesota Dept. of Natural Res. 500 Lafayette Blvd., Box 40 St. Paul, MN 55155-4001 (612) 296-6157			Ruffed, spruce: mid-Sept. through Dec. Sharp-tailed: mid-Sept through Nov.
Mississippi State of Mississippi Dept. of Wildlife, Fisheries & Parks P.O. Box 451 Jackson, MS 39205-0451 (601) 961-5300		Mourning: early Sept. through mid-Jan.	Nov.

Always consult state regulations before hunting.

Hungarian Partridge	Pheasant	Ptarmigan	Quail	Woodcock
	Early Oct. through mid-Dec.			
				Mid-Oct. through late Nov.
	Late Oct. through late Nov.		Bobwhite: late Oct. through late Nov.	Early Oct. through late Nov.
	Mid-Oct through mid-Nov.		Bobwhite: late Oct. through mid-Nov.	Mid-Sept. through mid-Nov.
Mid-Sept. through Dec.	Mid-Oct. through early Dec.			Early Sept. through early Nov.
			Bobwhite: late Nov. through Feb.	Late Dec. through Feb.

Always consult state regulations before hunting.

State Game & Fish Dept.	Chukar Partridge	Dove	Grouse
Missouri Missouri Dept. of Conserv. P.O. Box 180 Jefferson City, MO 65102-0180 (314) 751-4115		Mourning: early Sept. through early Nov.	Ruffed: mid-Oct. through mid-Jan.
Montana Montana Dept. of Fish Wildlife & Parks 1420 East 6th Ave. Helena, MT 59620 (406) 444-2535	Early Sept. through mid-Dec.	Mourning: early Sept. through mid-Oct.	Blue, ruffed: early Sept. through early Dec.
Nebraska Nebraska Game and Parks Comm. P.O. Box 30370 Lincoln, NE 68503 (402) 464-0641		Mourning: early Sept. through late Oct.	Sage and sharp-tailed: mid-Sept. through Nov.
Nevada Nevada Dept. of Wildlife P.O. Box 10678 Reno, NV 89502 (202) 688-1500	Early Oct. through Jan.	Mourning: Sept.	Blue and ruffed: early Sept. through Nov. Sage; late Sept. through mid-Oct.
New Hampshire Fish & Game Dept. 2 Hazen Drive Concord, NH 03301 (603) 271-3421			Ruffed: early Oct. through Dec.
New Jersey Division of Fish, Game & Wildlife 401 E. State St., CN 402 Trenton, NJ 08625 (609) 292-9450	Mid-Nov. through mid-Feb.		Ruffed: mid-Oct. through mid-Feb.

Always consult state regulations before hunting.

Hungarian Partridge	Pheasant	Ptarmigan	Quail	Woodcock
	Early Nov. through mid-Jan.	Early Nov.	Bobwhite through mid-Jan.	Mid-Oct. through mid-Jan.
Mid-Sept. through mid-Dec.	Mid-Oct. through mid-Dec.			
Early Nov. through Jan.	Early Nov. through Jan.		Bobwhite: early Nov. through Jan.	Mid-Sept. through mid-Nov.
Early Oct. through Jan.	Early to mid-Nov.		Gambel's, mountain, scaled: early Oct. through Jan.	
	Early Oct. through Dec.		Bobwhite: early Oct. through early Dec.	Early Oct. through. mid-Nov.
	Mid-Nov. through mid-Feb.		Bobwhite: mid-Nov. through mid-Feb.	Mid-Oct. through late Dec.

Always consult state regulations before hunting.

State Game & Fish Dept.	Chukar Partridge	Dove	Grouse
New Mexico New Mexico Dept. of Game & Fish State Capitol, Villagra Bldg. Santa Fe, NM 87503 (505) 827-7899		Mourning, white-winged: Sept. through Dec.	Blue, ruffed: Sept. through Oct. Prairie chicken; early to mid-Dec.
New York New York Dept. of Fish & Wildlife 50 Wolf Drive Albany, NY 12233 (518) 457-5690			Ruffed: late Sept. through Feb.
North Carolina North Carolina Wildlife Resources Comm. Archdale Bldg. 512 N. Salisbury St. Raleigh, NC 27611 (919) 733-3391		Mourning: early Sept. through early Oct.; late Nov. through mid-Jan.	Ruffed: mid-Oct. through Feb.
North Dakota North Dakota Game & Fish Dept. 100 N. Bismarck Expressway Bismarck, ND 58501-5095 (701) 221-6300		Mourning: early Sept. through late Oct.	Ruffed, sage, sharp-tailed: mid-Sept. through Dec.
Ohio Ohio Dept. of Natural Res. Fountain Square Columbus, OH 39205-0451 (601) 961-5300	Early Nov. through early Jan.		Ruffed: mid-Oct. through Feb.
Oklahoma Oklahoma Dept. of Wildlife Conservation 1810 N. Lincoln P.O. Box 53465 Oklahoma City, OK 73152 (405) 521-3851		Mourning: early Sept. through Oct.	Prairie chicken: mid-Nov. through Dec.

Always consult state regulations before hunting.

Hungarian Partridge	Pheasant	Ptarmigan	Quail	Woodcock
	Early Dec.		Gambel's, bobwhite, scaled: mid-Nov. through mid-Feb.	
Early Oct.	Early Oct. through Dec.		Bobwhite: early Nov. through Dec.	Early Oct. through mid-Nov.
	Mid-Nov. through early Feb.		Bobwhite: mid-Nov. through Feb.	Mid-Nov. through early Jan.
Mid-Sept. through Dec.	Late Oct. through Dec.			
	Early Nov. through early Jan.		Bobwhite: early Nov. through early Jan.	Late Sept. through late Jan.
	Early Dec. through early Jan.		Bobwhite, scaled: late Nov. through mid-Feb.	Late Oct. through Dec.

Always consult state regulations before hunting.

State Game & Fish Dept.	Chukar Partridge	Dove	Grouse
Oregon Oregon Dept. of Fish & Wildlife P.O. Box 59 Portland, OR 97207 (503) 229-5403	Early Oct. through end of Dec.	Mourning: Sept.	Blue, sage, ruffed: late Aug. through early Jan.
Pennsylvania Pennsylvania Game Comm. 2001 Elmerton Ave. Harrisburg, PA 17110-9797 (717) 787-4250			Ruffed: mid-Oct. through late Jan.
Rhode Island Rhode Island Division of Fish & Wildlife Oliver Stedman Gov't. Center 4808 Tower Hill Rd. Wakefield, RI 02879-2207 (401) 277-2774		Mourning: early Sept. through mid-Jan.	Ruffed: late Oct. through Feb.
South Carolina South Carolina Wildlife & Marine Resources Dept. Rembert C. Dennis Bldg. P.O. Box 167 Columbia, SC 29202 (803) 734-3888		Mourning: early Sept. through mid-Jan.	
South Dakota South Dakota Game, Fish & Parks 445 East Capitol Pierre, SD 57501 (605) 773-3485	Mid-Sept. through mid-Dec.	Mourning: early Sept. through late Oct.	Ruffed, sharp-tailed, prairie chicken: mid-Sept. through mid-Dec.
Tennessee Tennessee Wildlife Res. Agency Ellington Agricultural Ctr. P.O. Box 40747 Nashville, TN 37204 (615) 781-6500		Mourning: early through late Oct.; early through late Dec.	Ruffed: mid-Oct. through Feb.

Always consult state regulations before hunting.

Hungarian Partridge	Pheasant	Ptarmigan	Quail	Woodcock
Early Oct. through Dec.	Mid-Oct. through late Nov.		Mountain: late Aug. through early Jan; valley: mid-Oct. through late Nov.	
	Late Oct. through late Nov.; late Dec. through early Jan.		Bobwhite: late Oct. through late Nov.	
	Late Oct. through Feb.		Bobwhite: mid-Oct. through early Dec.; mid-Dec. through end of Feb.	Late Oct. through early Dec.
			Bobwhite: mid-Nov. through Feb.	Late Oct. through late Nov.
			Bobwhite: early Nov. through mid-Dec.	
			Bobwhite: Sept.; mid-Nov. through Feb.	Late Oct. through late Nov.

Always consult state regulations before hunting.

State Game & Fish Dept.	Chukar Partridge	Dove	Grouse
Texas Texas Parks & Wildlife Dept. 4200 Smith School Rd. Austin, TX 78744 (512) 389-4800		Mourning, white-winged: early Sept. through mid-Nov.	Prairie chicken: mid-Oct.
Utah Utah Division of Wildlife Resources 1596 West North Temple Salt Lake City, UT 84116 (801) 533-9333	Early Sept. through Jan.		Blue, ruffed, sage; early Sept. through Nov.
Vermont Vermont Dept. of Fish & Wildlife 103 So. Main Street 10 South Bldg. Waterbury, VT 05677 (802) 244-7331	Late Sept. through Dec.		Ruffed: late Sept. through Nov.
Virginia Virginia Dept. of Game & Inland Fisheries P.O. Box 11104 Richmond, VA 23230-11-4 (804) 367-1000		Mourning: early Sept. through Dec.	Ruffed: early Nov. through early Feb.
Washington Washington Dept. of Wildlife 600 Capitol Way N., GJ-11 Olympia, WA 98501-1091 (206) 753-5700	Late Sept. through early Jan.		Blue, ruffed: early Sept. through Dec.
West Virginia West Virginia Dept. of Natural Resources 1800 Washington St. S.E. Charleston, WV 23505 (304) 348-2754			Ruffed: mid-Oct. through Feb.

Always consult state regulations before hunting.

Hungarian Partridge	Pheasant	Ptarmigan	Quail	Woodcock
	Early Nov. through late Feb.		Bobwhite, scaled, Gambel's, Mearns: early Nov. through late Feb.	Late Nov. through late Jan.
Early Sept. through Nov.	Early Nov. through early Dec.	Early Sept. through mid-Oct.	Gambel's: early Nov. through Dec.	
	Late Sept. through late Nov.		Bobwhite: late Sept. through late Nov.	
	Mid-Nov. through mid-Feb.		Bobwhite: mid-Nov. through mid-Feb.	Early Nov. through early Jan.
	Late Sept. through early Jan.		Valley, mountain, bob-white, Gambel's: mid-Oct. through early Jan.	
	Early Nov. through Feb.		Bobwhite: early Nov. through Feb.	

Always consult state regulations before hunting.

State Game & Fish Dept.	Chukar Partridge	Dove	Grouse
Wisconsin Wisconsin Dept. of Natural Resources Box 7921 Madison, WI 53707 (608) 266-2621			Ruffed: mid-Sept. through Jan. Sharp-tailed: mid-Oct. through early Nov.
Wyoming Wyoming Fish & Game Dept. 5400 Bishop Blvd. Cheyenne, WY 82002 (307) 777-7735	Early Oct. through mid-Dec.	White-winged, mourning: early Sept. through mid-Oct.	Blue, ruffed: early Sept. through Nov. Sage: late Aug. through mid-Sept.

Always consult state regulations before hunting.

Hungarian Partridge	Pheasant	Ptarmigan	Quail	Woodcock
Mid-Oct. through early Dec.	Mid-Oct. through early Dec.		Bobwhite: mid-Oct. through early Dec.	Mid-Sept. through early Nov.
Early Oct. through mid-Dec.	Early Nov. through early Dec.			

Always consult state regulations before hunting.

State Game & Fish Dept.	Chukar Partridge	Dove	Grouse
Alberta Alberta Dept. of Forestry, Lands & Wildlife Petroleum Plaza, North Tower 9945 108th Street Edmonton, Alberta T5K 2G6 (403) 427-6733			Blue, ruffed, sage, sharp-tailed: early Sept. through early Dec.
British Columbia British Columbia Ministry of the Environment Parliament Buildings Victoria, BC V8V 1X5 (604) 387-5429	Early Sept. through late Nov.	Mourning: early Sept. through late Nov.	Blue, ruffed, sharptail: early Sept. through Dec.
Manitoba Manitoba Dept. of Natural Res. 1495 St. James St., Box 24 Winnepeg, Manitoba R3H 0W9 (204) 945-3730			Ruffed, sharp-tailed: early Sept. through mid-Dec.
New Brunswick New Brunswick Dept. of Natural Resources, Maritime Forestry Complex P.O. Box 6000 Fredericton, NB E3B 5H1 (506) 453-2440			Ruffed: early Oct. through mid-Nov.
Newfoundland & Labrador Newfoundland & Labrador Wildlife Division, Bldg. #810 Pleasantville, P.O. Box 4750 St. John's NF A1C 5T7 (709) 576-2630			Ruffed: late Sept. through April
Nova Scotia Nova Scotia Dept. of Lands & Forests, Wildlife Division Toronto-Dominion Bank Bldg. 1791 Barrington St. Halifax, NS B3J 2T9 (902) 424-5935			Ruffed: early Oct. through mid-Dec.

Always consult state regulations before hunting.

Hungarian Partridge	Pheasant	Ptarmigan	Quail	Woodcock
Early Sept. through early Dec.	Early Sept through late Dec.			
Early Sept. through Dec.	Early Oct. through late Nov.		Bobwhite, Gambel's, Mearns mountain, scaled, valley: early Oct. through late Nov.	
		End of Sept. through March.		
Early Sept. through end of Feb.				

Always consult state regulations before hunting.

State Game & Fish Dept.	Chukar Partridge	Dove	Grouse
Ontario Ontario Ministry of Natural Res Outdoor Recreation Group Whitney Block, Queen's Park Toronto, Ontario M7A 1W3 (416) 965-4251			Ruffed, sharp-tailed: late Sept. through mid-Dec.
Prince Edward Island Prince Edward Island Fish & Wildlife Division Dept. of the Environment P.O. Box 2000 Charlottetown, P.E.I. C1A 7N8 (902) 892-0311			Ruffed: early Oct. through early Dec.
Quebec Quebec Dept. of Recreation, Fish & Wildlife Place de la Capitale 150 East Saint-Cyrille Blvd. Quebec City, P.Q. G1R 2B2 (418) 643-2207	Early Aug. through Dec.		Blue, ruffed, sharp-tailed sage: late Aug. through Dec.
Saskatchewan Saskatchewan Parks, Recreation & Culture 3211 Albert St. Regina, Saskatchewan S4S 5W6 (306) 787-2930			Ruffed: early Sept. through early Dec. Sharp-tailed: late Sept. through early Nov.

Always consult state regulations before hunting.

Hungarian Partridge	Pheasant	Ptarmigan	Quail	Woodcock
Late Sept. through mid-Nov.	Late Sept. through mid-Dec.			
Early Oct. through late Nov.				Early Oct. through early Dec.
Mid-Sept. through mid-Nov.	Early Aug through Dec.		Bobwhite, Gambel's, Mearns, scaled, mountain, valley: early Aug. through Dec.	
Late Sept. through mid-Nov.	Early Oct. through mid-Nov.; early to late Dec.	Mid-Nov. through March		

Always consult state regulations before hunting.

Index